RELATING TO OTHERS

SECOND EDITION

Steve Duck

OPEN UNIVERSITY PRESS
Buckingham · Philadelphia

Open University Press
Celtic Court
22 Ballmoor
Buckingham
MK18 1XW

email: enquiries@openup.co.uk
World wide web: http://www.openup.co.uk

and
325 Chestnut Street
Philadelphia, PA 19106, USA

First Published 1999

A catalogue record of this book is available from the British Library

ISBN 0 335 20163 6 (pbk)   0 335 20164 4 (hbk)

Library of Congress Cataloging-in-Publication Data
Duck, Steve.
    Relating to others / Steve Duck. — 2nd ed.
      p. cm. — (Mapping social psychology series)
    Includes bibliographical references and index.
    ISBN 0–335–20164–4 (hardbound). — ISBN 0–335–20163–6 (pbk.)
    1. Interpersonal relations. 2. Social interaction. 3. Courtship.
I. Title. II. Series.
HM132.D827 1999
302—dc21   98–36950
                                        CIP

Typeset by Graphicraft Limited, Hong Kong
Printed in Great Britain by Redwood Books, Trowbridge

RELATING TO OTHERS

MAPPING SOCIAL PSYCHOLOGY

Series Editor: Tony Manstead

The second edition of this book is offered
in grateful recognition of the genetic contribution of
John Duck, yeoman (died 1604)
and his widow Margaret Duck (1550–1624)
of Goathland, Yorkshire, England,

'obstinate recusants'*

* various transcripts of North Yorkshire Quarter Sessions Court, Helmsley, Malton and Northallerton 1600–1623

CONTENTS

PREFACE

The field of research into **personal relationships** was just beginning its tremendous (and predicted) growth when the first edition of this book was published in 1988. The growth has manifested a number of strengths that are also unusual, compared to the normal routine comings and goings of academic fashions. It is unusual by being a truly interdisciplinary enterprise; it is unusual by having changed its style of work quite dramatically in the last ten years, from a focus on the psychological interior of informants to a focus on the behavioural interactions of two people influencing one another across time; it is unusual because of the immense rapidity of its growth; it is unusual by reason of the power it has to speak to issues in real people's everyday lives. It is also *very* interesting: very few of us can read the research on relationships without learning something that captivates and intrigues.

Nevertheless, it is my belief that from time to time specific topics in social psychology just happen to become the target of dramatic surges of interest, and that this happens almost unaccountably as the Zeitgeist, or spirit of the times, dictates – rather like popular music and the fashions of different generations. As I have argued elsewhere (Duck 1980a), that Zeitgeist is shaped by people, rather than being some disembodied theoretical ghost in the animated research machine. It is the decisions, actions and personal interactions of theorists and researchers – and their students – that promote some fields of activity while causing others to decline. At its roots, then, all research is basically a relational activity that occurs between scholars who talk to, meet, and interact with one another via the media of journals, conference papers, emails, books and personal talk, though it has often been presented as the lone activity of scholars working late and alone in immense libraries or laboratories. Thus the enterprise is characterized by much that this book describes in the course of its attempts to understand and depict the roots of relating to others. The relationships of scholars to one another are simply one form of relationship that may be studied, and as such are influenced by the Zeitgeist of relationships as much as by the Zeitgeist of scholarship. The field of personal relationships research is lucky enough not only to have a Zeitgeist made up of interesting problems to address but also to be populated by a notably young and vigorous group of researchers. For example, the average age of the first two Presidents of the *International Network on Personal Relationships* is 45 years, whereas for other organizations it is about 20 years older. Such scholars are likely to be in the peak of vigour in their professional lives and to be active ambassadors who make the field attractive to those working in other fields. I was therefore legitimately optimistic in the 1988 edition that the growth of interest in personal relationships was destined to make it a key area of research in the 1990s in its own right although the *Journal of Social and Personal Relationships* now receives a very high number of citations in other journals. However I was wrong to overestimate not the extent of its expansion within ten years, but its infusion into other fields, which is only beginning. So I will cheat on my earlier prediction: the *next* ten years will nurture even more growth and scholarly collaboration across disciplines. 'Personal relationships' will also become a recognized academic discipline in its own right offering courses in relationship studies in an increasing number of universities. But more than this I firmly believe that many disciplines will come to recognize – from within their own methodological cultures and theoretical traditions – the fundamental ways in which relationships infiltrate almost every aspect of social life and human experience.

The youthfulness and vigour of the researchers working in this field in part explains the movement towards interdisciplinarity (Acitelli 1995). Since these people were trained in a time when universities were pushing the disciplines towards one another, many of the active workers are open to the notion that different disciplines can work together to help solve the issues raised in a particular topic of study (Acitelli 1995; Fincham 1995). The question of the interdisciplinary nature of the enterprise is a hobby horse of mine and, as I noted in the first edition, something I have been working hard to turn into a self-fulfilling prophecy. Let us first follow Acitelli (1995) in distinguishing multidisciplinary from interdisciplinary work: *multidisciplinary* work involves many different disciplines and theoretical or methodological styles independently applied to a given topic ('Disciplines at parallel play' in Acitelli's elegantly sardonic phrase); *interdisciplinary* work on the other hand involves, at best, cooperation between experts from different disciplines and, at the very least, awareness of, and respect for, the contributions of different disciplines to a collective activity. There are many examples of such cooperative work to be found in the various series in close relationships that have published works by people from social psychology, developmental psychology, sociology, communication studies, family studies, and other disciplines. Also testament is the publication since 1988 of two editions of the *Handbook of Personal Relationships* with sections devoted to the different constituent disciplines of the canon of work in personal relationships that increasingly often cite research across supposed disciplinary boundaries. That this canon extends beyond the reach of any one discipline is far clearer now than it was in 1988 when the first edition of *Relating to Others* was published.

The issues in the explanation of personal relationships go far beyond the reach of one discipline, even if that discipline is social psychology, as acknowledged by leading social psychologists Berscheid (1995) and Fincham (1995). The issues are too complex for any one discipline to have all the answers and any biases of a particular discipline's approaches are readily supplemented or advantageously corrected by the contributions of other scholarly partners in the research enterprise. In a sense, then, the study of personal relationships is its own motto: the study of relationships works best when scholars relate to one another and are willing to step outside the confines of their own disciplines in reality as well as in prefaces.

There are many kinds of books that can be written 'about' a field. At one extreme is a handbook detailing the research that gets done and giving as comprehensive as possible a review of the past and future of the discipline (Duck *et al.* 1997a; Duck *et al.* 1988). At the other extreme are the popular books that simplify the research to make it accessible to interested laity who have no particular training in the discipline but are driven by general concerns or a desire for greater information about a given topic. Somewhere in between there are introductory texts, which are of different sorts, too. One kind fits an area into a broader perspective, such as I tried to do in my *Human Relationships* (3rd edition) (Duck 1998), which places the study of relationships in the context of, and in relation to, the rest of social psychology. The present book, on the other hand, is intended to introduce the area of personal relationships on its own and in its own right, assuming some broader framework in which the readers will locate it from their own experience and training. I am focusing here on the research strictly in this field and so am aiming at students with some knowledge of social psychology already, or at least some awareness of its principles, even if the reader starts from a background of communication science or family studies or sociology or developmental psychology or health and leisure studies.

This, however, is a book in a series mapping social psychology – and is intended *primarily* for student social psychologists, therefore. As indicated above, I would not mind one bit if those in communication or sociology or family science or any other discipline also got something out of it. Nor would I mind if researchers rather than students found it useful in its structuring of the literature on relationships. Indeed, this would rather reinforce my belief that the topic is a uniter of disciplines and interests, as well as a focus of human experience. As a social psychologist myself by training, but one who has moved towards communication, I must be honest and state that I fervently believe that allowing the sole dominance of social psychology (when the field was narrowly conceived as dealing only with first impressions or initial attraction) was unwise for the field and helped us to see and understand only some of the major issues. It is only because progress in the social sciences is typically not only built on previous work but also goes far beyond it that we are now seeing the dramatic advances detailed throughout this book. However, this book is for those who might start out thinking otherwise. The book shares some of the traditional emphases of social psychology, to be sure. Much of the work discussed here is based on studies of white, middle-class students giving self-reports or reacting in laboratories; most of it is about *voluntary* relationships (i.e., not about relationships between prisoners and guards, professors and pupils, couples and in-laws or kin, for example); there is practically nothing here about children's friendships (but see Duck 1993b). Although I cover **courtship**, there is less here on marriage and on parent–child relationships than there is in *Human Relationships* (3rd edition) (Duck 1998). Those omissions do not trouble me, given the scope that the book was contracted to have, although it clearly does not cover all the fascinating and profound relationships that could be studied. (Two editions of the *Handbook of Personal Relationships* amount to some 1500 pages and do not exhaust the topics either.)

Given these admitted limitations, the book offers a perspective on the study of personal relationships that is broadly based on the historical development of the discipline from its roots in social psychology towards the broader canopy that it now supports. The book notes the early work on attraction to strangers through the work on physical attractiveness and then moves on, as the field has done, to consideration of the broader behavioural and cognitive contexts within which relationships are performed, in terms of continuing real-life relationships that develop or deteriorate, taking account of social context and communication patterns as well as the internal emotional experience of the individuals in a particular dyad. My hope is that this will show not only the contribution made by social psychology to the study of relationships but also the ways in which social psychology can learn from, and build on, the work of other scholars.

This field is so exciting because it is now progressing and proving its worth as a scholarly pursuit. It is, I believe, poised for major recognition and growth within and across several disciplines. My 'first edition opinion' that it would be the major field in social psychology within ten years proved a little optimistic – but it is getting there. The next ten years seem sure to elevate it to that position as its ramifications in such topics as attitude change, narrative, self-presentation, social cognition, and even jury decision making become more evident (Duck 1998). My colours thus incautiously nailed to the mast, I now invite you to see for yourself whether you will agree with me.

Steve Duck

ACKNOWLEDGEMENTS

I am grateful to many people who helped me with this book. Foremost of them all is Chris Brenneman, who worked like a Trojan in spite of my infamous handwriting, and never let me down once on impossible deadlines or unreasonable tasks while she also completed all the possible and reasonable ones ahead of time. I really could not have managed to do the book without her unstinting help and assistance (and quite often guidance and correction as well).

Roz Burnett did an excellent job of reading the draft of the first edition and producing well-judged and extremely helpful comments that made the book a better product than it would otherwise have been. Dan Perlman also read the final MS (as I thought) for the first edition and made such careful, attentive and well-judged comments, coupled with such good guidance for revisions, that I could not ignore them and just had to write the 'final version' again. Mollie Condra and Tony Manstead also read and commented on the drafts and I benefited very greatly from their thoughtful and detailed advice. Joanna Lawson also helped me with both final versions of the manuscript and Linda Acitelli discussed many of the ideas and concepts, offering excellent advice and drawing my attention to literature I had overlooked. I am grateful to all of these people for their help.

I also hereby acknowledge with thanks the permission of Academic Press Inc. to reproduce Figure 4.1 (from page 67 of S. W. Duck and R. Gilmour (eds) *Personal Relationships 2: Developing Personal Relationships*, Academic Press, 1981), Figure 6.1 (from page 16 of S. W. Duck (ed.) *Personal Relationships 4: Dissolving Personal Relationships*, Academic Press, 1982) and Figure 7.1 (from page 169 of S. W. Duck (ed.) *Personal Relationships 5: Repairing Personal Relationships*, Academic Press, 1984). Finally, I acknowledge the gracious permission of Guilford Press for me to borrow extensively from my article with Harriet Sants in Chapter 8. Some of the ideas there were first published in Duck and Sants (1983) 'On the origin of the specious: are personal relationships really interpersonal states?' (*Journal of Social and Clinical Psychology*, 1: 27–41).

ONE

THE ROLE OF RELATIONSHIPS
IN LIFE

That personal relationships and friendships are important to us is obvious. We need merely to reflect for a moment on the sources of our greatest pleasure and pain to appreciate that nothing else arouses the extremes of emotion that are experienced in the course of personal relationships with other human beings. If formal evidence were needed, however, it is to be found in a report by Klinger (1977) which surveyed 'inner experience and incentives in people's lives'. The clear leader was people's relationships with one another: almost everyone indicates that it is important to feel loved and wanted. It is also important to have available sources of help in disasters (Kaniasty and Norris 1997) or during emotional crises and transitions (Trickett and Buchanan 1997), but beyond such instrumental functions, relationships are simply just a 'Good Thing' (Duck *et al.* 1997b; Heller and Rook 1997). Relationships with friends, kin, children, or a same-sex or opposite-sex partner make life meaningful (Duck 1994a), whether the relationships are good or bad (since even enemies can give meaning and purpose and goals to life; Wiseman and Duck 1995). Equally, there is now considerable evidence that the presence of a close confidant helps to stave off not only depression (Sarason *et al.* 1997) but also other clinical problems (Hooley and Hiller 1997) and certain physical ailments (Heller and Rook 1997). Although the picture is not one-sided, since relationships have a down-side that we shall also explore, it scarcely needs argument to establish the importance of relating to others.

Poets, novelists, playwrights, philosophers – and many others besides – have studied relationships in an effort to discover why they matter, how they work, and how to improve their quality. Even Ancient Greeks like Aristotle and Roman orator–philosophers like Cicero had something to say about relationships with other people, particularly friendships – and their thoughts are still used by those who study the rhetoric of desire and the language in which liking and loving are expressed (Poulakos 1997). Despite all the years devoted by such thinkers to the problems of explaining and improving friendships, marriages and social relations in general

– even international relations (Goodwin 1998) – we are only just beginning to find out the answers to broad questions about success of relationships in our own personal lives. Common sense is not a good assistant here: it offers merely uncertainties and conflicting advice ('Opposites attract' yet 'Birds of a feather flock together', for instance). Such maxims should prompt us to ask a host of more complex questions. Not only should we begin to ask which factor matters most, similarity or oppositeness, but also what sorts of similarity or oppositeness, and in what way do they matter? Do they cause initial **attraction** or do they promote good relationships in the long term? What sort of relationships do they affect? How are they 'done' in real everyday life relationships? How does similarity or oppositeness lead to behaviours or communications that create different sorts of relational experiences in people? It is perhaps because common sense is not much help that questions about the proper way to conduct everyday relationships seem to constitute the bulk of issues raised in problem pages, self-help courses and intimate confessionals, and TV chat shows and soap operas, as well as occupying the minds of all of us at some time or another.

THE DEVELOPMENT OF THE FIELD OF RESEARCH IN PERSONAL RELATIONSHIPS

Like early research, ordinary human beings tend to think first of using a magnetic metaphor to explain the basic workings of relationships ('attraction', 'repulsion'). Unconsciously, such metaphors move our thoughts towards the inherent (psychological?) properties of persons that work to draw them together, perhaps against their better judgement. Dating agencies continue to make money from this commonly accepted assumption (Goodwin 1990), but the model of the processes of relating contained in the metaphor is really quite displeasing when you think about it: that people are unwittingly pulled towards one another's inherent and pre-existing characteristics, willy-nilly. It regards relationships as implicitly independent of interaction, co-construction, mutually responsive behaviour, or shared understandings derived from active conversation. It represents relationships as separated from necessary management of routine and ritual; distinct from silly things like playfulness and joking; strategic activity; and as unconnected to matters of structuring of leisure. In short, it leaves out most of the other things that humans do in everyday life, and so it serves to caricature social and personal relationships as the unthinking domain of reactive magnetism. By contrast the present book will give consideration to all that such a metaphor leaves out.

Recent research does likewise and places initial judgements of attraction in a more complex picture of the operation of a variety of psychological (Acitelli *et al.* 1993), sociological (Allan 1993, 1998), social–contextual (Wood 1993), and dynamic (Planalp and Garvin-Doxas 1994) influences on relationship conduct, that we will explore. These include relational aspects of memory (Miell 1987), self-presentation and identity management (Spencer 1994), meaning construction (Duck 1994a), and the material or financial resources available to the participants (Allan 1998). For example, think how difficult it is for adolescents to find a material *place* to conduct their romances, or reflect on how complex it is socially to make a first date continue over to a second date (Sprecher and Duck 1993), a continuation that is by no means as automatic as an attraction metaphor implicitly suggests.

An easy criticism of the early attraction work that has led to the types of change we see now is that it fossilized the effects of magnetism by freezing the moment of attraction to one specific judgement. The work I shall review here is much more likely to investigate the dynamics of relationships and the continuously unfolding nature of relationship experience in real life and real time (Duck 1990, 1994a; Shotter 1992). Recent work also attends to *process* across time and hence to the dynamic aspects of the conduct of interactions, making the point that relationships are variable experiences in time rather than unrelentingly constant or repetitious ones – our interactions with friends may have definable recurrent themes but are not exactly the same each time we meet them (Duck 1994a) – we all have bad days even in the same relationship.

While psychologically important work on the social judgements that surround initial attraction is still carried out, as we shall see in Chapter 2 (Baldwin 1993), there is now more work on the processes of developed relationships like marriage (Fletcher and Fitness 1993) and this book will focus on the ways in which social psychology broadens the scope of analysis well beyond initial attraction. Researchers now look at the structuring of cognition into 'memory organization packets' about relationship development (Honeycutt 1993), or the development of **relational culture** (Wood 1982), or the interplay of various relational **schemas** (Andersen 1993), or the role of relationship awareness and talking about relationships in the conduct of the relationships themselves (Acitelli 1993). In the last ten years there has also been significant recognition of the fact that third parties influence the form and structure of relationship development or partners' management of conflict (Klein and Milardo 1993), and the fact that a person's relationships of one type affect their relationships of another type – for example the types of dates which adolescents select are strongly affected by the friendship groups or cliques to which they belong (Berndt 1996). Also we can investigate the influence of a network on a specific dyad (Milardo and Wellman 1992); look at maintenance of relationships (Dindia and Canary 1993; Canary and Stafford 1994); consider how only some relationships decline (Duck 1982a; Orbuch 1992); and reflect carefully on the mundane, trivial, everyday conduct of communication in relationships (Duck *et al.* 1991; Dindia 1994; Spencer 1994).

Social scientific work on relationships has become more concerted relatively recently – since about the early/mid-1980s – as it attacks such aspects of relating to others. All the same, work on specific sorts of relationships, like attraction, dating, and marriage, has a longer history in many separate disciplines such as social psychology, communication, family studies, sociology and clinical psychology. Indeed, in the grand historical context, the scientific scrutiny of social and personal relationships has been so recent a development that it is still in its early childhood, though this has proved to be a vigorous one with a huge expansion of growth in the ten years since this book came out in the first edition. For example there is now an *International Network on Personal Relationships* and a *Journal of Social and Personal Relationships*, with other organizations and journals and two sets of interlocking relationship conferences. The development of work with approaches that are *multidisciplinary* (respecting the work of many different disciplines) and *interdisciplinary* (carried out by different disciplines cooperating) – a distinction carefully drawn by Acitelli (1995) – has come about as scholars in different academic departments have been able to read and discuss each other's work together in these same places rather than hunting all over the place for it in different journals and conferences. As a result it has become obvious how each disciplinary group looks differently at relationship issues and yet can contribute valuable insights to the work of the others.

By such work many common-sense assumptions have been put to the test in empirical research, the truths thereby being separated from the half-truths and the cosy errors, as I shall try to show in the rest of this book. The work that I reviewed ten years ago in the first edition of this book (Duck 1988) focused noticeably on the *individual* and on structures of cognition and personality. Thus it often implicitly supposed that relational success could be predicted from the pre-existing attributes of the participants – for example that two initially similar people were destined inevitably for marital bliss where now recent researchers would focus more on the realities of prenuptial contracts (Winters 1997) or previous histories of interaction in courtship (Notarius 1996).

This change of approach comes about as scholars have realized that they had assumed that such characteristics as physical attractiveness somehow 'created' special relationship behaviour and yet had not taken the process approach to research that actually looked at the 'somehow' and explained how it worked. Scholars are now looking at the ways in which relationships are actually conducted in real life, something I called for in the final chapter of the 1988 edition of this book. A final development, of necessity, is as an antidote to the deliriously cheerful early emphasis on the delights of relationships that we used to see (e.g., Argyle 1987). Research of recent years has discovered the dark side of life generally (Cupach and Spitzberg 1994) and of relationships in particular (Duck 1994b), including consideration of enemyships (Wiseman and Duck 1995), relational anger and shame (Retzinger 1995) and the management of the daily routine relational hassles that we all experience (Bolger and Kelleher 1993), or the drag of long-term relational obligations (Stein 1993).

In our everyday relationships, friendship quite obviously involves *binds* as well as *bonds*, in Wiseman's (1986) elegant play on words. The delights and benefits of friendship are offset by oppressive obligations that are not occasional and unexpected happenings once or twice in the life of a relationship, such as, for example, providing help in moving house or offering comfort during bereavement. They are real daily consequences of the need to *do* relationships. We are often required to coordinate two timetables, two sets of preferences and needs, or two sources of demands that are created by the uniting of two otherwise independent beings into one relational entity. Of course, such accommodations have psychological consequences and are difficult to do, not simply pleasures of relating to others.

Adding a strong theoretical overlay to such observations, Baxter and Montgomery (1996) show that most relationship activity represents the activity of (and the need to address) dialectical tensions rather than the simple linear causal forces implied in the old attraction literature. For example, friends feel a need to balance out the desire for disclosure and openness against the desire for privacy and the right to retain secrets and so avoid vulnerabilities. Friends must perpetually balance the tension between, on the one hand, a desire for connectedness and interdependence – inherent in a relationship – and, on the other hand, the desire for autonomy and independence – inherent in individuality. Such tensions are not brought up to the table and resolved once and for all in a tempestuous conflict, but are instead constantly in the background requiring (re)negotiation and thermostatic adjustment throughout the life of the relationship.

As will be apparent from the suggestions for further reading at the end of this chapter and subsequent chapters, there is now no shortage of excellent social psychological and other social scientific works devoted to such deep and continuous processes of personal relationships. Whereas work used to focus mainly on why we are attracted to strangers (e.g., Byrne 1971; Duck 1977; Berscheid and Walster 1978), it now extends to investigation of methods of exploring real-life, long-term relationships (Acitelli 1993, 1997; Duck 1994a; Baxter and Montgomery 1996; Baxter *et al.* 1997; Duck *et al.* 1997b). It looks at the features that identify 'best friendship' and distinguish it from, say, casual acquaintance or marriage or 'ordinary' friendship (see Fitch (1998) on the ways in which relationships are 'spoken in to existence' or encoded in the everyday speech patterns of partners; or Davis and Todd (1985) on the paradigmatic features, like loyalty and trust, that make some relationships what they are; or Wiseman and Duck (1995) on the ways in which enemies conduct their relationships). It deals not only with the problems of relationship dissolution and decline (Duck 1982a; Hagestad and Smyer 1982; Orbuch 1992), but now also with the dark sides of relationships that are normally present even in relationships that work well (Cupach and Spitzberg 1994; Duck and Wood 1995) such as hurtful messages (Vangelisti 1994), troublesome patches (Levitt *et al.* 1996) and the other 'stratagems, spoils and serpent's teeth' that can afflict even generally positive relationships (Duck 1994b). This is a big change from the work available for review by the first edition of the book, and it is a change that makes research on relationships radically more realistic and relevant to everyday life experiences.

These dramatic changes in topical focus in the last ten years are, I think, a direct result of the increased accommodation of researchers to the concerns and techniques of other disciplines. Also, ten years ago most social psychological research was laboratory-based, although calls for 'real world' studies were routinely made and ignored (Clark and Reis 1988). It has since become significantly more sophisticated in adopting a range of laboratory and discourse-based approaches (Billig 1991). Such research typically takes a relatively traditional social psychological approach (often being carried out as survey research or laboratory study, for instance). Yet there is also a move towards field observation; for example, Fitch (1998) studied the ways in which people in Colombia subtly differentiated their daily life relationships through use of different everyday speech patterns and styles of address. Researchers look also at the relating of personal characteristics to actual experiences in friendship and social participation. For example, Duck *et al.* (1994) studied the social participation of lonely persons, finding, in a study where lonely people observed others' inter-actions and also saw tapes of their own interactions, that lonely people usually see social interaction – their own and other people's – as more negative than do non-lonely people. Gaines and Ickes (1997) examined the role of a person's race or ethnicity in friendship and Werking (1997) has opened up the study of non-romantic cross-sex friendships which are actually quite common parts of everyday life. She successfully demon-strated that there are strong norms for people in cross-sex relationships to 'explain themselves', since everyone otherwise assumes that the friend-ship is really a repressed or disguised *sexual* relationship.

Progress is becoming rapid as researchers move from the style of work that locked itself in the laboratory environment and have now begun to explore life as it is lived 'out there' (see Chapters 1 and 2 here, as well as Burnett *et al.* 1987; Duck 1994a; Fincham 1995, for fuller discussion of these points and the reasons for recent changes in the style of research). Nowadays scholars are much more inclined to look at real people doing real things in real life, instead of relying so much on controlled studies of special people doing special things, though to our discredit we still do plenty of that also (Duck *et al.* 1997a). Researchers also now recognize the importance of the fact that being a friend or being a spouse inducts us into a *role* – the role of friend or spouse – and attachment to the role itself can be attractive: for example, in the film *Muriel's Wedding*, Muriel wanted to *get married*, not to marry a specific person. Thus 'being a friend' is more than being able to name friends: it involves a role relationship to some-one else along with rights, such as confidences and information about personal secrets, and obligations, such as the duty to help a friend in need even if that is inconvenient (Wiseman 1986; Stein 1993).

A book such as this – especially since it is intended to be concise – therefore has quite a task before it in giving a fair representation of the historically important work while keeping the present styles in mind, since they are such different extensions of what came before. (Fuller dis-cussions by various authors are available in the two editions of the *Hand-book of Personal Relationships*, 1988 and 1997.) While you will read here about the laboratory research that characterizes much of social psycho-logy, you will also be introduced to the more varied techniques that derive from other disciplines and take us further into the real world where people carry on their daily lives. These other disciplines have important contributions to make but, of course, they do not tackle precisely the same questions nor use precisely the same techniques as social psycho-logists do. Sociologists, family scientists and communication scholars do not think in the same terms as social psychologists and therefore approach problems and their solutions differently. But just as an athletics team will not win the Olympics if it consists only of high-jumpers and nobody who can sprint or throw a javelin, so cooperation between dis-ciplines is needed to increase our knowledge of relationships on wider fronts (Acitelli 1995).

This book will therefore cover more research than that narrowly encompassed in traditional social psychological research and associated traditional social psychological textbooks – not only because social psychologists do not believe that they know all there is to know about relating to other people (e.g., Berscheid's (1995) call for a sociologist or anthropologist to take a lead), but also because social psychological research can benefit from the contributions of other disciplines as much as vice versa. On the other hand, I emphasize the social psychological approach, tinged strongly with communication and family theory. That is to say, I am writing about the ways in which people think about social events, the nature of interpersonal behaviour face-to-face, the individual and social forces that affect communication in social interaction, and the thoughts, feelings and actions that make up the process of relating to others. All the same, I am not disputing the positioning of such judgements in a broader context of social action and economic circumstances which materially affect the ways in which relationships are carried out – whether, for example, they are carried out in the home, for well-off people, or in public places, for the economically challenged who cannot afford to invite people back to their homes and have too little space to make it feasible or too few resources to offer meals or entertainment there (Allan 1998).

Such an approach can be applied in a general way to relating to others, since many researchers believe that there are general principles in social and personal relationships, even if there are also particular defining characteristics for each sort of relationship. Thus, while we shall see that casual and best friendship are somehow the same, they are also different in some respects. For example, both involve interaction, mutual liking and, probably, trust, yet best friendship also manifests levels of intimacy and concern for one another that are less evident in casual friendship. Equally, while dating partners do many things, and are many things, to one another that married couples, close friends and acquaintances do and are, there are qualities that nevertheless differentiate these four sorts of relationships despite the fact that they all have the same backcloth. My argument throughout this book will essentially be that the differences and the similarities in the functions of relationships are both to be found in the extent to which, and the ways in which, the lives – and particularly the meaning systems – of the two partners are intertwined.

LIFE'S RICH PAGEANT OF LITTLE THINGS

In order to understand more clearly just why it is that relationships are voted the most important aspect of our lives in the general sense noted at the start of the chapter, we need a clear picture of the role of relationships in our everyday lives in a particular sense (Duck *et al.* 1997b). Even if we all believe that personal relationships are a 'Good Thing', how do they work in reality? How does friendship map onto everyday life? What do friends actually do for us? Is our time with others spent looking meaningfully into a mystical sunset, or is it spent whining, laughing, musing, drinking coffee together, talking about our shopping needs, arranging to play tennis, worrying, and gossiping about colleagues at work? Also, in

coming to understand the significance of relationships, we need to understand more clearly the role of everyday life events in our relationships.
However grand our motives are supposed to be by philosophers and religious writers, at bottom most of our daily life is mundane ('the long
littleness of life', as Frances Crofts Cornford called it) – and it is that
process of social living that social psychology should be all about, not
simply what people do in special, interesting, and involving circumstances
in laboratories. We therefore need to explore the underpinnings that social
relationships provide for the rest of social behaviour (see Duck 1994a for
the full argument of this point).

It is very clear, but often under-appreciated, that daily events are typically centred on and intertwined with our relationships in remarkable
ways. It is so obvious as to be *un*remarkable that many of our most
significant meetings are with friends or family; many of our major concerns are about relationships or about the people with whom we share
them; many of the most fearful and life-shaking crises concern the separation of ourselves from our friends or relatives (e.g., divorce and separation
from children, bereavement, estrangement, leaving home, going to college, the ending of love affairs or the death of a beloved friend). More
subtle, more important, and less clearly understood than these dramatic
and cataclysmic instances, however, are the other more frequent and
typical cases, where apparently minor daily events impinge upon our
relationships and vice versa (Duck 1994a). For example, daily life at work
or at play brings us into contact with many people we like and dislike
only moderately (Winstead *et al.* 1995). All the same, they affect our
enjoyment of and attitudes to life or may create **divided loyalties** between
the demands of friendship and the duties of the workplace, especially if
one friend is the other's boss (Zorn 1995). We gossip about other people
(Bergmann 1993; Duck 1998), we form our relationships, we share our
experiences in ways that seem to enhance our psychological health and
our sense of well-being (Heller and Rook 1997) – and we do it through the
medium of relationships. But not all of this results in lofty enterprises.
The boring human chores that make up much of our everyday existence
have also to be incorporated into our relationships as do pleasant but
seemingly unimportant things. Thus we go shopping with a companion,
or for a walk with a lover, get others' advice about what to buy or to wear,
or ask a friend's help in shifting a piano or call our mother or read a story
to a child. We eat meals with friends and relatives; we watch television
with companions; we make both big and small decisions with the advice
of confidants; we wash the dishes and cook with or for intimates; we take
our leisure, play our sports, watch TV and go to the movies with friends.
We even go to classes with people whom we know, arrange our timetables
around shared human needs like food, and organize our lives around
joint ventures and projects like leisure and sports, or shared desires, like
sex. We structure our relationships in various ways to accommodate our
daily human requirements for staying alive, keeping our bodies functional
and healthy and stimulating or recreating ourselves. We can dramatically
see how important such mundane and taken-for-granted things are as soon
as one partner becomes chronically sick, and these routine, apparently
trivial things become very tough, hard work or disrupt the conduct of

social life to the extent that they even threaten relationships. The management of the routine and the trivial and the taken-for-granted certainly makes relationships very much different experiences for [people with] chronically ill partners than they were before the illness, as the people might have to revise their daily timetable in order to perform medical procedures, might need to sleep a lot, or retire to the bathroom in the middle of conversations or during love-making or otherwise restructure their availability for social interactions that had previously been predictable and easy to arrange (Lyons *et al.* 1998).

Whereas all this may seem trivial to us (and certainly used to seem trivial to researchers), a moment's reflection will show us that relationships are affected by these things in deep, not minor, ways. For one thing, many of our trivial daily tasks and ventures require not only joint planning and agreement about priorities, but coordination of personal schedules that may otherwise be more or less unrelated (Clarke *et al.* 1986). The less involved two people are, the more it is difficult to manage such coordination of their unrelated daily lives and yet as we get to know someone better we not only want to spend more time with them but we usually become more accessible to them as part of the role. This can bring obligations and duties and restrictions (Wiseman 1986; Stein 1993). We are supposed to 'be there' whenever a friend needs us and any unavailability has to be explained and excused. Non-availability is unfriendly and undermines the sense of relationship, yet as Baxter *et al.* (1997) point out, friends are very often confronted with divided loyalties and forced to choose to spend time with A rather than B, thus essentially prioritizing one relationship over the other rather than fulfilling the obligations to both. Even so, the necessary discussion or planning of time may be beyond the ability of the partners or may get them into heated discussion that could affect the future of the relationship or its development. For instance, couples frequently get into conflict about when they should be ready to go out or the amount of time that can be devoted to work and the amount to leisure together. Couples argue about the coordination of desires for sexual behaviour or where to go out, or who does what around the house, or whose turn it is to go out shopping or what TV programme to watch (Duck and Wood 1995), but the ways in which they perceive (as well as manage) these conflicts can be exceptionally important to the future of the relationship (Crohan 1996). These conflicts can be major or trivial or can start trivial and turn into something bigger. Conflicts are most definitely not irrelevant to satisfaction in the relationship. They may even affect the whole nature and course of the relationship, despite the fact that they seem superficially to be utterly immaterial to it.

As a related point, consider that the creation, organization, or development of a relationship may place the two persons in conflict with other people or with other parts of their life – as when the birth of a child brings the new parents into conflict while they attempt to adjust to the new forms of their relationship (Crohan 1992, 1996; Trickett and Buchanan 1997); or when one person falls in love with someone at work in contravention of stated university policy about student–instructor relationships; or when one likes a person of whom one's parents disapprove (Huston and Schwartz 1995); when a friendship or love affair is so strong and important that it makes one reluctant to take an offer of a promotion or a new job (Crouter and Helms-Erickson 1997); or when one's friendship with a work colleague interferes with one's ability to be an effective manager of the person's work (Zorn 1995). Crouter and Helms-Erickson (1997) also indicate some of the strains between work and home life created in dual career couples but also within families in general. We will look further at this matter in Chapter 2.

An understanding of relating to others will therefore derive not only from the events that clearly take place within a relationship (e.g., what makes one person feel liking for another, or the intimacy level in a relationship). It will come from a broader view that looks at the events and circumstances that impinge on the relationship from outside, such as the pressures of daily living, the **contexts** and circumstances that affect the relationship, the influence of being in a network of other people within which the relationship occurs, and the effects of belonging to a particular culture, with its own rules and definitions of relationships (Fitch 1998), as well as its own forms of social influence from social networks (Milardo and Allan 1997) to TV, media and printed sources (Duran and Prusank 1997) or relational constraints imposed by such social or economic forces as class or lack of money (Allan 1998). In short, I will argue in this book that it is necessary to explore not only the interior, cognitive, and affective elements in a relationship but also the exterior context in which relaters lead their daily lives. I regard the simple and ordinary business of living as an important element of this context (Duck 1993a).

There is very little in everyday life that could not be relevant in some way to a person's experience and enjoyment of personal relationships, given the above remarks. One way of looking at it is to recognize that the sharing of close relationships involves the sharing of practical daily lives, not just feelings, and that lives are made up of all that humans think, feel, experience, and do (Duck 1990; Bolger and Kelleher 1993).

Moreover, relationships do not just happen in a vacuum: they occur in a context provided not only by cultural, social and economic factors (Allan 1998; Fitch 1998) but also by various human needs that relationships satisfy (Weiss 1998). All these forces direct relational behaviours, but so do exterior elements that impinge on people's choices and freedom to exercise them, such as the prevailing cultural rules (which, of course, can become internalized or accepted as 'obviously true'). To focus this a little, however, I shall identify three main areas of concern that seem to be especially relevant:

1 the interior – cognitive/emotional elements of individuals;
2 the exterior – factors and influences like time, economics, and culture;
3 other factors – such as individual skills at relating, the role of chance, opportunity and coincidence in relating.

INTERIOR NEEDS AND CONCERNS OF HUMAN BEINGS

Some people – very shy people, for example – don't actually like relating to other people much (Bradshaw 1998) and some people prefer solitude to company either as a general principle or at particular times of need. Sometimes everyone likes a bit of peace and quiet and sometimes we respect others' needs to withdraw from sociality (e.g., during bereavement or on honeymoon). So we should not begin thinking about relating to others as some universal desire. Nor should we make the mistake of seeing it as some deliriously besought goal that everyone wants to do all the time to the full extent of their being. Indeed as Bradshaw (1998) demonstrates, some high-shy people are successful at relating only if they have a person with them whom they know well and whose presence makes them feel comfortable or who acts as a social surrogate and, as it were, is sociable for both of them. Thus when this chapter starts to delve into the basis of relating to others, try to keep in mind that the general rules are always going to be too broad to cover every specific case or every particular way in which people choose to relate. One rather important additional reservation to bear in mind is that our 'standard belief' about the causes of love or friendship is probably totally wrong or at least overstated: I mean the assumption that love and friendship are the result of an individual's feelings or emotions. Let us explore this now.

We naturally assume that the most important factor in our relationships is whether we personally like, dislike, or feel neutral about the people we meet. It probably also occurs to us as natural that feelings would be the most important factor in the growth and development of relationships. However, this view is insufficient. For one thing, our feelings are affected by various human needs and social circumstances (cf. Wright 1985a, 1985b, for a list of the needs identified by his long and impressive research programme, discussed here in Chapter 3). For another, our knowledge structures or ways we think about relating may influence the sorts of relationship that we seek out and the reactions that we have to intimacy (Andersen 1993; Fletcher and Fitness 1993). Also McAdams (1988) showed that some groups of people have strong needs for warm, close interaction with others while some people do not, and that the two groups' friendships are patterned in ways that reflect those underlying needs. Latty-Mann and Davis (1996) indicate that persons' experiences in childhood attachments to their parents can influence the extent to which they seek or are satisfied with similar partners when they are themselves mature – whereas a previously much more common assumption in relationship research is that similar people *always* get on better. Furthermore, Putallaz *et al.* (1993) indicate that parents' memories of their own childhood influence the ways in which they choose to bring up their own children, either emphasizing things they enjoyed as children themselves or steering their children away from things they found unpleasant – a factor extending even to issues of whether they abuse their children or are violent in the home.

In short, even if we focus only on people's feelings towards others, these are not 'absolute' influences on relationships but depend on, and are influenced by, personality, memory, experience, cognitive structures, personal needs, explanatory styles, and past relational experiences. Furthermore, our feelings do not alone create relationships, for other reasons. For instance, we may feel that we like someone but may be uncertain about their corresponding feelings for us, so we decide not to act on our own feelings. Thus, Duck and Miell (1986) found that individuals starting relationships were very uncertain about their partner's feelings for them and tended to underestimate the stability of the relationship and their own role in it. It is as if people acted on the assumption that it is the other person who controls, and is responsible for the existence of, the relationship, and that if the other person changed his or her mind then the relationship would disintegrate, whatever they thought of it themselves. People saw others as their friends rather than claiming to be sure that they themselves were someone else's friend.

Alternatively we may fall deeply in love with someone but feel inhibited in showing it because of what our friends or colleagues – or even the law – might think about it (Allan 1993; Klein and Milardo 1993; Milardo and Allan 1997). Also we may feel that we want to develop a relationship but go about it in an unskilled way or be too shy to make the right moves in the right way (Miller 1996; Solomon and Samp 1998). These are some – only some – of the reasons why feelings alone are not enough to make relationships.

Another factor to consider in exploring the detailed and specific practicalities of daily life communication is the way in which they are driven by effort after meaning (Duck 1994a). Humans have a need for structure in life and a way of achieving this is by having projects to accomplish. Little (1984) has pointed out that we all have both mini-projects and maxi-projects that help to structure our lives. We may, for example, be concerned about petty, pressing matters like a need to tidy the house before guests arrive, or to get good grades on a class assignment. Alternatively, we may be focusing on a more impressive life project like 'Be a better friend to Linda' or 'Teach Gabriel to read' or 'Learn to express emotions to Ben' or 'Behave more assertively with Diane'. Such projects probably occupy a lot of cognitive capacity and intrude into our social concerns and social behaviour in ways that direct and influence what we do or think. For instance, the urgency of a small project may prevent us from taking long enough to deal with a friend's need for advice or help on a given occasion. Or our pressing thoughts and concerns may keep creeping into our conversation with a friend. Or anxieties about a project to purchase a car may affect the ways in which we happen to structure our time with friends during the day, or could influence the ways in which we choose to act in a given meeting with a new acquaintance (for instance, by preventing us from being very friendly and 'available'; Baxter et al. 1997).

As such, everyday projects obviously have an impact on our social and personal relationships both directly and indirectly. Although the possibility that they do so is rarely studied, such concerns are likely to be important specific motivations and direct influences on much of our social behaviour (Little 1984). They make up a large part of being human and, as such, go with us wherever we go and enter into all our social interactions.

Inclusion

A major project that we need to fulfil and for which we seek others' company is need for **inclusion** and acceptance (Weiss 1998). Needs of human beings for inclusion amount essentially to a need to be part of a social structure, a need to feel we belong (Baumeister and Leary 1995), a need to experience life as a part of a community or network of others, however small that community may be (Weiss 1998). Each of us has desires for membership of pairings, groups and networks, and a large part of our concern in friendship development is for establishment of such inclusion. Inclusion ratifies our identities as people (Duck *et al.* 1997a) – that is to say, it shows us that we are acceptable to other people in the things that we do, the ways that we think, the emotions that we feel, the concerns that we have and the solutions that we propose to problems in our own and others' lives (Duck 1994a; Duck *et al.* 1997b; Weiss 1998). Inclusion gives us a social value, the chance to evaluate ourselves by comparing ourselves and our reactions with other people and their reactions. Inclusion also gives us a chance to see ourselves as important to at least one other person in the world. To be included is to be accepted and to be accepted is (both implicitly and explicitly) to be approved. Exclusion is a social means of registering disapproval. It says, 'We don't want you; you're no good; you're not acceptable as a human being.' That is why it is painful to feel left out and why loneliness hurts so much: it conveys the message to the rejected or lonely person that he or she is not to be included, not to be accepted, not worth very much to anyone else (Tornstam 1992).

There are large research programmes that have investigated the differences between individuals in their need for inclusion or need for **affiliation** (e.g., Mehrabian and Ksionzky 1974; Brock *et al.* 1998) and it is clear that there are differences between people. For example, Goldstein and Rosenfeld (1969) found that neurotics, to a much greater extent than other people, find it difficult to tolerate dissimilarity in other people and find it stressful – at least to begin with – to affiliate with others who are not from the same background as themselves and who do not share the same attitudes: they find dissimilarity inordinately threatening in early encounters. It is also clear that there are effects of circumstances, with people generally preferring to be in the company of others when they are under stress (Schachter 1959). Such matters could well take up a whole chapter or take us into the issue of **social support** and its psychological nature (Hobfoll and Stokes 1988; Heller and Rook 1997; Sarason *et al.* 1997; Lyons *et al.* 1998). My purpose here is introductory rather than exhaustive, so I emphasize that my point is only that the need for inclusion is generally important to all of us, however that basic importance is affected by personal idiosyncrasies, ecological stress or circumstantial variation (Weiss 1998). Humans *like* relating to others.

Similarity

Another consequence of the uncertainties of social life is that we prefer, to a greater or lesser extent depending on personality style, similarity to dissimilarity (Duck 1994a). We generally have a preference for the familiar and normative over the unfamiliar though this makes life difficult for some people such as gays and lesbians who are often harried for being 'different' (Huston and Schwartz 1995). Yet similarity is not just a prefer-ence but something that gets enacted in practical life (Duck *et al.* 1997b) and from the 'field of availables' (that is all the people we encounter), we ultimately pick from a 'field of eligibles' (that is, the group of people who are realistic possible choices for us). Such a pool is already much filtered by social factors like economics and educational level: we tend, as a matter of social fact, to meet more people from our own economic, educational and religious groups. Thus Kerckhoff (1974) notes that married partners typically come from the same race, the same social class, the same reli-gion, the same socio-economic background, the same intelligence level, and the same educational context. It is even likely that persons will marry others who live within a very small distance from themselves (Fischer 1982; Blumstein and Schwartz 1983). Preference for the similar and the familiar over the rest manifests itself in the tendency to mix and associate with people from the same background as ourselves: we prefer other people with attitudes similar to our own, and we feel comfortable with people who share some of our characteristics like race, or socio-economic status (Kerckhoff 1974; Whitbeck and Hoyt 1994). It is axiomatic in research on friendship and relationships that we seek out others who have something in common with us, but it is not always recognized that this is probably based on our need for inclusion and our concerns that we be members of a community of equals (Weiss 1998), as well as on the results of daily cir-cumstances and social practices that tend to bring similar people together in similar places (Duck *et al.* 1997a).

Memory for social experience

Although social forces and practices of daily life serve people's needs, an individual's memory for social experience serves human needs too. The ways in which we remember social events, social interactions, friend-ships and relationships are important because memory not only records experience but also organizes it in ways that are personally relevant and meaningful (Umberson and Terling 1997; Grote and Frieze 1998). In our memories of relationship events we can make such memories into chains of grief once we lose a person as a partner (Harvey *et al.* 1995), or we can be selective in our memory of lovers' qualities, making them rosier than they really are (Hendrick and Hendrick 1993). Memory is not, as we often naively assume, purely 'photographic' but is organized actively in ways that conform to our social needs (Ross and Holmberg 1992). As Grote and Frieze (1998) have shown, even memory for love is often recalled in a way that is biased to be consistent with what we are presently doing, thinking or believing anyway – for instance, love is experienced as more 'selfless' later into a marriage but more 'erotic' early in a marriage. Moreover, Miell (1987) showed that the present state of a relationship influences our memory for its original development, with the recent history of the rela-tionship (specifically the last three days) tending to colour a person's recall of the more distant history of the relationship, such that pleasant recent experiences cause a rosy glow to suffuse the rest of the history. Also recent turbulence creates a more negatively loaded recall of the rest of the relationship. Felmlee (1995) noted that those things that romantic partners liked about one another can later be recalled as reasons for break-up – with the 'loyal reliable' person being later seen as 'tediously predictable' and 'unexciting', for example. When breaking off relationships we may be more likely to remember the negative side of the relationship and to de-emphasize the positive if we are keen to get out, but we may cling to the positive and de-emphasize the negative if we hope desperately to stay in (Harvey *et al.* 1986). In short, relational events are not perceived neutrally and are not remembered neutrally.

Memory for social experience thus serves a constructive purpose in shaping our relational lives (Duck and Sants 1983; Edwards and Middleton 1988; Duck 1994a). It does this in obvious ways as well as less obvious ones. For example, we swear never to make the same mistake as we did in a failed relationship *ever again* and so we structure our relational behaviour in ways calculated to avoid the same cycle, as Putallaz *et al.* (1993) showed for parents raising their children in ways intended to avoid the negative experiences the parents had when they were children. On the other hand, when partners reminisce, they can use memory as a symbolic form, a way of reminding one another of the strength of a relationship and its significance to both of them. Thus they are not just recalling its history but are positively celebrating and perhaps idealizing it (Werner *et al.* 1993). Moreover, Edwards and Middleton (1988) have shown that parents use photograph albums to help children reminisce about their early years and use that time as a point for emphasizing the role of others in the family, identifying key members of the group, re-emphasizing family ties and so forth, creating a sense of belonging rather than simply rehearsing memorable facts, people, and places. Thus memory for relationships serves to *create* the relationship in people's minds or to reinforce it, celebrate it, or to change its nature, not just to *record* it.

In short, from all of the above we have to conclude that friendship and relationships do not involve just simple emotions or special sorts of behaviour but also involve practical experiences that are embedded and 'situated' in our ordinary lives and memories (Bochner *et al.* 1997). The study of relating to others is thus an integral part of the study of human functioning in general since as people we take our human concerns and our regular styles of thinking and behaving into relationships with us when we go.

EXTERIOR FACTORS

Human life has a structure that comes not only from the cognitions, projects, and concerns of its participants but also from the social context in which we are embedded, which can even influence the form of relationships that are considered acceptable. Expressiveness of feelings has in modern times replaced instrumentality and service to others as the yardstick of intimacy, for example see Allan (1998). Whereas our ancestors forged relationships built upon mutual cooperation and assistance, today we expect people to pour out their souls instead. All of us are inevitably included in a human structure, a society, a civilization, a network of other people, a language system with its terminology and implications for describing friendship, a rule system indicating how to behave in relationships as different as friends and lovers (Allan 1993; Wood 1993), but also governed by laws about the conduct of relationships (e.g., you may not marry your grandparent nor neglect or endanger your children without incurring legal sanctions).

It is not possible to work, learn, eat, stay healthy, or do much else without other people, even if we wanted to. This social fact has two sides to it. We not only learn 'facts' or norms about relationships from associating with other people; we also learn how to use and interpret those facts and to operate on them to translate them into socially acceptable behaviours. Simmel (1950) pointed out that people often evaluate their relationships not just 'for themselves' but also relative to prevailing cultural norms and standards. These are available in a variety of sources such as newspapers or TV programmes or from gossiping with neighbours. We are liable to compare our own friendships or marriages with 'The 10 signs your relationship is in trouble' in a magazine, for example. Klein and Johnson (1997) and Klein and Milardo (1993) indicate the ways in which friends, neighbours and relatives can act as guardians of such social rules by exerting direct influences on the ways in which two people conduct their relationships, by directly admonishing them about it or giving advice. Even gossip (or fear of being gossiped about) can restrain or direct our relational behaviour, which we might all have first thought was a purely personal thing (Bergmann 1993; Duck 1998). Clearly then our membership of society affects our social life and necessitates our doing certain things, like talking to other people, and this shapes our behaviour in 'appropriate' ways, makes us accountable to others and makes us aware of, and responsive to, societal concerns and attitudes. These are not just abstracts but impinge on and influence our formation, maintenance, and termination of relationships: for instance, we are often concerned about 'what the neighbours or our parents will think' when we enter or dissolve relationships with particular people (Klein and Johnson 1997) and we take that into account over and above our own personal feelings.

Cultural context

We all know that we live in a culture but are as unaware of the fact that this experience affects us as we are aware that 'foreigners' *are* affected by one. Yet newspapers, TV, neighbours, friends and partners steer us to live our relationship with them in particular, culturally accepted, ways (Fitch 1998). Our location in a culture presents us with particular styles and types of acceptable relationships that may be quite different from those acceptable and familiar in other cultures. For instance, those of us who inhabit Western cultures would often say that we would not consider entering arranged marriages or marriages where we did not love our partner. However, Collins and Coltrane (1995) found that nearly 50 per cent of Americans marry for reasons *other than* love and Kephart (1967) found that over two-thirds of women then surveyed said that they would marry a man they did not love as long as everything else were satisfactory. Many of us would perhaps not recognize – or accept – that marriages are actually 'arranged' by religion, social position, wealth, class, opportunity and other things over which we have little control, even within our own culture. Nor is everyone aware that parentally arranged marriages in some cultures are gladly entered into, and are considered to be perfectly normal, natural relationships that are anticipated with pleasure.

There are many ways in which our culture or societal membership exposes us to 'proper' ways to conduct relationships (Allan 1993; Milardo and Allan 1997; Duck 1998). For instance, the media in our culture expose us to certain representations of relationships that are implicitly represented as desirable, acceptable, or preferable, compared to other forms of relationship. Soap operas and popular magazines alike display certain sorts of relationships rather than others (Duck 1998), implicitly give us examples of how these relationships should be conducted, and can even serve as models for the course and content of the relationships in our own lives. In an early consideration of the influence of media on our perception of relationships, Kidd (1975) examined popular magazines of the 1950s, 1960s and 1970s and researched the kinds of advice given about relationships. The typical style in the 1950s was one based on the implicit assumption that there is a single right or wrong way to conduct relationships and that persons with problems could be given specific and universally applicable advice on how to act in them. For instance, it was claimed that 'a man can feel kinship with the gods if his wife can make him believe he can cause a flowering within her' so the 'worthiest duplicity on earth' was for a woman to fake orgasms (Kidd 1975)! Further, readers of such magazines were regularly presented with problem scenarios such as 'What is this husband doing wrong?', 'How can this marriage be saved?', 'Where must a man have feminine traits?' and 'What does a wife's paycheck do to her marriage?' In such cases the outline of the problem would be presented and the readers asked to judge what should be done. A panel of experts would then provide *the* 'correct answer' and point out a few major steps that should be taken. The notion was that there could be one correct solution for all problems, irrespective of the individuals concerned.

By contrast, in the late 1960s, the same magazines were suggesting that the appropriate ways to solve relationship difficulties involved the couple negotiating its own solution to its own problem, communicating with one another, and openly expressing their feelings and emotions, rather than concealing them or – worse – faking them. In these later views, universal rules for solving relational problems were not endorsed (except for the notion that 'open communication is always good'). As we will see in Chapter 2, more recent work has confirmed and yet subtly amended these views, but the changes are readily influential on the conduct of relationships within that culture.

In addition to the ideas that we may unconsciously assimilate by reading magazines, many indications about relationships are available from television. For instance, many people model their own behaviour on the actions of players in soap operas, not only adopting their mannerisms but even taking on their styles of conducting relationships. Rubin *et al.* (1985) examined the possibility that lonely people might watch television in order to find out more about the proper way to conduct relationships, but found that lonely people watch more news programmes and fewer 'soaps' than do non-lonely persons. Such lonely persons have parasocial interaction with newscasters – that is to say, they verbally greet the newscaster, respond to sign-off comments, argue volubly with points made by the TV commentators – and even refuse to undress in the bedroom if the TV is on and a newscaster is talking to them! Cortez (1986) showed that some newscasters get letters asking for advice on the best colour to paint the viewer's living room, or reporting that the viewer will be going on holiday shortly and that the newscaster should not feel offended if the viewer is not watching during that week! It has also been shown that viewers prefer newscasters who act in a talkative and jovial manner with the other persons on the team, and that newscasters are preferred if they are slightly humorous and acknowledge and address other members of the team (Horton and Wohl 1956). Clearly, then, those of us in affluent Western societies obtain information about relationships from the media, and some people use media personalities as substitutes for 'real' friends.

Networks and the relationship of relationships

Such exterior cultural influences are important in themselves but so too are the influences that we derive from groups and our membership of them. Our lives are lived in communities – and communities influence their members (Milardo and Wellman 1992) both directly by the making of rules and laws (e.g., about who may marry whom) and indirectly through the social pressures inherent in our social interconnectedness with specific other people and the rules and norms for behaviour in various relational settings (Klein and Milardo 1993). Thus, our behaviour is likely to be influenced by our concerns over the moral reactions of colleagues to what we do. Societies and groups maintain these influences by such means as **gossip** – or fear of being gossiped about – and various forms of intervention in relationships whether by direct advice and admonishment or simply by 'being there' so that we are aware of their liability to make moral commentaries on our relational behaviour (Bergmann 1993; Duck 1998).

Our relationships do not happen in a vacuum and often have their origins created, or their limits set, in other relationships. Attraction is only quite rarely something that happens in a social vacuum. Parks and Adelman (1983) and Adelman (1987) have shown that lovers are often introduced by matchmakers or mutual friends. Also, our involvement in some relationships affects other relationships we have. For example, when we marry a person of our choice, we automatically become sons-in-law or daughters-in-law to specific people over whom we had no choice and vice versa: they are our in-laws because of their pre-existing relationship with our spouse. Young and Acitelli (1998) also show how experience in some relationships early in life influences our perception of other relationships later in life, specifically perceptions of other people. Using a probability sample of people who were in committed relationships, these authors found that secure individuals felt positively about their partners irrespective of marital status but insecure individuals perceived partners more positively as a function of level of public commitment (i.e., marriage). Finally, as Romeo and Juliet dramatically discovered, membership of a particular group, family or gang can restrict freedom of choice among other relationships: if you are a Montagu you may not marry a Capulet, however strong the mutual attraction. In sum, then, our membership in some relationships has mutual impact on other relationships in which we find ourselves (Dunn 1997); the circle of our acquaintances affects our opportunities to meet others, the range of knowledge to which we are exposed, our views of acceptability of certain types of behaviour, and our own evaluation of ourselves (Milardo and Allan 1997; Fuendeling 1998).

OTHER FACTORS

A final human element that influences relationships and our conduct of them as ordinary human beings is that they take place within the rest of our lives – where we may have a job or leisure interests, for example, that sometimes use up time that close partners may expect us to share with them. Another issue is that relationships occur in our life cycles and are affected by the influences that in turn affect us during the life cycle (Adams and Blieszner 1996; Bedford and Blieszner 1997). For one thing, this means that our immediate concerns for relationships change and develop as time passes, with older adult friendships being different from the friendships of younger people (Adams and Blieszner 1996). For example, a person's relationship with parents changes in nature across the life cycle (Stein 1993; Cooney 1997), as the two generations gradually change the balance of dependence on each other, parents eventually becoming dependent on their children instead of vice versa. The relationship needs of a newly married couple are different from those of a couple who have just had a first baby (Veroff et al. 1995), which in turn differ from those of a couple whose youngest child has just left home (Dickens and Perlman 1981). Thirty-year-old males seek more same-sex friendship patterns based on the workplace, while twenty-year-old males are more actively seeking cross-sex relationships outside the workplace, for example (Reisman 1981). The influences of the life cycle serve to direct and affect our relationships and our relationship choices in ways over and above personal emotional choices or preferences.

Other relevant categories of influence on relationships and the behaviours that we display in them are such things as personal skills in social contexts, shy people differing markedly from non-shy people not only in styles of relational performance but also in terms of means of attracting other people in the first place, as already noted (Bradshaw 1998). We cannot assume safely that all persons seek or accomplish friendships in the same way, or that everyone has equivalent needs or skills. These differences need to be explored (see Chapters 2 and 3 for further consideration of this point).

Finally, chance and coincidence also play a much underrated role in friendship and social relationships (Perlman 1986), since all relationships basically depend on the fortunate coincidence of the right sets of circumstances. Many 'perfect partners' just find that one lives in Bismarck, North Dakota and the other in Sydney, Australia, or good friends or partners may have to endure long-distance relationships that cannot be made to work through frequent face-to-face contact (Rohlfing 1995). Likewise, the 'ideal' other whom one meets and falls in love with on vacation may well be unable to join one when one returns home. Eiser and Ford (1995) found that 24 per cent of holidaymakers aged 16–29 engaged in casual sex at an English seaside resort, yet with a strong tendency towards indifference about a continuing or developing relationship after the holiday and Herold *et al.* (1998) confirmed a similar pattern for North American undergraduates on spring break. Recently research on long-distance email relationships (Lea and Spears 1995) has also greatly increased, and the ramifications of email relationships are just beginning to be examined and understood by means of direct questioning of the attitudes, behaviours and forms of communication used by people using 'chat-rooms' or MUDs (Multi-User Dimensions) and MOOs (Multi-User Dimensions, Object Oriented) (Parks and Roberts 1998).

When relationships work out, therefore, it is often because circumstances worked out favourably *in addition to the fact that* the partners liked one another. There are plenty of examples where a contextual set of circumstances conspired somehow to prevent an otherwise idyllic relationship from developing. Therefore we need to be aware of the role played by circumstances, society, timing, and the rhythms of daily life in relating to others (for example, using a diary log method, Duck *et al.* 1991 found that there is more conflict on a Wednesday than on other days of the week).

SUMMARY AND IMPLICATIONS FOR THE REST OF THE BOOK

I have tried to show that 'relating to others' is a much broader topic than it first appears. It was once conceived as being restricted to such issues as why we are initially attracted to someone else. It is particularly true that our 'first pass' views of relational activity are not really workable. For instance, the idea that intimacy is an individual characteristic or a simple relational feature has had to be reconsidered (Acitelli and Duck 1987; Prager and Buhrmester 1998). Researchers have opted for more interactively focused models that combine individual psychology with awareness of communicative behaviour (Reis and Shaver 1988). Our 'first pass' ideas will, as we go through the book, focus more on processes of relating to others and take account of the extent to which a relationship, like life itself, is always a form of unfinished business (Billig 1987; Duck 1990). The 'ongoingness' of relational life is also an important psychological frame for the way in which specific relational behaviours are conducted (Duck 1990) and this fact itself provides a set of avenues through which the social psychological, communicative, and sociological study of relationships has developed. Also, as I have emphasized, there is a continued effort to explore connections between early life experience of relationships and later life experience (Bartholomew 1993; Beinstein Miller 1993).

A full understanding of these issues would involve us in comprehending the contribution of many research disciplines other than psychology, but if one restricts oneself predominantly to social psychology then that too creates a broader enterprise than has previously been conceived (Fincham 1995). For example, many traditional areas of social psychology, such as persuasion and attitude change, are in fact based on relationships, since we make special dispensations when friends try to influence us, or we might be willing to do friends a favour where other people would have to persuade us hard. Duck (1998: Chapter 5) also explored relationship underpinnings of everyday persuasion – not how to change 'big' attitudes about nuclear war or smoking, but how to persuade a partner to 'get serious', for instance. Questions about attitude change can also concern everyday life behaviour ('how to make an enemy like us', for example (Wiseman and Duck 1995)), and attribution theory can be understood as dealing with such issues as 'how to help someone understand why a partner left them' (Frederickson 1995), or 'the role of **relationship awareness** in creating the sense of relationship' (Acitelli 1993)). The issue of the role of personality in friendship takes us further afield; it is not just about the way in which two personalities 'match up' on paper but how people with similar personalities make relationships *work*. Finally, influences of friendship systems and social networks are daily, practical, and interactive events, not special abstract occurrences that happen only at moments of crisis. Even a sense of others' reliable alliance is created from daily interaction, not from their reaction once a crisis actually happens (Leatham and Duck 1990). We could explore the rules of behaviour in relationships or the communication patterns that differentiate talk between friends from talk between strangers (Planalp and Benson 1992) and that takes us into the social psychology of language or into communication studies, where much is being done on such questions (Planalp and Garvin-Doxas 1994; Krauss and Fussell 1996).

I have also tried to show that recent approaches to the above topics are centrally concerned with the development of a new methodology for studying the advanced subject matter. As the work done in laboratories is supplemented by work with real couples (e.g., Acitelli *et al.* 1993), so too are experimental manipulations of hapless subjects being supplemented by ethnographic participant observations of life on the streets (Fitch 1998), studies of playfulness (Baxter 1992), everyday behaviour (Duck *et al.* 1991) and the real 'dirty hands' immersion in what is really going on out there (Allan 1998).

The latter approach recognizes the significance of the fact that relationships are things that people *do*, not just things they *have*. To paraphrase Karl Marx, people make their relationships but not in circumstances of their own choosing. As we will see later in the book, there are many ways in which people not only conduct but also celebrate their relationships, not only in practices like giving presents at birthdays, but even in the language forms and in rituals and in lots of little sorts of behaviours that reinforce the existence of the relationships day by day.

The study of friendship and relationships, then, far from being a small and narrow topic focused on attraction to strangers – as the research area was conceived 20 years ago (Berscheid and Hatfield 1978) – actually uses and develops much of social psychology, sociology, family studies, and interpersonal communication. One could employ almost all of the research in those disciplines to enhance our understanding of relating to others. Equally – and equally valuably – one could use much of the new research on human relationships to enrich our understanding of social psychology more generally in areas such as persuasion, altruism, group decision making, and social perception (Duck *et al.* 1997b). After all, what is the basis of social behaviour and interpersonal communication if it is not relationships with other people (Duck 1998), and what is the source of human happiness and misery if it is not to be found in our friendships and social relationships? You may recall that it was with precisely that issue that this chapter began.

ANNOTATED FURTHER READING

Canary, D. J. and Emmers-Sommer, T. (1997) *Sex and Gender Differences in Personal Relationships*. New York: Guilford, explores the evidence for and against the existence and prevalence of differences between men and women in relationships.

Duck, S. W. (1998) *Human Relationships* (3rd edition). London: Sage, is a supplementary textbook designed to fill out the gaps in standard social psychology textbooks, which typically do not devote enough attention to human relationships. It contains other chapters on persuasion, social psychology and health, and on family relationships.

Duck, S. W., Dindia, K., Ickes, W., Milardo, R. M., Mills, R. S. M. and Sarason, B. (1997) *The Handbook of Personal Relationships* (2nd edition). Chichester: Wiley, is the second edition of the only handbook of research in personal relationships. It contains some 30 chapters, covering such research areas as communication, social support, developmental psychology, social psychology, and sociology and family studies.

Hinde, R. A. (1979) *Towards Understanding Relationships*. London: Academic Press, is the text from which most people date the origin of the field of personal relationships. A classic account of the nature of relationships and of our needs in its study.

Prager, K. J. (1995) *The Psychology of Intimacy*. New York: Guilford, provides an interesting account of the nature of intimacy in a variety of settings and fills out the idea that intimacy is an emotion or a pattern of self-disclosure.

Werking, K. (1997) *Just good friends: cross-sex friendships*. New York: Guilford, offers a pioneering exploration of the nature of non-romantic relationships between the two sexes, an increasingly significant kind of relationship in many people's lives.

CONTEXTS OF RELATIONSHIPS

There are many ways of relating to others: we may be kin to some, casual acquaintances of others, close friends of some, the marital partner or steady date of one, the father/daughter/mother/son/sibling of others and the working colleague of a few. However we must not overlook the fact that these various instances of relating occur in a broader social and cultural context that recognizes and accepts certain sorts of relationships and ways of doing them while failing to recognize and accept others. For instance, in cultures that embrace Confucianism there are five named types of relationships, each exemplifying a particular quality:

1 father–son (closeness);
2 emperor–subject (right and duty);
3 husband–wife (distinctness);
4 elder–younger (order);
5 friend–friend (faithfulness).

Even in Western cultures certain relationships are acknowledged and others denied: for example marriages are not permitted between people of the age of six and there is no simple name for the relationship between the parents of an adult who remarries and the existing children of the person to whom the remarriage takes place (though Ganong and Coleman (1998) offer the term 'step-grandparenthood'). Also there are marked differences in the ways in which cultures and individuals count behaviours as 'intimate' (Register and Henley 1992), something that did not even receive attention in the 1988 edition of this book (and indeed the Berscheid *et al.* scale to measure closeness was not published until 1989). Furthermore, as Chapter 1 indicated, we are surrounded by insistent messages that tell us how to be good at those relationships that a given culture recognizes. Not only do childhood fairy tales tell us how romances are to be idealized, but friends and neighbours offer their guidance and advice when we ask for it – and sometimes when we do not. In addition, the direct effects of the social embeddedness of any dyadic relationship are also relevant (Klein and Milardo 1993); a group of people in a community or network can affect the shaping of marital conflict (or its resolution) by commenting and advising on it. Likewise, the network has an impact on dyadic conduct, or groups and clique memberships affect adolescent friendship choice and conduct (La Gaipa 1982). Furthermore some 60 per cent of romantic partners are introduced to one another not by the exercise of open 'free choice' but by the intervention of mutual acquaintances or third parties. This is not the contextless 'attraction' celebrated in films and in the early attraction literature. Decontextualized 'attraction' does not often happen and instead the connections between group and dyadic activity are at least as important as individual social judgement alone.

However, Chapter 1 also began to develop two other notions that built on the implications of this latter point: (a) the significance of the performance of relationships by *doing* them; (b) the strains and conflicts between different needs or demands in relationships – whether at the level of competing loyalties towards different relationships (to spend time with kids or to be alone with spouse?) or at the level of conflicts between different sorts of relationships – for example, the problems of managing a marriage in the context of other relationships and duties at work, a problem increasingly faced by dual career couples (Zvonkovic *et al.* 1994).

Researchers have looked at many sorts of voluntary relationships including relationships of blended families (Coleman and Ganong 1995); cross-sex non-romantic friendship (Werking 1997); romantic or friendly relationships in the workplace (Dillard and Miller 1988; Zorn 1995); relationships between cooperative neighbours (O'Connell 1984); relationships between prisoners and guards (Hepburn and Crepin 1984); sibling relationships (Dunn 1996); parents and children influencing each other (Pettit and Lollis 1997); children relating to other children (French and Underwood 1996); and adults' relationships with their parents (Lewis and Lin 1996); to say nothing of the vast literature on various types of family relationships (Fisher 1996). These cannot all be covered here in the space allowed and I will focus on voluntary intimate relationships, often with a hint of romance. However, just as a wicked thought to bear in mind for later, you might like to consider whether marriage is a voluntary relationship or not. The *choice to marry* is voluntary, presumably, but once the marriage is a few years old, it is in reality a much less 'voluntary' relationship than one might think, since getting out of it is attended with a great deal of social and legal baggage. Thus when we talk about 'voluntary relationships', we need to recognize not only that the exercise of apparently free choice is always tempered by the social realities and constraints that surround us, but also that, once exercised, some choices are then disabled and cannot be easily or straightforwardly remade. To that extent, therefore, their consequences become non-voluntary.

Another point to bear in mind as we become more sophisticated about relating to others is the assumption that two people in the same relationship experience it equivalently. We typically tend to assume that there is equivalence in the **voluntariness** of the two partners or equivalence of intimacy between partners or equivalence of knowledge about the partners (indeed the very measuring of 'the' intimacy level in a relationship presumes that sort of equivalence). In fact, however, a parent–child relationship, for example, is much less voluntary for the child than for the parent – for instance, a parent who leaves a child can be sued for support money but cannot be forced back into the home, whereas children who run away usually can be, if caught. If nothing else, this example tells us that we need to be thoughtful about assuming that there is equivalence of any of these things in any relationship and it alerts us to the important difference in power, information, and feeling between partners in the same relationship, in different social contexts. The important point behind this, however, is that relationships are not objective and neither is intimacy level of a relationship, nor are many of the other concepts that social scientists would like to assume in order to measure them easily. Of course it would make our jobs easier if they were objectified and immovable, just as it is easier to study animals staked out on a slab in a biology lab. However, at least as exacting is the biological or ethological/behavioural observation work that goes into studying animals or relationships in living form in their natural habitats and circumstances. It is *because* it is more difficult to study something fluid and non-objective that this is also a more exciting place for social psychology to sharpen its tools and hone its techniques.

Even so, there was early work attempting to objectify the differences between types of voluntary intimate relationships. For example, Davis and Todd (1985) report on a procedure for classifying personal relationships according to the **prototypes** or 'paradigm case formulations' that common folk – and other theorists – use to distinguish between stages or types of relationships in the ideal case (for example the extent to which a particular relationship involves acceptance, trust, confiding, or support). Argyle and Henderson (1984) believed that certain universal 'maintenance' rules apply to all relationships (e.g., 'respect other's privacy') and special interpersonal reward rules apply to intimate relationships (e.g., 'express affection').

More recent work, however, has indicated that it is not that simple. Kamo (1993) compared relationships in the USA and Japan and found that different ideals and conceptions of a relationship as fundamental as marriage existed in the two countries. Accordingly partners' judgements of their marital satisfaction matched with their judgements of their position relative to their cultural ideal, not relative to some 'absolute' or universal rules. Baxter and Montgomery (1996) also note that simple rules about privacy actually do not work simply, since relationships are usually hotbeds of tension between partners' wishes for 'openness' when they also have needs for 'privacy', or for 'autonomy' when they also want to be 'connected and interdependent'. Vonk and van Nobelen (1993) even found that people do not describe their 'self' in universal ways in relationships but modify the roles they use to expound self according to whether the partner is female or male. Lin and Rusbult (1995) even found that the notion of 'commitment' was expressed differently in Taiwan and the USA, and in cross-sex as compared to dating relationships.

Thus old schemes for classifying and distinguishing relationships are historically important but limited ways to look at the dynamics of relationships. Indeed they often were unsuccessful in taking into account such basic 'contextual' issues as race (Adelmann *et al.* 1996; Fujino 1997) or gender (Demo and Allen 1996) or age (Aldous 1996; Kovach and Robinson 1996; Folwell *et al.* 1997), or whether the relationships were sexual or platonic (Kaplan and Keys 1997; Werking 1997). As soon as work on relational dynamics developed vigorously in the 1990s, researchers became more and more aware of the subtle differences created within different contexts (Duck 1993a; Fehr 1993). Regan *et al.* (1998) conducted a prototype analysis to explore men's and women's cognitions (knowledge and beliefs) about the nature of romantic love. The most commonly generated characteristics were trust, sexual attraction/desire, and acceptance/tolerance. They found that sexual desire was one of the prototypical features of love that endured across contexts but also noted that the prototype was falsely recognized by some subjects given different circumstances to consider. Further, as Spitzberg (1993) importantly notes, behaviours like respecting privacy or showing affection are not absolutely appropriate in themselves but only in context and in relation to the actions of the partner. Sometimes even telling lies is a *good* relational behaviour (especially such examples as being polite about another person's terrible new clothes, or lying about the nature of a forthcoming meeting arranged with one's partner in order to conceal a birthday or anniversary surprise). My prediction for the next decade is that the qualification of apparently general rules for relating to others will become more significantly developed in the scholarly work as researchers strive to understand context and the ways in which it modifies the broad generalities we have accumulated in the research until now.

MEETING PEOPLE

However many types of relationships there may be, and however general rules should be qualified, they all start in the same broad way – as a meeting between strangers. This is even, in some special sense, true for parent–child relationships, but I will focus here mostly on friendships. A task for researchers has been to discover why it is that some pairs become friends while numerous other first meetings do not develop into a friendship. (Interestingly, as Delia (1980) pointed out in a neglected but very insightful paper, researchers have typically focused much less on the equally interesting fact that most meetings do *not* develop into intimate relationships and that the trajectory for most relationships is to *non*-intimacy – for example, with neighbours, shop assistants we meet regularly and even some workmates.) One interesting topic for readers and researchers to ponder would thus be an exploration of the ways in which we keep people at a distance or are strategic in sapping and resisting the growth of intimacy. Clearly, we somehow not only choose to allow some potential relationships to develop while nixing others, but we also select our friends from the range of people that we meet – and so the real questions for us here are, how and why do we choose to develop relationships with some people and not others?

By means of the mechanisms outlined in Chapter 1, some choices are taken for us by the pre-selecting that practical circumstances and the realities of everyday life actually do for us to reduce the 'field of availables' (Duck 1997b) – that is to say, the range or field of persons who are really available for us to meet is actually constrained by the realities of life: we normally do not look for deep relationships with waiters or check-out clerks because we might reasonably expect that it will not work out in most cases; we don't try to date every wonderful person we meet because they may not accept and we'd feel bad, or because we may already have a steady partner. There is considerable pre-selection, in any culture, of the sorts and types of people that we meet or become aware of or tend to 'regard' or treat as realistic possibilities for relationships (Rodin 1982). As noted in Chapter 1, they are mostly from our own race, our own religion, socio-economic group, intelligence level and educational background and for various reasons those are also the people that we find most initially attractive as a group. (One reason for this fact is that similarity of such things makes communication easier since we share common assumptions; another reason is that similarity is 'simply reassuring'; a third is that we meet basically similar people more often because of the way society is structured; Duck *et al.* 1997a.) So our own personal choices have less to do with attraction at that point than do other forces over which we have no control. Equally we are more likely to be interested in being attracted to other people in some contexts rather than others (for example we are more 'affiliative' and inclined to seek others' company when we are anxious (Schachter 1959); when we have just left a close relationship or moved to a new neighbourhood (Shaver *et al.* 1985); when aged between about 16 and about 26 (Bailey 1988); when we are not in a hurry (Perlman 1986); if we can afford the expenses of conviviality like drinks and food (Allan 1998); and if the relationship is not felt to be in need of cautious public conduct in front of other people, as is felt by some gays and lesbians (Nardi and Sherrod 1994)). Also of course the political and cultural context in some societies can influence the occurrence of some behaviours we take to be necessary for relationships, such as open self-disclosure. Goodwin (1995) indicates how self-disclosure is affected by political circumstances and the social context created by concern that others might report one's privately expressed views, whereas Mamali (1996) also notes that fear of betrayal in communist societies had a frequently chilling effect on the behaviours that we otherwise take for granted as signals of intimacy, like honest discussion, and the expression of personal vulnerabilities.

Also, although face-to-face meetings will be the focus of discussion here, do not overlook the fact that they are by no means necessary preliminaries to acquainting nor the only way in which we become aware of others. Many relationships are conducted at long distance via telephone or correspondence or all-too-infrequent face-to-face meetings (Guldner and Swensen 1995). Increasingly often these days, relationships begin, or are conducted, on email (Lea and Spears 1995) and Parks and Roberts (1998) have discussed the ways in which this occurs through virtual environments on the Internet, like MOOs (Multi-User Dimensions, Object Oriented). In a study based on self-reports of 235 Internet respondents describing their chat room use and 155 also completing a survey on off-line relationships, Parks and Roberts (1998) found that almost 94 per cent of surveyed Internet users had formed ongoing personal relationships using MOOs, some of which relationships had led ultimately to face-to-face interaction. Some people may benefit from use of email as a way to overcome shyness, lack of access to suitable pools of others (e.g., because of living in a very small town or working alone), lack of time, stigmata (like handicaps or overweight), or special needs (such as alternative life-styles). Others use personal ads or video-dating techniques for getting to meet people in ways that weed out certain types of other people and construct a smaller **'field of eligibles'** (the group of *suitable* rather than merely 'available' people) as noted in Chapter 1 (Hatala *et al.* 1998). These are modern-day technological equivalents of the introduction by means of visiting cards and third parties that was customary a hundred years ago (Rothman 1984). By all of these means, both obvious and non-obvious, technological and basic, social and personal, our freedom of choice may be restricted or expanded or changed for good or ill.

Given such, often unrealized or unnoticed, constraints on or expansions of our choices, what are the answers to the questions of what makes us attracted to others from among the whole set of people who are our **'field of availables'**? What makes them specifically members of the much smaller field of suitable people ('field of eligibles'), or out of that smaller field the people we actually want to get to know (**'field of desirables'**)? In the popular culture, there are several dozen different and competing answers to such questions, ranging from 'dress for success' through 'opposites attract' and 'birds of a feather flock together' to 'beauty is only skin deep' and 'it's not what you say but the way that you say it'. Each of us probably cherishes a different type of answer to the questions, and if you want a review of this material (now bypassed to a very large extent by the focus on new issues to do with the conduct of relationships in everyday life), the first edition of this book provided one (Duck 1988). Chapter 2 of that book reviews the research on physical appearance and attraction and although good work on those issues is still being done (e.g., the discussion by Clark *et al.* (1998) of the effects of weight on attractiveness), its importance in understanding relating to others is now painted on a broader canvas. New work looks at the practical conduct of relationships, not at the relatively static factors once thought to cause them to come into existence.

IS BEAUTY ONLY SKIN DEEP?

All the same, one cannot escape the force of the assumption that attraction is somehow related to attractiveness! It feels as if the more physically attractive people are 'really' more attractive generally. Questions about the effects of beauty have concerned the human species for thousands of years and we still have the sneaking suspicion that the initial cause of attraction is physical appearance (Kenrick and Trost 1997). Recent theorists are less concerned with the old issues of listing the cues that make someone physically attractive than they are with the reasons why physical attraction would matter at all. Kenrick and Trost (1997) carefully review the evidence that physical cues (and other relational behaviours) are attractive or consequential because of their evolutionary significance – for example, those who are regarded as physically attractive are typically those who have the characteristics that would guarantee breeding success.

Twenty years of research have shown that the idea that beauty has a positive effect on relationships with other people is only partly true, but as the first edition of this book lamented, much of the work on this topic was done using photographs, not the real decisions of everyday life where physically attractive people may have other commitments or be inadequate at social interaction or may be smelly/conceited/stupid or may be socially inaccessible to those who would choose them if they could (cf. Romeo and Juliet). When real people are studied and rated while interacting with strangers (as Stiles *et al.* (1996) did using an analysis of videotapes of 38 previously unacquainted mixed-sex dyads who met in a waiting room and were unobtrusively observed as they interacted) the interactions of physically attractive persons were rated as more disclosing, intimate and satisfying than those of unattractive people – whether or not the attractive people were interacting with another attractive person.

Other studies typically evaluate physical attractiveness by means of facial characteristics rather than other parts of the body, although some of the earliest systematic work on the topic of beauty (see Perrin 1921) distinguished between **static beauty** (and, incidentally, included ratings of attractiveness based on nails and teeth) and **dynamic beauty**, in terms of 'nice' behaviour. There have nevertheless been studies where silhouettes of whole bodies were rated for attractiveness (e.g., Beck *et al.* 1976) from which it is found, for example, that women prefer, in those circumstances at least, men with firm, prominent buttocks and large chests. However, a questionnaire survey of some American psychology students (Franzoi and Herzog 1987) found that body shape as a whole is relevant to both men's and women's ratings of physical attractiveness, with upper body shape being most important in judgements about men and overall weight being most important in judgements about women. In an impressive variation on this theme, Alicke *et al.* (1986) created composite slides from faces and bodies photographed during two summers at a swimming pool (the kind of scientific research job we would all like to have). They were able to create slides with attractive bodies and unattractive faces, the same attractive body with an attractive face, and so on, by means of photographic processing techniques. Their study then proceeded by showing the slides to an audience of subjects who rated them and showed that faces affected ratings of intelligence, sociability and morality while bodies influenced ratings only of sociability and intelligence!

Given the above strong hints about the difficulty of investigating the question realistically, it nevertheless seems entirely probable, on first sight, that the more physically attractive members of the community will also be the more attractive socially, however unfair or unpalatable this assumption may be from the point of view of social democracy (Berscheid 1981). All the same, we have all met physically attractive people with the intelligence and personality of a couch, and we all know that the way one can relate to such persons is more important to satisfaction in a relationship than is their outward appearance alone, at least if one is looking for a long-term relationship.

To accept that beauty creates long-term success in relationships, even if it does increase a person's social opportunities, is not very appealing or complete. Many people react negatively to beautiful people, envying them or resenting them or fearing to approach and invite them into relationships because it is assumed that they are involved in lots of satisfying relationships already or have higher standards and will be more rejecting. This belief seems to be unjustified in reality, however, for Reis *et al.* (1980) have shown that the level of a woman's physical attractiveness is not predictive of her level of social participation. Furthermore, as I argued in the first edition (Duck 1988), relationships are not created by the mere 'chemistry of partner attributes' – i.e., they do not spring into life from the mere mixing together of positively valued social attributes, such as beauty or attractive personality. Instead, relating to others involves interaction and social processes that can override the effects of initially positive responses to superficial characteristics or immediate aesthetic reactions to external appearance. What physical attractiveness may do, however, is influence the range of persons who regard themselves as available to us (and vice versa) and there is research suggesting (however undesirable the fact is) the relative importance to women of their own physical attractiveness, both in the short and the long term (Freedman 1986). However, other research shows that in longer term real-life relationships, physical attractiveness seems to have a greater effect on men's relationships than on women's (Reis *et al.* 1980). The research taken as a whole seems to show that it works mostly at the point when preferences are expressed, specifically in the case of date selection in a laboratory study. Neither is the (assumed) effect of attractiveness on long-term relationships fully supported by other parts of common sense: most people seem to believe that physical attraction is only a little relevant to our choices of friendships and dating partners, but that, beyond that, it is personality and attitudes that account for success, stability, companionship and depth in relationships. It would be extremely unflattering to hold the belief that even if people do make choices on the basis of others' appearance alone, they also let the whole course of their relationships be dictated by such a factor.

LOOKING BENEATH THE SURFACE

Most of us assume, therefore, that there is more to life and relationships than physical attractiveness – for instance, that rich and successful people or highly intelligent ones will be more attractive than their opposites, whether or not they are physically attractive. Most social psychological research assumes that the whole panoply of a person's attributes, reward value and negative qualities will be brought to bear on the assessment of their ultimate social value and worth, even if particular attributes get mentioned more and attended to more often in the dating scene. For instance, recent work assumes that people are attractive because of what the attractive cues *mean* rather than how they look (Duck 1994a), or how the attractive cues lead to inferences about other unobservable cues, or how they lead to certain sorts of behaviours in relationships that are enjoyable (Burleson *et al.* 1996) or carry positive implications for the later development of the relationship (Acitelli *et al.* 1993).

In some intriguing work on the advertisements that people place in the personal columns of newspapers, several researchers have examined the kinds of 'advantages' that advertisers proclaim themselves to have in the partnership stakes. As Lynn and Bolig (1985) noted, this way of meeting partners is increasingly respectable and more frequently used nowadays than it once was, and Hatala *et al.* (1998) confirm that it is widely used by would-be daters who are gay or HIV positive. We should note, in caution, that the method is used more by middle-class, white 'yuppies' who can afford to place such ads or join dating agencies and we need to be cautious in generalizing too broadly. Indeed Goodwin (1990) showed that, at least in a study of a British population, members of dating agencies had a higher than average educational level with higher status jobs. They also had lower social skills.

Cameron *et al.* (1977) and Harrison and Saeed (1977) investigated the kinds of statement made by men and women who placed ads. Their research questions were: What do advertisers note as their best 'selling points'? Are men and women likely to advertise the same sorts of advantages? Rasmussen *et al.* (1998) found that both heterosexual and homosexual advertisers basically looked first for partners within the same range of age as themselves. Cameron *et al.* (1977), however, had found a remarkable tendency for advertisers' other claims and requests to conform to cultural role expectations then in force: that is, men tended to stress status as an attractive characteristic, while women mentioned their appearance more often. Harrison and Saeed (1977), on the other hand, found that women were very likely to seek financial security, to stress the need for sincerity and genuineness in replies and to ask for dates with men older than themselves. Men usually asked for attractive partners who were younger than themselves and who were looking for a long-term relationship such as marriage. Lynn and Bolig (1985) indicated that women made more references to the personality traits, education and careers of themselves and their prospective partner, while men mentioned physical appearance and interests or activities that they enjoyed.

In the market place for setting up meetings with strangers, then, personal advertisers clearly play towards cultural beliefs

1 that certain features of themselves are more relevant to attraction than others;
2 that these features are related to age, physical attractiveness, and wealth; and
3 that these are basically predictable from the traditional norms held in a society about the relative gendering characteristics of 'men' and 'women'.

Hendrick (1988) regards the particular traits of 'masculinity' and 'femininity' (or 'androgyny' – a mixture of the two) as self-ascribed qualities that are functional for the initiation of relationships – making it feel to the individual that it is either 'appropriate' or 'inappropriate' to take the initiative in relating or to 'offer' certain properties or qualities in relationships. Thus it would be likely that men who feel that they are 'masculine' and women who feel that they are 'feminine' would be more likely than androgynous individuals to advertise themselves in terms conforming to sex stereotypes and would be less likely to mention characteristics atypical of their ascribed sex: for example, we might predict that they would be likely to mention their appearance if they happen to conform to the male–female stereotype physically. Indeed, Koestner and Wheeler (1988) indicated that, at least in personal ads, the two sexes tend to 'offer' the attributes that popular culture suggests will be attractive to the other sex. Women 'offer' slimness and physical attractiveness and 'seek' taller men, for instance, while men 'seek' women who are slim and shorter than themselves, while they 'offer' their own height and social status in such ads.

Are such things as outward appearance, wealth, status and age *really* more important to most people than are personal qualities? We should recognize the special nature of the situation here, though, since advertisers have to present their positive side in a way that is both easy to assimilate and economical in terms of space. What is actually going on is that such needs encourage people to play concisely towards cultural norms and stereotypes. On the whole people get plenty of messages from their culture about things that matter in relating to others, and so they develop reasonably clear ideas about the sorts of cues that should be mentioned in ads, because they know about the values placed by their culture on certain cues relative to other cues.

CULTURAL AND NETWORK CONTEXTS

Although we may be tempted to think of cultures as evident only in *other* people (the French, Filipinos, 'foreigners'), the temptation is simplistic. We are all in, and of, a culture. Equally meretricious is the idea that a culture is an abstraction that has no real parameters; in fact 'the culture' (in the abstract) vigorously reinforces itself through the activities, opinions, and moral sanctions of those we know and trust. Friends, spouses and – most of all – in-laws tell us how to 'do' our relationships, whether by direct advice or by gossip, by playing on our fear of being gossiped about or through the general moral accountability that comes with being a member of a society. We have to account to others for what we do (Shotter 1993), even in personal relationships (Klein and Milardo 1993; Klein and Johnson 1997).

Through activities of unseen significance such as gossip (Bergmann 1993), societies reinforce certain forms of relational behaviour as against others – for example, no-one gossips about someone whose marriage is perfect and conducted honourably, though people frequently gossip about others who conduct relationships against moral conventions ('I hear he's having an affair . . . !'). Although it is easy to overlook the significance of the quiet ways in which such forces operate, they do work in everyday life very powerfully (Duck 1998) and gossip is a very strong way of enforcing certain types of behaviour (Bergmann 1993). A particular force is the activity of those we know best: friends, family, and neighbours. As Klein and

Milardo (1993) and Klein and Johnson (1997) indicate, relatives and friends reinforce the ways in which a relationship 'should' be conducted. Individuals often consult friends and confidants about their relationships and although it feels to us as if we are simply asking advice, the received advice is very likely to reinforce cultural norms (Fitch 1998). A person's network therefore serves not only to support a person in times of stress (Sarason *et al.* 1997) or to provide comforts of relationships and association in the rest of life (Leatham and Duck 1990), but also to reinforce norms of behaviour and act as society's secret guardian of behaviour, reinforcing what is expected and discovering what is not. Indeed Baxter and Widenmann (1993) conducted retrospective interviews with 101 university-level participants and showed that people sometimes conceal their romantic relationships from others in their network – or at least consider carefully whether to reveal such relationships to the network. Thus our nearest and dearest reinforce certain styles of behaviour and discourage others (Billig *et al.* 1988). Although we serve the same function for our own friends and may perhaps prefer to deny it, we also reinforce their behaviour by reifying the ideology of friendship, dating, or marriage that our culture prefers. Just as all politics are local, so all cultures are locally owned and operated. Culture works through the people we know and meet.

Even within a particular culture there exist varieties of acceptable forms of relationship based on, for example, sex (Canary and Emmers-Sommer 1997) or race (Gaines and Ickes 1997) or economics (Allan 1993). As Allan (1993, 1995, 1998) points out, the ways in which human beings conduct their relationships are shaped by their economic circumstances and are not the result of pure choice. For example, those with relatively abundant finances can entertain other people at their homes, which are probably quite spacious and well furnished, provide their guests with dinners and fine wines, play sophisticated music on the CD player in the background and provide a place for the guests to park the car, whereas those with modest resources cannot do any of this. Thus, Allan (1995, 1998) argues that wealthier individuals tend to 'perform' their relationships within the home, arranging meetings with friends to occur there, whereas those with lower or marginal economic resources tend to perform their friendships in public places (such as bars or pubs). Although this seems on the face of it to be a relatively small point in some ways, it is in fact fundamental because the places in which relationships are carried out will clearly have effects on the ways in which they are carried out and developed. As people having affairs have been known to report (Weiss 1998), the unavailability of private space for performing intimacy can become a management issue that scuppers the relationship, for example, and those in long-distance relationships regularly report that the absence of a place to have face-to-face interactions is a strain (Rohlfing 1995; Sahlstein 1998).

Allan (1998) goes beyond these observations to make the point that the very form and nature of friendship in different economic groups can be quite acutely different as a function of the facilitation or difficulties experienced as a result of financial circumstances and their consequences. The broader role of place in the performance of relationships is a well-established point and the place itself shapes the way in which the relationship is experienced and celebrated (Werner *et al.* 1993). This point also connects to the ways in which the social network knows about and acquires evidence or opportunity for moral assessment of relationships: if relationships are done in public places then other people can see them and hence opportunities for concealment are reduced in those persons with fewer economic resources (hence the growth of the role of the car – specifically the back seat – in the conduct of illicit relationships in recent times; Bailey 1988!).

Although all these embedding influences and circumstances surround our choices of partners and offer guidance on the workings of relationships at some point, the issue still appears to comes down to individual exercise of choice or preference, and then to exercise of that choice in the practical reality of relational conduct. Perhaps it is more likely that personality characteristics and attitudes – the depth of a person's humanity – are the real key to success in attracting strangers into relationships because they predict such behaviour in the down and dirty real lives of partners. How well does that idea work as an explanation of attraction?

BEYOND THE OUTER LIMITS

The first edition of this book described the older research on the idea that similarity of attitudes might create positive feelings in partners as an appealing one that generated a lot of research (Byrne 1997). In essence, it provides empirical support for the view that when dissimilarity of attitudes is rewarding – for example when the similar person is normal, and sensible, and holds rare attitudes with which we agree – then we will find similarity to that person attractive in proportion to the reinforcement value that the attitudes provide (Byrne 1997; Duck 1998). Obviously we like others to be somewhat similar to ourselves – but not to share our faults – although few of us would want our friends to be exact replicas of ourselves in all respects. The real question is whether such matching of attitudes or personality really matters in the functioning of relationships. Historically research on attraction tells us that it matters. In order to understand why it matters and when it doesn't, we need to look more deeply at what such similarity *means*.

Some types of personalities are thought to be more attractive than others even before we see how the two personalities of the separate relational partners intertwine for good or ill (Crohan 1992, 1996). For example, our culture values outgoing sociability rather than shyness, and for this reason extroversion is regarded more favourably than introversion. Thus extroverted strangers are rated as more attractive partners than are introverted ones (Hendrick and Brown 1971), or secure ones are rated more attractive than insecure ones (Latty-Mann and Davis 1996). This is a general judgement of extrovert/introvert personalities reached by observers who have not interacted with the specific person and it is based only on the reading of some personality scales completed by the individual – a strictly one-sided set of circumstances. The task there is comparable to showing a person a photograph of someone else and asking what the viewer thinks of the person – and just as misleading. Nevertheless we should bear in mind that on first sighting or first encounter we are unable to process the 'depth' of someone's personality and so we have to focus on surface appearances. Thus, extroverts are likely to be rated as more attractive than introverts if we take simple measures of *initial* attraction. If we explore the issue more thoroughly, then we find that such general descriptions of a person are less important, as an acquaintanceship proceeds, than are behaviours and practical realities of working on a relationship (Duck 1994a). Partners will undoubtedly get more concerned with the depth of one another's personality structure and attitudes as time goes by – it is what 'getting to know someone' really means in everyday parlance. They will also start to consider the ways in which the two persons' personality and attitude structure match up together (Duck and Craig 1978) – whether or not the partners are similar, for example, or whether the two of them can work out a way to get along specifically, independently of the type of personality that each has.

Even if such research primarily focuses us on the effects of personal characteristics upon attraction to others, it has also recently placed such cues in the context of cultural prototypes or schemas for interpretation. For example, a particular shape of face is not itself attractive unless a cultural schema defining 'attractiveness' says it is (Andersen 1993), and we have only to look at the film stars thought to be stunningly attractive in the 1920s to realize that schemas of beauty and attractiveness change over time even within cultures. Thus a person's attractiveness as a basis for relating to others can be understood not in absolute terms but only relative to some cultural prototypes or some personal meaning system that makes that particular item 'attractive' in those circumstances at that time to that person. Likewise characteristics such as loyalty and other features felt to be lovable are so only relative to a cultural prototype and a person's own schema at the time (Planalp 1985; Fehr 1993). Indeed as Felmlee (1995) showed, the same person can describe the same characteristics of the same target person as attractive *and* as flaws, depending on how their relationship with the target is going at the time. When we are falling in love with someone, we see their reliability as an asset and their unpredictability as exciting, but when we are falling out with them the reliability is by then described as 'boringness' and the unpredictability as 'irresponsibility'.

We would be unwise, then, to see personality simply as pure information about someone else; the independent personalities of the two individuals cannot simply be matchable in the absence of any information about their interaction together as people (i.e., their success in relationships cannot be predictable from knowledge of them as individual personalities). Also the different layers of personality are, at best, differently relevant over the term of an acquaintanceship (Duck and Craig 1978; Duck 1990). The most significant role over time is played by our evaluation and experience of the other person's reactions towards us. These reactions depend on and are influenced by the long-term conduct of the relationship and partners' attempts to make the relationships work. Ruvolo (1998), for example, examined the well-being and general happiness of individuals from 317 newly-wed couples (161 African American couples, 155 white couples) in the first year of marriage and again in the second year. She found that the higher a person's well-being at an early point in marriage, the more likely it was that the partner would have higher well-being at a later time.

These important contexts – whether social, personal, or temporal – for the previous research on the absolute value of certain cues to attraction are significant and important. Researchers have in the last ten years become much more sophisticated about the relationship of physical attraction, personality and attitudes, in the abstract, to the *meaning* of physical attractiveness, personality and attitudes in the everyday life functioning of relationships. The fact that someone is good-looking does not mean you will find them to be a good partner: in any case, the person may already have a partner. Thus in contextualizing relationships instead of focusing on the hopes, cognitions and feelings of one person out of two, the research of recent years has at least gone some of the way towards a more complex depiction of the everyday realities of relating to others.

SUMMARY

This chapter has placed context around the ways in which relating to others occurs in real life within a vibrant social network of interactions with real other people – people we know. As such it supplements and gives perspective to older studies on physical attractiveness, personality, or attitudes as elements of persons that were once thought to 'make them attractive' or else 'make relationships happen'. Something may have been learned from the older studies on such matters as these though not probably as much as was (and still sometimes is) claimed for them in terms of their implications for understanding fundamental human sociality. All too often the reaction of students to a photograph, an attractive laboratory assistant, or the information on a personality questionnaire was used as the basis for far-reaching claims about the basis of friendship or relationship satisfaction or endurance of personal relationships. Only slowly has the appropriate caution about such specificities begun to come more into evidence.

ANNOTATED FURTHER READING

Allan, G. A. (1998) Friendship, sociology and social structure. *Journal of Social and Personal Relationships*, 15, 685–702, offers a fascinating analysis of the ways in which economic and social structural circumstances influence the nature and conduct of friendship.

Byrne, D. (1997) An overview (and underview) of research and theory within the attraction paradigm. *Journal of Social and Personal Relationships*, 14: 417–31, provides a review by a key figure in early attraction research, of the 'bogus stranger' paradigm for studying initial attraction.

Fitch, K. L. (1998) *Speaking Relationally: Culture, Communication, and Interpersonal Connection*. New York: Guilford, contributes a fine analysis of the ways in which forms of culture influence the experience of relationship and vice versa.

Kenrick, D. T., and Trost, M. R. (1997) Evolutionary approaches to relationships, in S. W. Duck, (ed.) with K. Dindia, W. Ickes, R. M. Milardo, R. S. L. Mills and B. Sarason, *Handbook of Personal Relationships* (2nd edition) (pp. 156–78). Chichester, UK: Wiley, furnishes an analysis of the evolutionary and sociobiological underpinnings of attraction and relationship formation.

THREE

DEVELOPING RELATIONSHIPS AND DEVELOPING PEOPLE

The previous chapter assumed that relationships were based on, and created by, more than just the matching or juxtaposition of partners' attributes. It tried to show how the idea of such matching was influenced by cultural models of relating but that the processes that became important were actually only indistinctly derived from the matched characteristics behaviourally anyway. Other cultural models of the development of relationships are also unavoidably inherited, as it were: as a result of our cultural membership we tend to believe some things rather than others about the reasons why relationships develop. We don't, for example, believe that relationships are caused by the 'friendship mosquito' or that a loving relationship is a likely outcome of a ritual cleansing followed by the eating of ground almond paste. Westerners also tend to be sceptical of the idea that persons in arranged marriages can actually love one another. Within our own cultural system, development of a relationship instead seems to be something that 'just happens' once we start to feel positive about someone else. That development is, however, itself strongly contextualized by a number of important social and personal influences, some of which have already been discussed in earlier chapters.

All the same, relationship development can feel as if it has an inevitability about it that is mostly derived from our increased liking for, and acquisition of knowledge about, our partners – and vice versa. The more the relationship develops, the more we get to know about our partner and, conversely, the more we get to know about them, the more the relationship develops. It might also feel to you as if another aspect of the development of a relationship is growth of intimacy, to do with greater feelings of relaxation, more bending of the 'relationship rules', greater familiarity, greater physical intimacy, and greater psychological closeness – among other things. Most important, though, is the fact that as we become closer to a partner so we also do things with partners that we do not do with other people: we choose to spend our time with them and we go to places with them, coordinate our lives and leisure and do things as a unit, forsaking all others, and choosing to spend time with the partner instead of with other people (Hendrick and Hendrick 1997). This is true whether we begin dating (Milardo *et al.* 1983) or develop other relationships that can divide our loyalties about the way we spend our time or which place us under stress about whether to pursue the relationship or a career (Zvonkovic *et al.* 1994). Much research on relationships looks at friendship and much at courtship. While the research issues in the two cases are sometimes different, there are nevertheless common principles, such as the issue of practical management of time and its distribution among relationships, and I shall focus here on the similarities while devoting a whole chapter (Chapter 4) to the special questions and special research that deal with courtship. You might also spot some differences in the processes on which the research focuses in the two cases, since it is simply not true that research explores the same processes in different sorts of relationships: there is usually a confounding of the type of relationship and the aspects of relating that are accessed.

WHAT ARE WE TRYING TO DEVELOP WHEN WE DEVELOP A RELATIONSHIP?

What develops when a relationship develops? It is easy to imagine that a lot of what happens is 'all in the mind' or is all about expansion of feelings for someone, yet as Baxter and Widenmann (1993) noted, we often face choices about whether or not we tell people that we are developing a relationship (we would keep affairs secret; we may not tell people we are dating someone), so there must be a social management and a practical side to the whole issue. Also, as Baxter (1992) demonstrated, using transcriptions of interviews of a stratified random sample, the development of a relationship takes place within a metaphorical context provided by the language in which our social psychology of relationships is based. That is to say, people's thoughts about relationships, their cognitive **schemata** for understanding them and their ways of explaining their emotions are channelled by particular metaphors for describing relationships. 'Growth' of relationships is one such metaphor and it encourages us to look for things that 'grow' or 'develop' in quantity, like love, which we typically describe as increasing in quantity over time when a relationship is developing. Typically there is also an underlying idea of the development of a relationship being a metaphorical journey of discovery and finding out more about each other, tiring of the relationship when the newness and discovery wear out. The 'effort' that it takes 'to make a relationship work' is another metaphor, and relationship development as an uncontrollable force is a third ('The relationship engulfed us totally'; 'It was like I was drugged or something. I just couldn't help it'). These metaphors are useful ways for relaters and social psychologists alike to use in describing relationships and the change that occurs there across time. Such metaphors are particularly suited to a science that *measures* things and can therefore assess change in quantitative terms by measuring changes in the *amount* of something (increases in intimacy, for example). All the same it is necessary to attend to the fact that metaphors channel – as well as expand – our thinking (Duck 1994a). If a research team thinks of 'pathways to marriage', as, for example, Huston *et al*. (1981) did, then it will be natural for the team to start looking for 'turning points' on those pathways and to talk about 'goals' of relating and to identify 'marker posts along the way' and to write about 'changes in direction'. Other teams with different metaphors by contrast write about the market place, cost-benefit analysis, alternative choices, behavioural (consumer?) options, and the kind of brand loyalty represented by commitment (Berscheid and Lopes 1997). Yet other relational scholars instead see relational change in terms of transformation rather than quantitative movement (Conville 1997) or in terms of an entirely new 'drama' composed of modified 'acts' of self-presentation (Leary and Miller 1999) or in terms of the 'construction' of something different out of other available 'materials', using roles differently or honing one's skills or using parts of self differently (Carl 1997).

All the same, let us stick – at least at first – with the most commonly employed metaphor, recognizing it for what it is, a metaphor. That metaphor usually sets us thinking in terms of growth and development, rather as an infant grows into a fully functioning adult that is recognizably the same and yet different from the original infant. Interestingly, other researchers in social psychology typically adopt metaphors of growth that are measured *quantitatively* and which assess change in terms of an increase in the amounts of something (for example increases in intimacy, increases in amounts of self-disclosure). *Transformational* models of growth are not used – for example, the growth that occurs when tadpoles turn into frogs or eggs turn into caterpillars and thence to pupas and then butterflies (Duck 1984a). Even so, as for infants, it is surprisingly perplexing to decide what it is that 'grows' as a relationship develops and how all the changes interrelate to show the finished result. Therefore social psychologists, family scientists, and communication scholars and sociologists have devoted considerable attention to exploring *what* it is that develops when a relationship 'grows' or 'increases'.

People certainly change their lives in major or minor ways to accommodate a new relationship, but the 'sense of being in the relationship' is what makes the real difference (Duck and Sants 1983) and couples often develop a story about where they first met (Duck and Pond 1989 – by the way, if you can think of any *new* jokes about this pair of authors, let me know). Such stories may be inaccurate or accurate, but that is less the point than is the fact that people regard the stories as meaningful and treat them *as if* they were true (Bochner *et al*. 1997). It is partly the emergence of such stories that indicates the time (often quite early on) when the partners realize that they are 'in a relationship' rather than just being two people who have met one another on a number of occasions and talked and done things together. Also, as Acitelli (1993) has noted, both partners talk not only to each other but *about each other to each other*: they develop a sense of relationship awareness and they think 'about interaction patterns, comparisons or contrasts between [self] and the other partner in the relationship' (Acitelli 1993: 151). The ways in which individuals think of themselves in the relationship can of course influence the ways they behave in the relationship, just as an awareness of being in a relationship affects partners' understandings of each other and their relationship. It is therefore necessary to consider what a relationship might be, so that we can begin to get an understanding of how it comes to be and how its change might be assessed.

According to Hinde (1981), the nature of relationships is determined by a set of features which change (in quantity) and intensify as the relationship proceeds. He argues that we can achieve some understanding of relationships by looking at where they are located on the following eight dimensions of assessment.

1 Content of interactions

Relationships derive much of their essence from the things that the partners do together: customer–waiter relationships differ from father–daughter relationships in the nature of the activities that occur within the relationship. For a father to charge his daughter for every meal or cup of coffee in the home, for instance, or for customer and waiter to hug and tell one another secrets or play hide-and-seek would violate the norms for conducting their respective relationships. The typically-enacted types of activity help to define the relationship and differentiate it from others. Naturally, as relationships develop (from acquaintance to close friendship, for example) so the partners will alter their interactions to embrace different content. They may talk to one another about different subjects or go to different places: indeed it is sometimes a quite significant escalation of a relationship for one person to invite another to visit at home or to invite talk about a previously taboo area – a sign of the breaking of a barrier and an indication of a desire to increase the intimacy.

2 Diversity of interactions

Some relationships do not involve a lot of variety. Student–instructor relationships, for example, are typified by interactions focused on a rather limited range of topics to do with academic life and typically do not involve going on picnics or talking about holiday travel plans or fears of death. Others, parent–child relationships for example, involve a lot of diversity – playing, instructing, comforting, protecting, educating, healing, feeding . . . and so on. Hinde (1981) therefore draws a distinction between **uniplex relationships** (where the types of interaction are limited in scope) and **multiplex relationships** (where the varieties of interaction are far greater). One way to classify and differentiate relationships, therefore, is in terms of the diversity of interactions that compose them: the more diverse the interactions, the deeper the relationship.

3 Qualities of interactions

Although the content of interactions is significant, the 'adverbial properties' (Duck and Sants 1983) are important too: it's not what you do but the *way* that you do it. A significant means of understanding relationships, therefore, is in terms of the qualities of the interactions that occur. We can assess these qualities by examining the intensity and style of interactions, the nonverbal signals exchanged, and so on. Intensity could be measured simply – for example, by checking whether the partners shout at one another or whisper in each other's ear. Style could be assessed in terms of the style of language they use (Duck 1998), the types and topics of self-disclosure (Dindia 1997), or the likelihood of using personal nicknames (Bruess and Pearson 1993). Nonverbal signals are also important: they are the bodily cues that accompany speech in socially significant ways – such as whether we look directly at someone when we speak to them or look down sheepishly, or whether we smile or frown when they talk to us (Keeley and Hart 1994). As social psychologists have shown for a number of years (e.g., Argyle 1967), **NVC** (nonverbal communication) constitutes a system by which intimacy is conveyed. For instance, high amounts of eye contact usually indicate intimacy, close physical proximity normally implies greater intimacy, and the two at once indicate considerable intimacy – which is why people who do not know one another look intensely at the floor, the indicator board, or the decorations of elevators in which they are compelled to stand close to each other.

4   Relative frequency and patterning of interactions

A deepening voluntary relationship tends to increase the frequency of meetings between the persons – although in long-distance relationships this function is usually carried out on email or by phone (Guldner and Swensen 1995). Other indices of increasing closeness are affection expressed verbally and nonverbally, the absence of conflict, and so on. An increased frequency of contact is usually a result of choice because we *want* to enjoy one another's company more often (Hays 1988). Another signal is the way in which interactions are patterned according to societal norms or the preferences of partners: thus, for a couple to make love more often than the social norm tells us something about their sense of duty to society's statistics, but tells us about their relationship or their sexual satisfaction *only if* we map it onto their expressed desires for sex. The answer to the question: 'How is their sexual activity patterned relative to the wishes of each partner?' reveals much more information about the nature of the relationship between the partners than is revealed by simple statistics about the absolute frequency of their sexual activity. Thus Blumstein and Schwartz (1983) show that even in happily married couples, frequency of intercourse varies between 'less than once per month' (about 6 per cent of couples happily married between two and ten years) to 'three or more times per week' (about 27 per cent of couples happily married for more than two years).

5   Reciprocity and complementarity

In some relationships I do the same sorts of things that you do. You say 'How are you?', and I say 'Fine, how are you?'; or you buy me a drink, and I feel obligated to buy you one. You invite me to dinner and I say 'No, you took me out last time, now it's my turn'. These are reciprocal actions based, superficially, on obligation: the more superficial the relationship, the more people keep count of whose turn it is to do the behaviour next. On the other hand, when I ask you for help and you give it, or you try to dominate and I submit, or you look sad and I try to cheer you up, then our behaviour is complementary: it is different behaviour but it goes together to make a perfect whole. In complementary behaviours people take account of each other's needs to a greater extent, and, accordingly, the relationship is felt to be less superficial.

6 Intimacy

There are two sorts of intimacy: physical and psychological. As we get to know someone better, so our access to their body and their soul increases. Friends, especially female same-sex friends, are permitted to touch one another more often and in a greater variety of parts of the body than are casual acquaintances (Jourard 1971) – the hands are available for almost anyone to touch, but knees, for instance, are parts reserved only for persons that we know quite well. The same applies to psychological intimacy: the more you know someone, the more you are granted access to their inner feelings, fears and concerns. It used to be believed that open **'self-disclosure'** (i.e., reporting on inner feelings) was a clear mark of the growth of intimacy but we now know a lot more about the importance of appropriateness of disclosure, and the other jobs that self-disclosure does in relationships (Dindia 1994; Spencer 1994) and so I will devote a whole section to it below.

7 Interpersonal perception

Individuals have views of themselves ('Myself as I am'), of other individuals ('X as I see her or him') and of such abstract entities as their ideal self ('Myself as I would like to be'). We can also hold views of 'Myself as my friend sees me'. Interpersonal differences in such perceptions could be the result of personality characteristics (Snell 1988) or could be the result of processes (Acitelli 1993). Kenny and Acitelli (1989) distinguish between *similarity* (when both partners' perceptions of themselves are congruent – A sees A the same way B sees B), *perceived similarity* (when one partner's perception of self is congruent with that person's perception of other – A sees A the way A sees B), and *understanding* (when a person's view of the other corresponds with the other's own views of self – A sees B the way B sees B). These variables relate to such important things as the likelihood of marital satisfaction and the general tenor and direction that it takes (Acitelli *et al.* 1993): 'A wife's marital well-being is more connected to how her perceptions relate to her husband's, while a husband's marital well-being is more connected to what each spouse perceives they are doing individually' (Acitelli 1993: 157). Thus we need to distinguish the separate perspectives of self and other (something that classic social psychological work in interpersonal perception has explored, Zebrowitz 1989) from the relationship between these perceptions and the perceptions by the partners themselves of their relationship – something generally affected by the fact that when people have a relationship (surprise!) they actually *talk* about it (Acitelli 1988).

8 Commitment

As individuals grow closer together, so, Hinde (1981) notes, their commitment to one another increases. The degree of commitment has often been used by researchers as a barometer of the strength of a relationship (Berscheid and Lopes 1997) although the complexities of the concept have admittedly not yet been adequately captured by self-report measures of the extent to which a person *feels* committed (Berscheid *et al.* 1989). It is often the case that a person feels both – and simultaneously – a commitment and a need for autonomy (Baxter and Montgomery 1996) or that commitment is expressed verbally but not effected in actions (Feeney *et al.* 1997), or that a person feels simultaneously committed to several different sorts of relationships (e.g., to friend, spouse, parents) and is occasionally faced with practical stresses that force choices between spending time with one relationship rather than another to which commitment has also and equally been expressed (Baxter *et al.* 1997). All the same, 'commitment' essentially means some sort of determination to continue and respect a relationship in the face of adversities or temptations (Johnson 1982). Examples are exclusivity, if the relationship is a sexual one, and a tendency to put the other person's interests on an equal or greater footing than one's own.

Hinde's (1981) scheme thus provides us with a set of dimensions on which to assess the nature – and by implication the development – of a relationship. We could measure casual, mid-range, and close relationships on the above dimensions and find key ways in which they differ systematically. We might ask whether close friendships show particular patterns of interactions or communication as compared to the other sorts of relationships, or we could track relationships through their lives and note the changes that occur (Adams and Blieszner 1996). When relationship development is charted, we do in fact find that much of friendship development is banal and repetitive activity rather than being a dramatic and intense increase in intimacies (Duck and Miell 1986; Duck *et al.* 1991).

Wright (1985a, b) proposes additional dimensions of friendship. For instance, a degree of voluntary interdependence is important, but so are the degrees to which each person can serve the other's needs, provide stimulation, and support one another's ego (**utility value, stimulation value**, and **ego support value**, respectively). Furthermore, a 'difficult to maintain' factor influences friendship: even if two people love each other, it is harder to sustain a relationship if one lives in the USA and the other in the UK. Additionally, the valuation of the person qua person (Wright 1985a) can be important (in other words, the extent to which we like that person as a unique individual).

All the same, the above general views of relationship development are quite one-sided, implying that people go into relationships and change their relationships rather than changing each other by being in a relationship. Aron and Aron (1997) note that relationships usually result in mutual self-expansion or mutual growth in identity and that it is the people who change rather than the relationship that they are in. One of the recent changes in the social psychology of relating to others has been a greater recognition of the *mutual* influence of the 'relationship' and the persons (Acitelli 1993) and hence the influence of relationships on the partners' sense of identity rather than just vice versa (Duck 1994a; Duck *et al.* 1997a). This is an important but subtle recognition, since it points out the *overlap* of people with relationships, rather than seeing a relationship as some imaginary separate entity that 'contains' people.

HUMAN FEATURES AND CONCERNS THAT WE TAKE WITH US INTO RELATIONSHIPS

We can see even from this brief selection of theoretical approaches, and those listed in Chapter 2, that there are several ways of addressing the interaction of personal identity and relationships (Duck *et al.* 1997a); one can focus on the behaviour of people in relationships, on the two people's cognitions of each other, or on various attitudes and behavioural dimensions that can be extracted by measurement scales and careful analysis of the experience of relating to others, or on the ways in which they work themselves together into a unit (Fletcher and Fitness 1993; Hendrick and Hendrick 1997; Weiss 1998). Since theorists take different positions and focus on different themes, proper critical assessment of the different themes requires a larger book (Duck *et al.* 1997a). However, it can be seen that we can explore a whole range of different elements in studying the development of friendship. It is not simply a question of just measuring growth in partners' feelings for one another.

One highly relevant aspect of friendships is that we enter them as human beings, with all the needs and anxieties that we have as human beings in general anyway. These are more likely to influence our behaviour and our styles in interactions than some of the pioneering research (and even present-day research) has been able to register. If our human concerns make us worry about other people's perceptions of ourselves, then it is likely that, for example, we shall try to gather information about other people's reactions and try to help them to reach the conclusions that we would like them to reach (Leary and Miller 1999)! However, the mixing of two perspectives together is not enough to make a relationship; rather mutual accommodation and understanding also have to be processually created (Acitelli 1993). Indeed, Bradshaw (1998) demonstrates that some very shy people fulfil their social needs deviously by going to places where their lack of social involvement will not be noticed (e.g., loud bars where their lack of participation is likely to be explained as a result of the noise) or by going out with a very socially active friend who will do enough social interaction for two people anyway!

Duck and Miell (1986), in charting the development of friendships, found extreme uncertainty about the other person's feelings towards oneself and the likely stability of those feelings. Friends adopt the view that the existence and future of the relationship depend much more than 50 per cent on the feelings and choices made by their partner. We seem to be aware of the risks of the other person 'going off us' and we are constantly concerned about it. The intriguing aspect of this is that both parties simultaneously do this and believe that the other person has control! Naturally these beliefs direct their behaviour and probably go a long way to explaining why there is such concern over gathering information about the other person: we need to check and 'round out' our beliefs about the likely endurance of the other person's feelings towards us and the extent of his or her commitment to our relationship.

Whatever it is that develops when relationships come into being, a relationship is clearly not a thing that exists independently of the persons who are having it. The persons and the relationship are mutually influential and all change together. Relationships are not simple containers (Duck 1994a; Baxter and Montgomery 1996), even though we are used to thinking of them that way and talk about being 'in' them as if they carry us around. It is also important to notice that 'turning points' in relationships may be significant points of psychological upheaval or adjustment or even turmoil, but they are as likely to be *stories* about such things as realities (Bochner *et al.* 1997). As noted earlier in the chapter, however, such notions are really thought-ways created by the metaphors we choose to use to describe relating to others. Although we are used to thinking of relationships as having stages, for example, that idea is basically just a handy way to think about them rather than being the way they can be shown to work (Honeycutt 1993). This fact seems likely to be one reason underlying the failures of social psychologists to find such stages (noted by Levinger 1996).

GETTING ACQUAINTED

The foregoing section abstracts the initial conditions for development of relationships – the expectations and concerns that we bring with us – and could be accused of representing it as something disembodied from our real-life actions in relating, just as most research has done (Berscheid 1994). We all know that when we meet new people we do not just *feel* something inside, we *do* something: for example, we take active steps to try to impress them, if we like them, partly as a result of the concerns in the above section, and we manage our social 'face' (Metts 1997). We also know that we think about relationships and people as we take baths or cook meals, so do the above theories really assume that relationships occur only when the two people are interacting face-to-face? Actually there must be a previous step.

When we look at the ways in which people help themselves to develop relationships we can identify several interesting features. First, but not well recognized in this context, is the fact that we must first choose whether or not to 'regard' someone as a possible partner. Rodin (1982) argued that the criteria for liking and disliking are not complementary or opposite ends of a continuum but in fact are completely distinct from one another. She argued that the first decision we make in viewing someone else is whether to eliminate them from our concerns. If we decide to 'disregard' them, we do not process information from them even if that information would be relevant to forming a relationship; if, however, we choose to 'regard' them, then we consider their attributes and their potential as relational partners. Thus, Rodin argues, we do not necessarily process all the information that others provide for us. If we have first decided that they do not count, then their behaviour and their personality characteristics will be disregarded: however likable these attributes may be, we simply will not notice or act on them. If we decide that we are interested, however, then the other's attributes will be processed to see how likable they are, or to what extent they would be good partners.

What do we need to look for?

Rodin's work indicates in a straightforward way that much of our initial activity relating to others is actually automatic, very fast, and affected by stereotypes, norms, the dramas of social life, class, and social convention. One strong convention prevents us from asking someone if they like us or telling someone directly that we like them. It just is 'not done' to turn to a stranger and say 'I think you are great' unless we are prepared to risk them saying 'So why should I care what you think?' Even feeling secure enough to say 'I love you' can take time. Because it is threatening to put our social selves so much in jeopardy, we also avoid risking a strongly negative answer to the question 'Do you like me?' by refraining from asking it straightforwardly. Kurth (1970) has suggested that this accounts for human indirectness in both indicating liking and assessing it. Typically, we use a lot of indirect nonverbal signals such as smiling, gaze, and eye contact to indicate liking without saying so, or else we ask a lot of questions and respond encouragingly to the answers, set up 'chance' meetings, and so forth. Not only the initiation but also the development of relationships progresses by indirect means: invitations to get more involved with someone are usually cautious and ambiguous (the phrase 'Would you like to come up to my place for coffee?' being an example where 'coffee' is sometimes a signal for 'a more intense relationship').

For this reason, though, we make life a little harder for ourselves because the process of signalling interest in or willingness to become involved with someone else necessarily entails some subtle, skilled, and often disguised efforts (Duck 1991). One under-researched means of doing this is by flirting and Sabini and Silver (1982) and Montgomery (1986) began scientific work on this topic. Sabini and Silver argued that the purpose of flirtation is to encourage the other person to acknowledge sexual interest, but to do so in such a way that the issue is not forced – i.e., to allow **'deniability'** ('Hey, I wasn't propositioning you; it was just a joke'), to play for time, and to enjoy the game for its own sake. Flirtation is therefore ambiguous – it has to be, because once it ceases to be ambiguous it is no longer flirtation and it becomes a blunt or direct relational (often sexual) proposition. Montgomery's work is complementary to this position, but also makes some useful distinctions. In a series of studies, she found that flirting serves a variety of purposes, the main one being to express friendship (although women see this function as more significant than do men, who, rather predictably, see flirtation as having more sexual overtones than women do). Flirting is also used to test the target's possible interest in a relationship: by flirting, a person indicates interest in a relationship through indirect means (i.e., by not actually asking a direct question) and, by responding positively and equally indirectly in a flirtatious manner, the target indicates willingness to accept the invitation. However, since the two sexes view flirtation differently, it is possible for crucial misunderstandings to arise and to cause serious difficulties when one partner intends a sexual message, has the message accepted because the target sees it as merely friendly, and then mistakenly acts as if a sexual acceptance had been received, rather than the friendly response that was in fact intended. Montgomery's (1986) work is important, therefore, not only because she opened up an approach to a neglected topic but also because of these intriguing new findings. (A possibility worth further investigation and pointed out to me by Paul Wright is that there may also be something of a self-affirmation attempt in flirtation: that is, there may be an attempt to test out one's own attractiveness to opposite sex others without any real intention of 'following through'. A long-married person may flirt with an acquaintance as a means of seeing whether the old magic is still there and a positive reaction from the acquaintance would be ego-boosting even if the whole thing went no further than the act of flirting.)

At the point where a full relationship might begin to be established, then, our main objectives are:

1 to appear in an attractive light to the other person;
2 to look for signs of approval and interest from the other person;
3 to signal our interest in that person;
4 to create opportunities for meetings where the relationship could be pursued.

Only one of these tasks is purely cognitive. At this point, then, our reactions to the other person are quite superficial, and as the relationship proceeds we need more information.

Active, passive and interactive strategies for information gathering

Once we have established our interest in a person and their interest in or liking for us, we can begin the information gathering that has been emphasized in much research, particularly in communication studies. We should not assume that this is always done directly, or even in the presence of the partner. We can reflect on our interactions with people, imagining or remembering and replaying a conversation and even planning what we hope or intend to do in the future (Duck 1980b). It can be argued that much relationship work takes place in private when we are on our own: it is simply called 'thinking', but its products can be future action, invitations to dates, letters, diaries, plans, and much else besides, all of which directly influence relationship development.

Berger (1993) has postulated a set of techniques and strategies by means of which we gather the kinds of information about partners that will help us to plan and build up a better picture of their personality and their suitability as a partner for us. Such strategies can be passive, active and/or interactive. Passive strategies are those where persons gather information by unobtrusively observing the target person. For instance, we may watch the person dealing with other people and thereby acquire information about his or her personal styles. Active strategies do not involve interaction between the person and the target, but the person does take active steps to gather information (e.g., by asking third parties questions about the target or by actively structuring the environment in such a way that it requires a reaction or response from the target). Interactive strategies involve direct interactions with the target other, such as conversation. They are not necessarily always a better method of acquiring information about a target because the target might deceive us or engage in impression management or other strategic action (Berger 1988). Indeed, Douglas (1987) finds that a primary type of information-seeking (87 per cent of all questions asked in acquaintance) is the use of demographic and opinion/preference information at the start of the uncertainty-reduction moves. As a matter of fact, the interactional performance of the other person is not much used as a source for initial **uncertainty-reduction**. However, speech between partners does take on particularities that are evidence of level of knowledge. For example, one acquires more shared knowledge, a greater level of ability to take common knowledge for granted in conversation, and a history of experiences together, which is recognized even by outsiders, who can distinguish the level of relationship between two speakers from their speech patterns alone (Planalp and Benson 1992; Planalp and Garvin-Doxas, 1994). Also partners develop codes that are intended to be obscure to outsiders and hence to exclude other people and act as boundaries around the relationship, too. They create **'personal idioms'** (Hopper *et al.* 1981), that is, personally meaningful language that serves to bind them together and simultaneously exclude other people. For instance, if a couple starts to use the phrase 'Time to do a Mr Johnson', it may mean to them 'I'm bored with this so let's leave and go home before it gets any worse' – but no-one else would know that and the couple can communicate the idea to one another without any risk of anyone else knowing what is happening. Thus the language serves as a binding and boundary-making mechanism even though on the surface it looks like a simple linguistic curiosity. In fact, therefore, the increase in knowledge about another person is actually *enacted* in the apparently inconsequential styles of talk between the people.

However, as Planalp and Honeycutt (1985) point out, this model is optimistic in so far as it assumes that all information will reduce our uncertainty about another person. Obviously, increasing amounts of information *per se* can increase uncertainty if the new information is contradictory or difficult to fit in with what we already know (e.g., 'S/he reads Plato in Greek and attends the opera, but now I find out s/he loves the Spice Girls'). Also the focus of the uncertainty-reduction has to be considered: increasing our certainty about a partner's faults is likely to be destructive, even if decreased uncertainty in this case may be good for us if it saves us getting into an unsuitable relationship. Sometimes, moreover, we might find out that a partner has lied to us, told our secrets to other persons or two-timed us in the past. This sort of information can, of course, increase our uncertainty about them rather than reduce it. However, it does reduce our uncertainty in other ways, in that it refines our judgements about their (un)suitability as partners, and might make us more certain that we do not want a relationship with them.

Douglas (1987) reminds us that relationship development is two-sided since both persons have a choice and take action to learn about one another. The information-gathering strategies of one partner alone cannot sufficiently explain relational action. Necessarily, we trade off efficiency (i.e., gathering all the information we need and doing so in the shortest possible time) and politeness which disallows efficient intrusiveness into other people's business or background). Douglas (1987) surveyed student subjects' strategies for coping with this and showed that this is particularly salient to individuals at the very opening moments of a possible relationship, where they are very keen to know about the possibilities of developing a relationship, yet cannot do so directly in a socially acceptable manner. He asked subjects to list the strategies that they might use to solve this problem and found that the general approach to this dilemma is a surreptitious testing of the other person's affective judgements and a search for unobtrusive clues to their liking of us. For example, one strategy is confronting (e.g., 'I put my arm around her: it made her say yes or no'), another is withdrawing (e.g., 'I stopped talking for a while to see if she was interested in picking up the conversation'), and another is hazing (e.g., 'I told him I lived 16 miles away and needed a ride home. I wanted to see if he was interested enough to go to all that trouble'). It is clear from Douglas's (1987) intriguing and innovative work that such affinity testing early in relationships is a major social task.

SELF-DISCLOSURE AND OPEN COMMUNICATION

One significant aspect to uncertainty-reduction focuses on the trustworthiness of our partner – is he or she the kind of person who can be trusted with our secrets? As Kelvin (1977) has observed, a key element in developing relationships is that we make ourselves more vulnerable. We usually tell our new partners increasingly secret or private information about ourselves and we do this both as a measure and an indication of our liking for them. However, that information – because of its very nature as private, secret, important, and revealing – puts a powerful weapon in his or her hands if he or she should ever want to harm us. Our vulnerability increases to the extent that we reveal ourselves to the other person – indeed, a paradox of relationships is that increased intimacy and consequent security also increase risk and potential threat (Derlega *et al.* 1993). A major concern of persons in dissolving relationships is precisely that the secrets revealed during the extended process of developing the relationship will be used to harm them or gain revenge for the breaking up of the relationship (Duck 1982b). In dealing with the invasions of privacy that are willingly permitted as relationships develop, we should keep in mind that this two-edged sword placed in the hands of friends can return in other contexts as a Sword of Damocles when we are dealing with the destruction of relationships instead of their creation and development (see Chapter 6).

None the less, an increase in willingness to disclose about self is a characteristic of relational development: a certain amount of intrusiveness or revelation is permitted and encouraged to develop as the relationship develops and this has been called 'self-disclosure' (Jourard 1971). As Sprecher (1987) has shown, in a survey of close partners, the important effects of self-disclosure come not from the amount that a person gives to a partner but rather from the amount that a person feels the partner allows to them, since this creates a sense of acceptance and is an excellent predictor of whether couples remain together over a four-year period (Sprecher 1987).

The older research has been criticized for too readily assuming tit for tat at early stages in self-disclosure, and too much directness and predictability in the way in which it occurs between people (Derlega *et al.* 1993). Indeed, direct questions are much more common in the early stages of relationships and are answered appropriately, then matched fairly often by a return question to the questioner about a similar matter. It is acceptable to probe directly about facts (e.g., where do you live?) or banal matters such as names and details of home town, type of job, and family or relational status (married or unmarried), but it is acceptable only to probe general opinions and attitudes at this stage, and the areas of questioning are usually restricted to non-intimate matters (Knapp 1984).

At these early points in a relationship, then, the range of topics is usually fairly neutral and public, with opportunities for great personal revelations reduced and restricted (Knapp 1984). Indeed great revelations at this stage are irritating and may well lead to negative evaluations of the questioner or discloser (e.g., to an assessment that the person is weird, unstable or a mere bus-load of problems looking for somewhere to park; Jones and Gordon 1972). At different stages of acquaintance, however (particularly the early stages), self-disclosure is expected and is prized: there is a **'norm of reciprocity'** (Gouldner 1960) in self-disclosure that results in partners matching their disclosures measure for measure, although this tends to wear off as the relationship progresses. While a global balance is still expected in long-term relationships, the specific matching up of disclosure with disclosure dies away. In many studies the subject's measure of intimacy in a disclosure has been rated by an experimenter and tested against the measure of intimacy in a disclosure returned by the subject's partner. Thus, 'My secret fears about my sexual inadequacy' would be typically rated by researchers as an intimate disclosure, whereas 'My favourite music' would be seen as personal information that is not truly intimate (Davis 1978).

In sum, then, the general work on self-disclosure notes social expectations about this potentially intimate sort of communication (Derlega *et al.* 1993):

1 you self-disclose if you want to be liked and approved;
2 the amount of self-disclosure must not be too much in the circumstances – particularly to start with;
3 self-disclosure should be matched to the intimacy level of the relationship (which could be changing – therefore self-disclosure can be used to escalate or de-escalate relationships);
4 one person reciprocates the other person's disclosures (and likewise can influence the growth or decline of the relationship);
5 self-disclosure changes and expands as the relationship grows.

We should not accept too readily the idea of information having fixed intimacy value. Not all information can be classified so easily and much of the intimacy value of a given statement will depend on the circumstances in which it is made, depending on context not on absolutes (Duck 1998): it is not as intimate to tell your doctor about your haemorrhoids as it is to tell an acquaintance. Also, Miell and Dallos (1996) have noted that intimate disclosures do not just come out of nowhere or have particularly special conversational status, but are also placed in contexts of other activity and norms of behaviour in subtle ways. For example, intimacy level of a relationship is often advanced by one of the partners strategically releasing more intimate information than is usual in the relationship and the other partner responding with equally (increased) intimate responses (see Miell 1984, or Miell and Duck 1986, for a summary). By careful testing of the likely response to such disclosures (e.g., by making an obscure, tangential, non-disclosing reference to the topic in general), the partners are able to assess whether it is safe to make the full disclosure, and so perform a secret test of the appropriate intimacy level for that relationship and of the partner's commitment to it. Indeed, the same piece of information can have different ratings and meanings, depending on the circumstances or the stage reached in relational development. Information that is highly prized in many settings, where open and frank information exchange is valued, can in other circumstances be regarded as highly negative and repulsive. Think about how you might react if a friend burst into tears and told you that he or she is worried about being unbalanced because the colour blue has suddenly become very frightening; now how might you react if a total stranger came up and said the same thing?

Strategies in self-disclosure

More recent work on self-disclosure (Derlega *et al.* 1993; Spencer 1994; Dindia 1997) has suggested that self-disclosure is built into everyday conversation in more complex ways than previously thought and also serves functions – and is itself carried out – in ways not formally recognized. For example, Spencer (1994) notes that a parent's self-disclosure to a teenager may not be carried out in order to increase intimacy but to educate the teenager ('When I was your age I was shy, too, and the way I handled it was . . .'). Dindia (1997) on the other hand suggests that self-disclosure is not so simple that it can be separated out as a specific event that either has or has not occurred. Rather it is a continuous process that is 'extended in time and is open-ended not only across the course of an interaction or series of interactions, but also across the lives of individuals as their identities develop/unfold, and across the life of a relationship as it evolves. The process of self-disclosure is circular: self-disclosure does not necessarily move from non-disclosure to disclosure in a linear fashion. The end-state of this process is not full disclosure . . . self-disclosure is contextual and is embedded in the larger processes of self-identity/human development and relationship identity/development' (Dindia 1994: 425–6). This position is strongly consistent with studies by Miell (1984) and Miell and Duck (1986), who showed the extent to which we use self-disclosure strategically in relationships. Miell's work used both interview techniques and direct observation of real encounters in a series of studies on this topic. One important finding from the research is that people 'float' intimate topics before they disclose about them seriously. For instance, someone may make a joking reference to exams in order to help them gauge the partner's reactions: if they get a sympathetically toned reaction then they will go ahead and make the full disclosure about their very intense anxiety about an exam; if not, they will not pursue the issue. It is also clear that we sometimes self-disclose not for its own sake but with the strategic purpose of inducing self-disclosure by the other person. Thus, because we know that there is a norm of reciprocity, we may make an intimate self-disclosure so that the pressure falls on our partner to make an equally intimate disclosure to us (Miell and Croghan 1996). Making self-disclosures oneself is also a way of relaxing the other person and can be an effective strategy in counselling or giving informal advice (Duck 1998). Thus when put in the context of everyday life, the role of self-disclosure becomes much more clearly a central, but not necessarily completely distinct, aspect of the daily conduct of relationships.

When does avoidance of self-disclosure help a relationship?

Although openness is highly prized in Western cultures and we are encouraged to disclose to our partners (indeed, we may be rejected by them if we are not willing to self-disclose), there are certain circumstances where it is inappropriate, as we have seen (e.g., too early, too much, too negative a reflection on the discloser's past or personality). Furthermore, as Baxter and Wilmot (1985) indicated, there are topics that create tension in relationships and which partners therefore avoid making the subject of self-disclosures. By means of **ethnographic interviews** the authors solicited accounts of topics that were 'off limits' in their current opposite-sex personal relationships. Results indicate that these 'taboo topics' can be such things as past, deep intimate attachments that the discloser has had (which carry the implication, therefore, that the discloser has had former deep attachments that did not survive – so this present deep attachment may go the same way too!). As another example, 'the state of our relationship' is a **taboo topic** which may launch a discussion that shows all too clearly that the partners have importantly discrepant or incompatible views of the nature of the relationship and its likely future – or future ending! For example, one partner may think the relationship is heading towards marriage, while the other has always regarded it as a casual relationship.

One thing we should not do directly, even at a later stage, is to ask too openly about the partner's commitment. It is taboo to focus too specifically on the current state of the relationship, the reason presumably being that if we ask too clear a question about it we may get too clear an answer – one we did not want or expect. However, uncertainty about the state of that relationship is of paramount importance and interest to people in relationships. So how do we solve that pair of conflicting problems? How do we find out the state of the relationship without actually asking? Baxter and Wilmot (1984) provide the answer: we use '**secret tests**'. In a study with three distinct stages, the authors first conducted ethnographic interviews in which respondents discussed a current or recent opposite-sex relationship. Next a cluster analysis and multi-dimensional scaling were performed on the resulting prototypical strategies. The third stage was a reanalysis of the interviews, examining gender and relational type in terms of the information-gathering strategies. The results are intriguing and informative about our human ways! If we want to know how much commitment our partner feels towards us, we find out indirectly by confronting him or her with tests, the results of which indicate the level of commitment in subtle ways. For example, we may dwell on the attractiveness of other potential partners and we secretly gauge the extent of the jealous reaction that we get from our partner as we tell the tale. If our partner becomes very jealous, we know that he or she likes us a lot. Another method stems from the implied results of a public presentation of the relationship: for instance, one might suggest 'Why don't you come down and meet my parents for the weekend?' To accept such an invitation is to be willing to have the relationship acknowledged by significant outsiders and thus indicates willingness to accept commitment to the relationship. These popular and familiar tricks and techniques are some of the ways in which we get the necessary answers to our questions without asking them directly. Even 'no answer', evasion, and 'playing for time' tell us something about the partner's commitment (or lack of commitment) to the relationship. However, it is also possible that the misunderstanding of the meaning or intention of the partner's response can lead us into a false sense of security or could produce an avoidance of direct discussion and communication which might ultimately be to the detriment of the relationship. Even if the secret tests are conducted, it does not, of course, follow that direct communications are thereby rendered redundant.

BEYOND COGNITION

Liking, trust, intimacy, and so on, are clearly important in the conduct of relationships, but are by no means the end of the story. For one thing, the individual's personality needs and his or her ability to interact skilfully both have an influence on sociability and social experience. It has nevertheless been very easy and meretriciously attractive to researchers to view relationships as simple creations of the feelings of two persons for one another, whereas other researchers have been seduced into the reduction of relationship conduct to sets of rules and skills (see Argyle and Henderson (1985) for a review). However, significant contributors to the success of the relationship – and indeed to the development of any sort of relationship at all – are the partners' aptitudes for conducting the negotiated action that is necessary for them to work together as a couple and to live together as partners. As we have seen here and in Chapter 2, the partners' individual thoughts and feelings – their identities – must become not only related but interconnected as a sense of relationship is built. In a smart phrase, the individuals move from two separate I-dentities to one We-dentity. While feelings and skills may be helpful stepping-stones on the road towards such satisfying relationships, even feelings lead to action and the intertwining of lives through joint action, talk, shared activities, talk, common leisure time, talk, sexual interaction, and a variety of other social behaviours that further enmesh the two partners into one another's everyday lives, including talk. To represent relationship growth as a purely cognitive or clinically decisive action is unfortunately and unnecessarily limiting. Appreciation of this point is increasing, however, and recent re-search is moving sharply towards a consideration of the unnoticed, uncon-scious, routine interconnectedness of the two partners' lives, including the influence of other persons and outsiders (Canary and Stafford 1994). The next chapter therefore examines the place where those influences and occurrences are most significant, the place where a voluntary relationship between two separate lives gradually transforms itself into a highly com-mitted (and, in a sense, involuntary) relationship that transforms these two people into one social unit: courtship.

SUMMARY

This chapter examined the ways in which development occurs in a rela-tionship and it pointed to the research evidence showing that such growth is not automatic, not smooth or linear, not based solely on intimacy or feelings, not based on cognitions or uncertainty-reduction alone, and not simply a matter of increasing the quantity of something (like intimacy). The chapter also emphasized the importance of a development of a sense of connectedness – 'we-ness' or 'we-dentity' – that is represented at the behavioural levels, not merely as the expression of some inner feelings or thoughts but as the essentialized nature of the relationship. In discuss-ing the cognitive side it made the point that perceivers are not simply passive processors of information but have active purposes in their social intercourse. It dealt with the strategies through which people manage the vulnerabilities of becoming intimate or of increasing trust and it considered self-disclosure as an element in growth of relationships. In outlining the view that a consequence of greater emotional involvement is greater enmeshing of two individuals' lives, it provides the basis for the following chapter on courtship progress.

ANNOTATED FURTHER READING

Acitelli, L. K. (1993) You, me, and us: perspectives on relationship aware-ness, in S. W. Duck (ed.) *Understanding Relationship Processes 1: Individuals in Relationships* (pp. 144–74). Newbury Park: Sage, is a chapter that offers an intelligent and novel analysis of the ways in which pairs of people come to interweave their different understandings of a relationship and, as it were, to staff the relationship with a whole network of subsystems of understanding.

Canary, D. J. and Stafford, L. (eds) (1994) *Communication and Relationship Maintenance*. New York: Academic Press, is an edited collection of original chapters exploring the various ways in which the maintenance of rela-tionships can be analysed and understood. The book is both unusual and instructive in making the assumption that this needs to be done.

Dindia, K. (1997) Self-disclosure, self-identity, and relationship develop-ment: a transactional/dialectical perspective, in S. W. Duck (ed.), with

K. Dindia, W. Ickes, R. M. Milardo, R. S. L. Mills and B. Sarason, *Handbook of Personal Relationships* (2nd edition) (pp. 411–25). Chichester: Wiley, is a chapter that reviews the research on self-disclosure in a vibrant and refreshing way and introduces some extremely interesting ways of understanding that process.

Miell, D. E. and Dallos, R. (1996) Introduction: exploring interactions and relationships, in D. E. Miell and R. Dallos (eds) *Social Interaction and Personal Relationships* (pp. 1–22). Milton Keynes: The Open University/Sage offers a good and exciting way of understanding the contexts in which relationships are conducted in the real world.

FOUR

DEVELOPING A STEADY AND EXCLUSIVE PARTNERSHIP

Most people develop a relationship with a life-partner at some point in their lives and most people therefore experience the form of relationship that, at least in Western cultures, is preliminary to a stable and exclusive relationship: namely, courtship. According to a survey I once ran in class, the average 22-year-old Iowan student has been involved in 3.45 such serious relationships since the age of 16 and the experience of developing them (and breaking them off) is quite familiar in that age group. While the earliest research on this topic examined the types of people who married (e.g., by recording their race, religion, economic class, and so on), more recent work has explored the processes of courtship itself and has been more concerned with courtship progress and courtship styles than with the broad social categories that are associated with stable or unstable marriages. It has also attended to the ways in which 'success' of an eventual long-term relationship can be predicted from the courtship phase (Notarius 1996; Sher 1996). The focus on long-term relationships of heterosexuals has also now been supplemented with discussion of gay and lesbian relationships (Huston and Schwartz 1995), including work on the stability and dissolution of such relationships (Kurdek 1991, 1992). Recent research on gay and lesbian relationships has added a sophistication to claims about relationships in general, with attention to a wider range of relationship types, and to the organization of community networks. Yet, as Huston and Schwartz (1995) note, we still know relatively little about gay and lesbian experience in serious relationships or networks of maintenance and commitment. Even in the heterosexual literature, most research looks only at young couples. Young people are not the only ones who marry, especially now that the increasing divorce rate releases older individuals to enter second marriages and create blended families (Coleman and Ganong 1995). The results of studies reported below, however, are invariably derived from subjects below the age of 30 and one can only assume that the results would have been different had the subjects been older. For instance, second marriages usually follow a briefer courtship than do first marriages (Coleman and Ganong 1995; Notarius 1996; Sher 1996) and older couples meet one another in different ways than do younger ones (for instance, older couples are more likely to advertise, use dating services, or meet through singles support organizations, as noted in earlier chapters.)

COURTING DISASTER: SOME EARLY RESEARCH APPROACHES

Because courtship is a halfway house between casual dating on the one hand and a stable, exclusive relationship on the other, a fairly natural assumption within our cultural belief system is that some force operates to drive it forward or give it momentum. Readers should note, also, the value judgements that are associated with this topic and this style of research into it. Those value-laden styles of thinking – which still pervade our common-sense view – assume that people who stay in relationships are 'successes' and people who leave them or are left by partners have 'failed'. Indeed Umberson and Terling (1997) analysed both in-depth interviews and survey data and showed that the symbolic meaning of relationships is a significant reason for the deep distress felt during their dissolution. As we shall see in Chapter 5, these value-laden judgements of success and failure are not only unfair but are often problematic for people in disturbed relationships since they feel a sense of incompetence. Such cultural judgements also can affect the feelings of those who enter non-normative relationships (Huston and Schwartz 1995). As we saw in earlier chapters, there are strong cultural endorsements for certain types of relationship conduct and these take some of the forms above – powerful yet not necessarily heavy-handed.

A corollary of this value-laden approach is that people celebrate lengthy relationships (e.g., by ceremonial marking of silver wedding anniversaries or re-enactment of vows; Braithwaite and Baxter 1995), since, on this model of partnership, the longer-lasting ones are the most 'successful' ones (Pearson 1996). On the other hand, overlengthy courtships are viewed with scepticism and a culture has its own views of the appropriate length of time between first meeting and exclusive commitment – not too short, not too long – although we shall see in this chapter that couples act differently with respect to this convention.

Our cultural models for relationships offer, as the engine for courtship progress and relationship 'success', the notion of love for one's partner: as love grows, this 'theory' would claim, so the relationship deepens and broadens; eventually the two partners realize that they were 'made for each other' and become exclusive or move into a live-in-lover relationship of some kind. Although this force has probably been implicit in many approaches to courtship progress, love is clearly experienced in a cultural context and is not a pure emotion felt and expressed the same way all over the world (Beall and Sternberg 1995). It is also experienced in a practical context and people who have affairs or people who are gay or lesbian or bisexual feel pressures not to reveal their love to 'outsiders' in public in the same way that single heterosexual people feel perfectly free to do (Huston and Schwartz 1995; Carl 1997; Shackelford and Buss 1997).

It is therefore impossible, in the present book, to do justice to the variety of approaches presently available about love, so I will have to select a number of points to make about a sample of the work. Some theories see love as a relatively unique emotion and they typologize its manifestations into different varieties that are broadly distinct from each other. Thus Lee (1973) and Hendrick and Hendrick (1993) identify and work with six basic types of love, ranging from self-sacrificing love of the kind shown by Christ and Gandhi to the passionate/romantic/erotic love shown by almost everyone else. Such theories essentially propose typologies based on profiles of the different sorts of the same basic emotion, without explaining its origins. By subtle contrast, some theories also create structural hierarchies by mixing other variables, like commitment, passion and intimacy, each of which is itself a different thing from love, but which can be mixed together with the others in order to create different forms of love (Barnes and Sternberg 1997). Barnes and Sternberg's theory proposes that the forms of love derive from independent psychological structures and processes that are brought together to create different clusters of love processes, and that each form of love results not from other forms of love but from entirely separate emotional/cognitive structures. Sternberg (1995) even views love as a story that people tell one another and outsiders about the properties of their relationship.

Zeifman and Hazan (1997) have recently reviewed the research suggesting that adult styles of loving may be similar to those noted by workers on childhood attachment. Ainsworth *et al.* (1978), working with children, proposed that there are three styles of attachment and many researchers have used these as their guide: *secure attachment* and loving are characterized by confidence and security in intimacy, while *avoidant attachment* and the avoidant style of loving are characterized by lack of acceptance of others, avoidance of closeness and discomfort with intimacy. The final style, *anxious/ambivalent attachment* and the anxious/ambivalent style of loving, are characterized by dependency and a certain amount of insecurity coupled with feelings of lack of appreciation. A fourth style suggested by Bartholomew (1990) is a result of differentiating avoidance of intimacy into two: a *fearful style* that is characterized by a conscious desire for social contact which is inhibited by fear of its consequences; and a *dismissive style* that is characterized by a defensive denial of the need or desire for social contact. Fuendeling (1998) indicates that such styles of loving are indeed associated with particular styles of regulating or responding to affect and emotion. Variations in such responses to affect are especially evident in the ways in which people direct their attention to specific aspects of others, appraise other people, and interact with others in emotional situations.

All such approaches ultimately assume that love – or ability to love in particular ways – is the product of mental operations in the context of emotional experience, while some other work does not necessarily explain where love comes from, but sees it as manifested in, and facilitated by, certain behaviours and circumstances. In the work on courtship that has preceded the recent work on the nature and description of love, theories about its nature are often undeveloped or implicit, and they broadly assume that we know what it is and that it promotes satisfaction and development in courtship. Adopting such an approach either explicitly or implicitly, much early research was devoted to the discovery of static or global factors that predicted love and assumed that this led more or less directly to courtship progress or marital success. Among a relatively unimaginative and predictable list of such factors are those briefly discussed in the previous chapter: the matching of partners' characteristics; the partners' demographic origin or background; and their personality characteristics, specifically the influence of partner similarities or individual differences that pre-existed the courtship.

Unsurprisingly, then, given its historical context, work on courtship began with such basic assumptions. It was assumed that courtship proceeds on the basis of two suitable or matched individuals falling in love with one another – however that occurs – and progressing gradually and thoughtfully through courtship and engagement to marriage. It was conceived as a slow, careful business that occurred between appropriately-paired adults roughly 22 years of age or more (Kerckhoff 1974). Essentially it was still held to be true, as Goffman (1952: 159) stated, that 'A proposal of marriage in our society tends to be a way in which a man sums up his social attributes and suggests to a woman that hers are not so much better as to preclude a merger or partnership in these matters' and that such attributes and attribute-matching were about all there is to it – a 'theory' currently espoused by dating agencies.

Early research therefore proposed essentially that the specific stimuli or characteristics of persons best predicted the progress of courtship or were the best correlates of ultimate stability and satisfaction in marriage. The question addressed by such research was: what sorts of people get into the most stable and happy relationships? The old answers tended to refer to religion, economic background, race, age, intelligence, and so on (Levinger 1965). It was repeatedly found, for instance, that couples who married young were likely to experience instability in marriage and had a higher risk of divorce, and indeed research indicates that, by 1985, 32.4 per cent of American women who first married before the age of 20 had divorced (Norton and Moorman 1987). There is also a relationship between incompleteness of a woman's education and likelihood of her divorce, since women whose education stops short of a degree or diploma are more likely to divorce than are those who expect to obtain a degree or diploma (Norton and Moorman 1987) – although when highly educated women do divorce, they are much less likely than are other groups to remarry, possibly because their education has enabled them to achieve a career position that facilitates greater economic independence. Low socio-economic status also predicts instability and unhappiness in marriage (although it predicts unhappiness almost everywhere else in a person's life, too). Couples who have experienced many different sexual partnerships before marriage are also likely to end up in unstable marriages (Athanasiou and Sarkin 1974).

More recent researchers have explored different sorts of stable relationships. For example, Cunningham and Antill (1995) have examined POSSLQs (People of Opposite Sex Sharing Living Quarters), the new term for cohabitation, a growing and widely occurring form of relationship. However as Cunningham and Antill (1995: 150) note: 'We know far more about the demographics and attitudes of those who cohabit than about the ways they weave their lives together, define the meaning of their relationships and, in general, go about the business of enacting connection.' Younger people are more likely to cohabit than are older people; the experience of parental divorce increases the likelihood of a person cohabiting; and women (but not men) who cohabit are more likely to divorce. There is also a disturbing tendency for increased violence in cohabiting relationships (West 1995). Cohabitors are likely to score lower on romanticism scales, but also are now much more likely to marry eventually, whereas 20 years ago cohabitors tended to be people with attitudes opposed to marriage and to score higher in measures of unconventionality (Cunningham and Antill 1995).

In tandem with studies about partners' demographic characteristics, past experiences and habits, researchers have looked at other global personal characteristics, such as personality factors, as predictors not only of original choice but also of 'success' in the eventual relationship (Notarius 1996; Sher 1996). These reviews indicated that the psychologically distressed, the neurotic, the highly ambitious individual and the person with a rigid defensive style were likely to be 'unsuccessful' in marriage, whether that meant a higher likelihood of divorce or merely higher levels of conflict (Gottman 1994). Notarius (1996), however, indicated that the skills of relating – the words, thoughts, emotions, and their management – are better predictors of specific outcomes of stable relationships than are demographic or other personal characteristics of the individual partners. Equally, the work of Veroff and his colleagues has looked at the ways in which two partners organize, manage, and conduct those relationships, in particular the question of whether the early stages of a relationship predict later outcomes (Acitelli *et al.* 1997). Veroff, Young and Coon (1997) extend this work by examining the situational circumstances and the behaviours and attitudes that contribute to the stability of early marriages and to the sense of marital well-being in individual partners. They explored the ways in which couples confront the tasks and problems specifically relating to the blending of their lives – a practical focus on the ways in which behaviour and attitudes create a working relationship that has particularly satisfying or unsatisfactory features and which ultimately lead to better predictions of 'success' or 'failure' of that relationship.

HOW 'COURTSHIP' GROWS: SOME BASIC VIEWS

To develop a 'courtship' (whether heterosexual or homosexual) you first have to be in it! The factors that influence *choice* of dates were discussed earlier and the present chapter focuses instead on the ways in which the partners *manage* the dating and the courtship process. Such management depends not only on the characteristics of individuals, the ways in which a culture predisposes couples to approach the enterprise, and the pathways or landmarks that it expects them to follow or pass, but also on the specific ways in which couples manage conflict, triumph, and disaster (Klein and Johnson 1997) and the manner in which they deal with other practical issues like the balance between the relationship and other life-concerns such as career (Crouter and Helms-Erickson 1997).

Conflict in courtship used to be regarded as a problem, pure and simple, and the researcher's job was conceived as directed to finding ways of reducing it (e.g., Haley 1964). Couples who fight and argue must be having a hard time (it was assumed), are doing something wrongly or unsatisfactorily, getting on one another's nerves and generally making one another's lives miserable. Therefore, conflict must be reduced and techniques were sought for dealing with conflict and minimizing its effects on the couple and their marriage (Gottman *et al.* 1976). Since conflict was regarded as an indication of instability in a relationship, its frequency was often used as a barometer of the relationship's stability or progress (Haley 1964). By contrast, Lloyd and Cate (1985) showed that some conflicts had beneficial effects on relationships. For example, when couples argued not about 'personal stuff' but about the ways in which to carry out the roles of partnership, their arguments led, as often as not, to a compromise or to a good resolution of the issue that then led to a smoother, more agreeable and more satisfactory conducting of the relationship. That sort of conflict was therefore ultimately beneficial and probably a necessary part of relationship growth. After all, there are a lot of types of issues around which conflict can be generated (ranging from 'Where do we hang this picture?' to 'How often and in what ways is sexual intercourse to occur?' to 'Who is to control the relationship?'). As these authors show, there are many components to the establishment of **routines** in a relationship that require resolution of differences between two persons: it is almost inconceivable that two individuals with different backgrounds would start out by doing everything in the same way, putting the knives in the same section of the same drawer, and so on. A large part of 'making a relationship work' is precisely the practical joint construction of a shared experience and routine (Duck 1994a). Thus not all conflict will hinder a relationship: some sorts of conflict promote relational growth by being a major part of the process of relationship creation. So the commonsensically 'obvious' point about conflict is not the whole truth.

By contrast, researchers looked at intimacy and assumed that it underlay successful relationships; the intimate feelings of men and women were assumed to be not only comparable but probably identical as far as scientific scrutiny was concerned, a view now cast into some doubt (e.g., Wood 1993). Only recently have new approaches to intimacy and distance begun to uncover sex differences and similarities in intimacy (Canary and Emmers-Sommer 1997) and it is clear that the progress of a courtship is affected by the degree to which the two individuals differ in their conceptualization and operationalization of intimacy. Instead of being a simple independent variable that operates on the dependent variable of courtship growth, intimacy is itself influenced by courtship progress and has complex interconnections with courtship development, courtship outcomes and subsequent marital 'success or failure' (Crohan 1996; Veroff *et al.* 1997).

Such research also assumed that one marriage was much like another and therefore that 'a marriage' was essentially the same kind of institution and the same kind of experience for everyone (remember the review of magazine advice by Kidd (1975) discussed in Chapter 1). Thus there could be 'perfect marriages' and the characteristics of good wedlock could be identified and held up for us all to try to copy. There was a traditional view of marriage that assumed that individual beliefs, individual expectancies and individual means of conducting the relationship were not relevant (Simmel 1950). On this view, where members of society are assumed to have uniform conceptions of courtship and marriage, there is a right way to do it and other ways are wrong, inexpert, or misguided (Prusank et al. 1993). Even that view, however, tacitly assumes that satisfaction with a courtship is not based simply on love, since couples will be able to compare themselves to the social ideal and could judge their satisfaction and success partly in terms of fulfilment of that ideal (Simmel 1950) or in terms of peer pressure ('Haven't you guys made it yet??'). Such views are fostered by very extensive literatures about romance, not only popular magazines, but also the very widespread romance novels available in supermarkets (Sterk 1986).

An alternative early idea was proposed by Murstein (1971, 1976, 1977) in an approach known as S-V-R theory (for stimulus-value-role). The notion here is that at first couples are influenced by one another's stimulus features (looks, for example) but subsequently concern themselves with the match between their values, attitudes, and so on. Finally, the important feature that concerns them is the role behaviour that they perform: for instance, whether their respective performances of the role of husband and wife complement one another sufficiently to make a satisfactory working unit for the total relationship. As Murstein's work attempted to show, it is important not only that a given husband and a given wife are each clear about the role of 'husband' and of 'wife' – whatever they happen to believe those roles involve – but that each of them is capable of performing the role as they see it. Furthermore, their views of 'husband' and 'wife' roles should be complementary ones in themselves. Thus, their behaviours in the role of 'husband' and 'wife', as they see them, should match well and the number of daily hassles between them should accordingly be reduced. Such an influence is a relatively late arrival in a given courtship, however, and the matching of partners' role concepts will be irrelevant to the success of the early stages of the courtship.

Clearly, some of the pioneering explorations of relationship development both answered some questions and raised other, more difficult, ones for future researchers to explore. Such work helped to uncover the difficulties with the belief that courtship success was determined by the two partners' attributes at the outset of the relationship, and that successful courtship is conflict-free, or, at least, that all conflict is bad and should be reduced if a couple is to have a satisfactory relationship. Later work by Veroff et al. (1997) and Ruvolo (1998), while accepting that different points of a marriage are different in style, nevertheless looks for continuities of styles of behaviour that lead to better adjustment to the unfolding nature of the relationship. Even in the case of longer term relationships that turn into marriage, the information that is gathered and developed about another person can have important behavioural consequences for the conduct of relationships and thereby on the satisfaction that partners have with the relationship or the ways in which they have conducted those conflicts. Ruvolo (1998) looks at feelings of well-being in partners in the early years of marriage and links them to outcomes of marriage – essentially the later feelings of one partner towards another, whereas Crohan (1996), using the same data, notes that the perceptions of partners affect the ways in which specific conflicts are carried out.

IS 'COURTSHIP' ANY DIFFERENT FROM ANY OTHER RELATIONSHIP?

If we look at a courtship as a process and as a *practical* issue rather than as a *state* of relationship or as a *type* of relationship, we can see that it has many parts and we can consider the research in that light – just as we can examine our own assumptions in the light of that new way of seeing things. First, courting or even long-term dating couples have special feelings for one another but only one part of the relationship involves that set of emotions. Courtship and marriage are probably the only types of voluntary relationship that have an exclusivity about them: part of the whole business of courtship is the cutting off of other sexual relationships and the devotion of oneself to a specific partner. Naturally, that fact has several important implications but also important to bear in mind is that as a couple develops increased closeness in relationships so, too, is it also trying out a new *way of life*, with which its other aspects of life must be fitted or accommodated.

Courtship typically takes place particularly at one period in the life cycle. Typically, courtship partners are aged between approximately 16 and 26. At each end of this age range social pressures are quite strong and the partners will be especially likely to be sensitive to a sense of it being 'too early in my life to commit myself just yet' or, alternatively, of 'time running out' as they approach the end of that time window (Hagestad and Smyer 1982). It is not just that one has feelings of love for a courtship partner, then, but that one is also aware of the appropriateness of the time to express and execute those feelings. Courtship takes place in a period which is known to last until a certain time of life after which the opportunity for courtship diminishes, as people see their 'marketability' for a first marriage or long-term partnership decreasing dramatically with increasing age. Often this makes partners think very carefully about such questions as 'Is this my last chance?' or 'Should I commit myself just now when other, more suitable partners may come along? I'm still young yet . . .'. It may be too early to get married to someone you love and have known for a year if you both still happen to be 20, but you might feel that the time is just right if you are both 25, even if the loving feelings are of the same strength in both cases. If courtship were about love and nothing else, these issues would not strike people as forcefully as they often do.

The importance of this point is accentuated by the special nature of courtship as a testing relationship *en route* to a known goal (long-term partnership) which allows partners greater leeway to end the courtship if it gets into trouble. When a **friendship** gets into trouble, the partners may just let things lie fallow for a while; by contrast, partners in a courtship will rarely be content merely to ignore or set aside troubles, problems or dissatisfactions with their relationships. Once they suspect that their relationship is not working they will probably at least talk about that (Acitelli 1988) and they may decide to end the relationship. Marriage is intended to be an exclusive relationship that lasts for life and the purpose of courtship is to test out a future marriage. Thus, if a courtship seems to be working enjoyably, one stays in it, yet if it does not work, one leaves in order to have a better chance to find a more congenial one. There are thus fewer half measures or quiet connivings in courtship than there may be with friends – who can fall out without the need to go through a formal or legal ending of the relationship.

The realization of interdependence that is often created during this testing causes other issues to surface. Because people recognize the track-like nature of courtship, they know where it is supposed to be leading (i.e., to marriage) and they know roughly how long it usually takes courtship to get to that goal (so several years would be 'too long' and three weeks would be 'too short'). It should come as no surprise to learn that partners in courtship very often break up at around 15–18 months into a courtship (Levinger 1965; Hill *et al.* 1976): by this time the relationship has developed to the point where it needs to be defined. The partners tend to see themselves as being confronted with a once and for all choice between marriage on the one hand, and terminating the relationship on the other.

COURTSHIP AND OTHERS' EXPECTATIONS

Another point about courtship has to do with the organization of the relationship (McCall 1988). Courtship, being a kind of recognizable relationship with a known social form and known expectancies (namely if it 'succeeds' then it leads to marriage or to live-in loving), has a certain predictability not only for the partners themselves but also for parents and friends. Once one partner has been introduced to the other partner's parents and friends he or she becomes enmeshed in the social network and its own characteristic set of expectancies about the relationship.

People in some sorts of relationships are treated by third parties as being in that sort of relationship in a way that leads to recognition and restructuring of expectations: for instance, they are invited out as a couple, not as individuals (Bendtschneider and Duck 1993). Furthermore, such social influences can take the control of the relationship out of the hands of the partners themselves and some actions in a relationship may be deferred (e.g., the partners may decide not to have sex yet) because of the fear that people other than the partner may find out, disapprove, or be upset. For instance, friends or parents may get angry or may disapprove if the unmarried courting partners enter obviously into a sexual relationship and, for example, want to sleep in the same bedroom when they stay at the parents' home. Equally, couples may be influenced by social networks to expect certain activities in their relationship. Christopher and Frandsen (1990), for instance, showed that couples sometimes approach their first sexual intercourse under the influence of friends' expectations that they will have sex. However, such influences can affect even the existence of the relationship as well as the behaviour in it; on the one hand is the claim of a 'Romeo and Juliet effect' that may occur in relationships where parents disapprove (Driscoll *et al.* 1972): i.e., couples may pull closer together in the face of parental opposition to the relationship, according to that study. Other authors are more qualified and claim that, whatever the immediate response, the ultimate result is that parental opposition (or very strong opposition from friends) is more likely to predict the break-up of the relationship (Parks and Eggert 1991). One thing that is certain is that the approval of other people is important and 'noticeable': whether we are eventually swayed by it or not, we cannot ignore it very easily. Indeed, Burger and Milardo (1995), who studied 25 wives and their husbands, explored the associations of spouses with kin and friends and their relationship to the four marital qualities of love, maintenance, conflict and ambivalence. They indicated that couples who are well integrated in their networks are also more stable as a couple.

The relational context provided by religious background can also be relevant here since, for instance, Catholics may progress more slowly in courtship or may stay in unhappy marriages for longer periods of time because of their religious convictions and the influence of these upon their beliefs about the conduct of relationships. As an extreme case, Catholic couples may remain married because they do not believe in divorce, even when they do not enjoy the marriage or even like their partner any longer (Newcomb 1986). Equally, couples may get into greater conflicts with one another because of differences in their religious beliefs about the sexual components of courtship and how those aspects should be managed (Cunningham and Antill 1995).

Organization of the relationship is also done with reference to cultural prescriptions, especially in preliminary relationships like courtship that have a testing function for some other ultimate form of relationship like marriage. Being in a known type of relationship for which strong social expectations exist, couples can, therefore, evaluate their progress towards normality and the approved endpoint or style of relationship (Fitzpatrick and Badzinski 1985). That is why people occasionally break off the relationship and give the reason that it does not feel as if it is progressing well (either too slowly – 'It wasn't going anywhere', or too quickly – 'It just got too intense too soon'; Baxter 1993). Part of the process of courtship furthermore involves the partners becoming attached to the socially defined role of 'being a couple', as well as coming to love the partner (Cate and Lloyd 1992). It takes a considerable amount of effort and accommodation for couples to work out the difficulties of becoming a couple that shares living space, develops routines for doing chores, accommodates one another's needs for privacy and for intimacy, and deals with the requirements of managing sexual interaction (Herold *et al.* 1998; O'Sullivan and Gaines 1998). For all of these reasons, the organization of a relationship can be problematic for courting couples.

OTHER ASPECTS OF COURTSHIP: (1) SEX (AND POSSIBLY VIOLENCE)

Courtship is different from friendship because it raises the issue of sexuality. Couples who fall in love may feel sexual needs that have to be dealt with in a way that satisfies them, yet does not upset outside observers. While promiscuity is tolerated in some societies, most have restrictive rules about sexual interaction. Persons or couples are not free to decide for themselves the limits of their sexual conduct and habits but are expected to abide by the formal rules of the society. They will attract censure from others if they fail to follow the rules. The norms about relationship conduct are not always formalized, however, and are often embodied in 'social pressure' from peers or parents, even in the form of gossip that can make a person's position awkward and thereby bring them back into line (Bergmann 1993). A couple's sexual habits are regarded as legitimate topics for gossip and peer pressure, such that couples will experience their own sexual needs not only in the context of the relationship itself but also in the context of the wider society (LaGaipa 1982). Conflict may be generated in couples by the societal context and its commentary on their behaviour as much as from within the relationship itself (Klein and Johnson 1997).

Even before courtship, it is evident that avoidance of a reputation for sexual promiscuity is borne in mind by persons indicating their availability for dating (O'Sullivan and Gaines 1998). A sample of 194 US college students (96 men, 98 women) completed surveys designed to examine uncertainty about engaging in sexual activity with a dating partner, the factors that influence eventual decisions regarding participation, and the perceived emotional and relational consequences of these decisions. The majority of students (81 per cent) reported at least one episode of ambivalence in the recent past. In over half the cases (53 per cent), respondents reported eventually rejecting their partners' sexual invitations, usually because of relationship or intimacy concerns.

In a study of 'the elusive phenomenon' of playing hard to get, Wright and Contrada (1986) showed that persons who were moderately selective in dating were viewed as more desirable than persons who were thought to be either generally non-selective or else over-demanding and highly selective in dating. What seemed to account for the attractiveness of such moderately selective persons is the attribution that the person is neither too hard to get through choice nor utterly available through choice: they choose to be selective, but not unreasonably so. Availability, then, is best when it is tempered by reasonable selectiveness.

After dating, and once courtship begins, the availability of someone for a date is obviously less of a deciding factor and it is sexual availability that becomes more significant. During courtship, obviously, the management of sexual behaviour is an increasingly significant aspect of the relationship. Christopher and Cate (1985) explored the different pathways to sexual intimacy taken by couples moving from first date through casual dating to considering becoming an exclusive couple to actually becoming one. Couples who pass rapidly through the progression (and who may even have sexual intercourse on their first date) experience not only greater feelings of love for one another but also much higher rates of conflict. For couples who move more slowly up the sexual intimacy scale, the increases in intimacy are also associated with increases in conflict, and it seems quite clear that intimacy and conflict go hand in hand in many ways.

Dating violence

As dating intimacy increases so too does violence between partners, as if the positive and negative elements in the relationship are jointly increased. In the case of married couples rather than dates, Kenrick and Trost (1997) suggest that violence occurs when it is in the reproductive interest of the involved persons – husbands who kill their wives most usually do so from jealous concern over reproductive rights whereas women who kill their husbands most often do so to protect themselves and their children. Accordingly Kenrick and Trost note that dating violence is less severe but more prevalent than spousal homicide. Although some studies (e.g., Makepeace 1981; Cate *et al.* 1982) report a figure around 20 per cent, Deal and Wampler (1986) report results of a survey showing that 47 per cent of individuals had experience of violence in a dating relationship at some point – the majority of such cases being reciprocal, with both partners being violent at the same time. We should be curious about why the figures disagree – and why disagreements are constantly noted and reported by reviewers (e.g., Cate and Lloyd 1992). Clearly there are some problems about the status of respondents' reports – not everyone wants to admit to perpetrating violence or being the victim of it – but there are also different definitions of it, some of it being 'symbolic' (such as threatening to hit or hurt someone, but without any real intention to carry out the threat). Not everyone who threatens violence actually does carry out the threat or even means the threat seriously or literally, as parents of young children often exemplify: the threat of punishment itself is often enough to induce obedience. Given such problems, still unresolved in this complex literature, it is interesting that Deal and Wampler's (1986) figures for non-reciprocal violence indicate that it was the male partner who was three times as likely to report being the victim, a finding very similar to that reported by Rosen and Stith (1995). There are various ways of interpreting this finding, one being that men and women differ in their expectations of being on the receiving end of violence and report only those cases where these expectations are exceeded. Another interpretation is that men, for some reason, feel more secure about admitting to being on the receiving end of violence. A third is that men regard more minor experiences as 'violence'. Fourthly, there could be a 'gendering effect', with female assertiveness being interpreted by a male partner as aggressive or violent, whereas the same behaviour in a man is perceived 'merely' as an expression of male assertiveness. A fifth possibility is that females do resort to physical violence when frustrated, because they have had fewer opportunities to engage in other, non-violent, forms of assertive display.

On a related theme, Marshall and Rose (1987) found that some 74 per cent of couples report having expressed violence at some point while somewhere around 60 per cent had received violence at some point in an adult relationship. Once one restricts the data to eliminate so-called 'symbolic violence' (threatening to throw or hit or else throwing or hitting an object rather than a person, for instance), the figures are 52 per cent and 62 per cent respectively – but that then refers to 'real violence' and is more in line with Deal and Wampler's study. Obviously these figures imply that violence is very common and a question we need to explore in future is whether the experience of violence is especially associated with certain points in a relationship or with particular styles of relationship management or certain types of partners. Rosen and Stith (1995) examined the experiences of 11 women who had been in abusive relationships and answer that issue by noting that abused women often experience preliminary seeds of doubt about violent episodes that go unrecognized at the time but are reported only in retrospect, once a 'last straw event' has occurred. Bookwala and Zdaniuk (1998) nevertheless indicated that interpersonal problems account for violence to a lesser extent than does a preoccupied type of attachment style.

OTHER ASPECTS OF COURTSHIP: (2) MARITAL EXPECTATIONS

A couple experiences not only expectations but also anxieties about marriage in a socially defined manner and in two separate ways: expectations about getting married and expectations about being married. First, Zimmer (1986) explored premarital couples' fears about marriage and found strong doubts about the possibility of maintaining security and excitement in the same relationship. Couples were also anxious about their ability to fulfil themselves. Obviously such fears might discourage couples from getting married. Second, Sabatelli and Pearce (1986) have shown that married couples have expectations about the 'proper' level of outcomes in the marriage and found that couples had very strong expectations about trust for a partner and less strong ones concerning privacy and communication about sexual relations. As we shall see in Chapter 6, such expectations often form a background for the break-up of relationships. Yogev (1987), in a survey of American couples, has shown that such expectations and perceptions also occur in relation to marital satisfaction in dual-career couples – an increasingly large subset of the populations in many Western societies. Despite the non-traditional behaviour of such couples it was found in Yogev's study that marital satisfaction is related to perceptions that spouses fit sex-role stereotypes. Both husband and wife see the husband as superior on most dimensions such as intelligence, competence and professional status, even in these essentially non-traditional couples.

ORGANIZATION OF THE RELATIONSHIP

Given all that is going on in the background, it is clear that courtships are not simply about the development of feelings for one another, even if that were a simple thing in itself. We should instead ask what it is that develops in courtship on the basis of all these expectations, attitudes, and differences in perspective. Researchers are now increasingly taking the view that what really happens is that people get themselves sorted out as a functioning couple (Veroff *et al.* 1997), although this is also accompanied by some important reorganization of thought, attribution, and cognitive schemas (Fletcher and Fitness 1993) as well as changes in the form of intimacy (Prager and Buhrmester 1998). As we explore courtship as an interpersonal process that is placed within a network context (Milardo and Allan 1997), and a set of other issues to do with work and everyday life in general (Chan and Margolin 1994), so it becomes clear that a major part of the process of courtship deals with the creation and organization of activities in the relationship, and such socially informative issues as whether the woman will change her surname on marriage (Kline *et al.* 1996). A considerable part of courtship involves the sharing of time together and, of course, the couple has to work out the means of achieving this for themselves. Huston *et al.* (1981) gathered recollections of courtship in 50 couples who were in a first marriage of 10 months' duration or less. The couples drew graphs to indicate changes in the likelihood that they would marry as they reviewed the period before they eventually did marry. After completing such a graph the subjects also filled out an activity checklist in respect of activities such as leisure, instrumental activity (such as shopping), and affectional activity. The research showed that courtship breaks down into four major types which differ not only in the speed with which the couple decides to get married but also in terms of their distribution of activity. Accelerated–arrested couples begin with a high level of confidence in the probability of marriage and then slow down their final progression to marital commitment. However, such couples are closely tied to one another emotionally and affectionally. They also spend most of their leisure time together and they typically segregate tasks and chores into those performed by the man and those performed by the woman. Accelerated couples start off somewhat more slowly but follow a steady track towards eventual marriage. They are typically the most close couples emotionally and also share many instrumental activities. Intermediate couples evolve slowly but steadily and do not really experience much turbulence or difficulty until the very end of the whole process. They are rather disaffiliated from one another, having weaker emotional and affectional ties; they spend considerable time alone, do not act particularly affectionately with one another and are quite separate and segregated in their performance of instrumental tasks. Prolonged couples are turbulent and difficult most of the time and their progress to eventual marriage is slow. Like the intermediate couples, they are quite unbonded affectionally, do not spend a lot of leisure time together, and typically segregate their roles in performing instrumental tasks.

So what is going on in these different courtships? In the longer ones the distinguishing feature is that the couple spends less time on joint activities and may not express strong feelings for one another consistently, either. The main point, however, is that there is an important integration between the development of feeling and the creation of joint patterns of activity for the spending of leisure time together.

As a part of the development of courtship, partners develop an approach to their relationship and have to make decisions about it. Surra (1987) has shown that couples in the different courtship types give different numbers and sorts of reasons for the development or decline of their relationship.

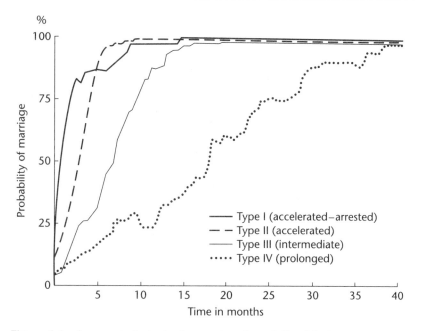

Figure 4.1 Average trajectories to marriage for relationship types
Source: Huston *et al.*, in Duck and Gilmour (eds) (1981: 67) Reprinted with permission of Academic Press.

Partners in the rapid, smoothly developing courtships not only become more closely interdependent and withdraw from the social network but tend to feel that the reasons for growth in their own courtship are similar to those generally expected to promote courtship growth. In other words the relationship grows because the person's expectations about relationships match well with his or her perceptions of what actually occurs in the relationship. Things are as they should be, so progress results. By contrast, couples with a slower rate of progress tend to ascribe responsibility for courtship progress to their own behaviours in the dyad; in other words they place responsibility not on expectations but on their own interactions such as conflict or self-disclosure patterns. Discrepancies between the two partners are more often cited as reasons for downturns in the relationship, in contrast to discrepancies between a person's own expectations and actual occurrences.

Although this chapter has dealt specifically with the issues that lead to the creation of a long-term exclusive relationship, and the next chapter deals with management of such relationships, I should remind readers that multiple forms of these relationships have now been investigated by researchers – indeed this is a point that opened the chapter. I have not covered them all because there are too many forms to discuss. Readers who are interested could follow up on gay and lesbian relationships, varieties of cultural relationships, different sorts of marriage, and other notions of marriage and family (e.g., extended family, family diversity) in the further readings listed at the end of the chapter.

SUMMARY

The notion that courtship progress depends only on the growth of feelings about a partner is clearly incorrect: many other factors are also involved. It is no use expecting couples to be successful in marriage merely because they are from similar backgrounds or have the same sorts of personalities. Their beliefs about marriage are as important as their behaviours in locking their lives together and sorting out the ways in which their time should be spent in one another's company. It is perhaps their practical management of relationships that is vitally important and much more so than are the initial individual characteristics that they bring into a relationship. As Carl (1997) and Conville (1997) noted, it is not so much the tools that a person takes into a relationship or creative work that define the end product as the way in which they 'make do and mend' *with* those tools. As we shall see in the next chapter, these matters also have important ramifications for the maintenance of relationships.

ANNOTATED FURTHER READING

A special issue of *Journal of Social and Personal Relationships* (August 1996) was devoted to the topic of family diversity and contains many interesting articles that follow up or expand on some of the points made in this chapter.

Fisher, S. W. (1996) The family and the individual: reciprocal influences, in N. Vanzetti and S. W. Duck (eds) *A Lifetime of Relationships* (pp. 311–35). Pacific Grove, CA: Brooks/Cole, explores the nature of a family and the functions that it serves, offering several different ways to look at this key set of relationships.

Huston, M. and Schwartz, P. (1995) Lesbian and gay male relationships, in J. T. Wood and S. W. Duck (eds) *Understanding Relationship Processes 6: Under-studied Relationships: Off the Beaten Track*. Thousand Oaks, CA: Sage, pp. 89–121, offers a strong analysis of the ways in which gay and lesbian relationships illustrate principles omitted from standard reviews of relationships and so propose a broadening of the ways in which relationships and relationship processes are defined.

Sher, T. G. (1996) Courtship and marriage: choosing a primary relationship, in N. Vanzetti and S. W. Duck (eds) *A Lifetime of Relationships* (pp. 243–64). Pacific Grove, CA: Brooks/Cole, offers an interesting perspective on the varieties of relationship options for courtship and marriage.

FIVE

MANAGING RELATIONSHIPS

Like a good government, good digestion or a good car, we do not really notice what it is that good relationships do for us when they are running well – unless they are running especially well. Yet relationships, like these other examples, seem to need maintenance, or else they fall into disrepair or turn into the kinds of skeleton relationships that are sustained only by the regular but infrequent means of exchanging Christmas cards or birthday greetings. Are the latter truly 'relationships'? Do relationships need maintenance or do they endure just because the partners like one another? Indeed, as Stafford (1994) asks, is 'maintenance' a stage in an intact relationship or a state of existence or a relative lack of change over time? As already outlined in several ways throughout this book, I think the issue of proper definition is captured by the exploration of the practical management of relationships in daily experience. Duck and Wood (1995) noted that relationships are such complex entities that they contain both good and bad, rough and smooth, sickness and health, richness and poverty. Thus it is not surprising that people find it to be a variable experience to have relationships, experiencing at different times a rough ride or a smooth one. All relationships have binds that go with the bonds (Wiseman 1986). Even more subtly, as Baxter proposes (1993, 1994; Baxter and Montgomery 1996), there is the point that relationships are *always* an experience of dialectic, that is, they *are* push–pulls between competing and opposing influences; it is their essence to be so. A relationship has an inherent contradiction between, for instance, a greater intimacy and the personal need for privacy, or between the interconnectedness of love and the individuals' needs to be autonomous. Thus all relationship conduct is an 'indeterminate [process] of ongoing flux' (Baxter 1994: 233) and 'a healthy relationship is a changing relationship in which a stable state is non-existent' (Baxter 1994: 234). A relationship is open-ended, unfinished business (Duck 1990).

Thus where the first edition of this book introduced the topic of relational maintenance, the present edition redescribes that as relational management, recognizing the insights of other scholars that essentially render the concept of 'maintenance as a stage of relationship' untenable. Continuous maintenance, or at least ongoing management, of the relationship *is the same thing* as 'having a relationship'. Our experiences of being in a relationship are experiences of managing the relationship, and it has to be *continually* managed.

Dindia and Canary (1993) discuss four common general concepts of relational maintenance that lead to this point:

1 keeping the relationship in existence;
2 keeping the relationship in a specific state or condition;
3 keeping the relationship in a *satisfactory* condition;
4 keeping the relationship in good repair.

Rather like a car, 'maintenance' means several things, from keeping it in good running order to smartening up the interior and the bodywork. In the present chapter I will look at several things that could be meant by 'relationship maintenance' and will translate all of them into issues of practical management. For instance, one clear sense in which researchers use the term 'maintenance' is to refer simply to the fact that the relationship endures, that it just keeps drumming along, and that partners ensure that, for example, a close friendship does not atrophy or become less close by reason of lack of contact or interaction. In another sense, 'relationship maintenance' could refer to the practical regulation of intimacy that prevents the relationship from developing a *greater* closeness and so stops any escalation. Thirdly, it could mean stabilizing a relationship that has been through a rough patch, though I will largely reserve discussion of that topic for Chapter 7 on relationship repair, while none the less recognizing that 'repair' and 'management' can overlap. As will become clear later in the chapter, the processes here centre on commitment, behavioural coordination and organization of routines, and so on, as well as affection and social skills in the management of conflict. However, people do not always manage or maintain relationships only by intentional means. As has been widely recognized, social constraints and family or network pressures can act as barriers to the break-up of relationships and so serve as maintaining forces, but these are not really management forces: they are influences that affect the ways in which a person or a couple may seek to manage a relationship but the forces do not in themselves *create* management so much as create the need for it. The couple has to do the management themselves within the constraints imposed by others or by social circumstances.

All the same, we sometimes stay in a relationship to avoid the social consequences of leaving or because of a felt moral pressure rather than because we actively enjoy and want to stay in the relationship for 'interior reasons'. 'What about the children?' and 'What will the neighbours say?' are psychologically powerful questions. Indeed, Johnson (1982) distinguished between 'personal commitment' (essentially based on a person's liking for the partner or the relationship) and 'social commitment' (essentially based on the perception of moral pressures, other people's views and societal forces). The present chapter is about the ways in which these intertwine but it deals with management of relationships that are not necessarily in trouble, and will emphasize the everyday activity of rela-tionships. A special issue of the *Journal of Social and Personal Relationships* was devoted to the matter of relational maintenance (Dindia and Canary 1993) and there is now a book on the issues of relationship maintenance (Canary and Stafford 1994) and a book on the issues of relational manage-ment (Duck and Wood 1995).

As has been repeatedly emphasized in the present book, relationships become integrally involved in the everyday lives of everyday folk and relentlessly intertwined with the everyday lives and activities that people carry out. One unfortunate consequence of early laboratory work on rela-tionships was that it unintentionally stripped them from their everyday contexts and the surrounding paraphernalia of life, like social networks and daily routines, or daily 'trivial' concerns, and focused only on the feelings and affect that people express. In real life, however, much hap-pens incidentally that keeps our relationships together – for instance, the routines of life make it easier for us to meet and coordinate our timetables (Duck 1994c). If we happen to live close to one another then the diffi-culties of maintaining the relationship are decreased and we can enjoy one another's company more easily than if the relationship is maintained at a long distance (Sahlstein 1998). If two parties have groups of mutual friends then meetings with them also bring the partners together. By contrast, long-distance relationships are more difficult to maintain (Rohlfing 1995) and relationships where one person has a chronic disability that interferes with routines of daily life are more difficult to manage in relationally satisfying ways (Lyons and Meade 1995). Also the management of blended families is complicated by such matters as the practical arrangements that are necessary for transporting children to the non-custodial parent(s) and coordinating timetables for that to occur (Coleman and Ganong 1995). Thus there are plenty of examples showing that practical realities that interfere with daily management of relationships have bad effects on the feelings that partners have about the relationship itself. These practical-ities of management are not inconsequential and can result in emotional overflow.

We take the routine aspects of daily living so much for granted that they seem 'obvious' and it is easy to underestimate their significance in keeping relationships 'maintained' or managed. Nevertheless, we begin to notice their relevance and significance once we come to the point where relationships break down (Morgan 1986) and people often report that 'trivial' interactions are not only necessary for keeping relationships going (Duck *et al.* 1991) but are part of what gets missed when a relationship ends (Harvey *et al.* 1995). The contrary is also true: when relationships break down, meetings forced by daily routines or the commonplaces of life and work become especially unpleasant – indeed, people will some-times leave a good job just to get away from a former friend or partner who has now become estranged, and in order to escape the daily routines that were previously pleasant and important. At that point the role of groups of friends also becomes especially clear and takes on a different character: you cannot avoid involving them in the break-up somehow or other (Klein and Milardo 1993). At the very least, friends will have to be told about the split; this can be an unpleasant task in itself, adding to the pain of separation and adding a social dimension that has to be taken into consideration.

Conversely the routines of daily life have an important place in relating to others through their provision of 'irrelevant' experiences that nevertheless have some impact on the conduct and maintenance of friendship. Circumstances and daily hassles happen to strain relationships independently of the feelings that the partners have for one another (Bolger and Kelleher 1993). For example, squabbles about daily chores can feed into the conduct of relationships, as can the ordinary hassles of daily life. A bad day full of irritations and frustrations can overflow into the relationship: anger generated by a frustrating day at work can spill over into frayed tempers at home. Chan and Margolin (1994) analysed daily log forms and mood check lists filled out by 59 dual earner couples on two consecutive days. Results showed that such spill-over from fatigue at work badly affected later moods at home and clearly indicated that the world of work and the domestic world are significantly intertwined. Such daily events can become the future weapons in a well-sustained battle or even a war that can strain a relationship ('Why do you always bring your work home with you?'). Equally, separation of partners when one of them relocates (e.g., moves home for occupational reasons) can place tremendous strain on the relationship, even though relocation should not always be taken personally and many long-distance relationships survive by telephone or email contact (Guldner and Swensen 1995; Lea and Spears 1995). Once again, then, we see that it is not feelings alone that keep a relationship intact, but something important about the way we structure our lives and manage the practicalities of everyday existence: these are not independent of 'relationships' that are conducted only on their own emotional level. Relationships intersect with the rest of life, because they are such a large part of its practicality.

Some of the routines of life keep relationships running as smoothly as a fill-up keeps a car running but, just as refills are not all that a car needs in the way of servicing, so too mere reliance on everyday routines is by itself inadequate to sustain relationships. Although much has been written on the skills of starting relationships, the real skills are those by which people manage and continue their relationships with one another (Dindia and Baxter 1987; Duck 1994c). Two friends are not just friends but are also individuals who have their own daily lives to lead, their own personal concerns and projects, their own daily problems to manage (Duck and Wood 1995). Their every waking thought is *not* about the relationship alone and researchers in the field of personal relationships could learn something useful from more vigorous and detailed plotting of the ways in which time is distributed in relationships. Just how much of the average day is spent on relationship tasks, such as planning meetings, preparing surprises, writing letters, making phone calls to friends, and all the other more mundane tasks of gossiping and relational management that take place through our helping friends with their daily tasks and personal concerns or projects? So far researchers have tended to accept the common belief (Rose and Serafica 1986) that most people regard their best friendships as self-maintaining and as being more or less entirely based on affection, and so they have seriously underestimated the damage done to relationships by incidental decreases in daily contact. Best friendships are expected to last in the absence of substantial maintenance in ways that close (but not best) friendships or marriages clearly do not. Casual friendships, at the bottom of the ladder of intimacy, are believed to require only proximity and frequent interaction between the two partners to sustain them. Yet it seems to me quite likely that different sorts of relationships require different sorts of management – or even are differentially affected by the need for management in the first place. Some seem to require virtually no management while others appear to require almost constant management. However, it is worth noting that persons may well underestimate the extent of any sort of work that they actually enjoy doing – in other words, in the most enjoyable relationships the same amount of management work may seem to involve less effort because it is more enjoyable (Duck and Wood 1995). By contrast, management work in the least enjoyable relationships may seem more full of effort because it is accompanied by a sense of self-sacrifice or self-discipline (Wiseman 1986; Stein 1993). These sorts of feelings could account for the fact that the most intimate (and so most enjoyable) relationships appear to require least effort – or are so perceived by the partners.

RELATIONSHIPS OVER TIME: MANAGING THE DAILY TRIVIA

Let us start by asking some questions about long-term relationships and how we think of them. Do they just develop to a given level and then plateau? If it takes all that work to get them to develop, what does it take to keep them there when they have peaked? Reissman *et al.* (1993) assessed the satisfaction of 53 married couples who were randomly assigned to engage in activities for 1.5 hours each week for ten weeks, the activities being defined by the couple as one of three categories: exciting, pleasant, or no special activity. The authors report that exciting shared tasks tend to draw people closer together emotionally but boring shared tasks can create a more general sense of dissatisfaction with the relationship. By contrast, Dainton and Stafford (1993) demonstrated that shared tasks and shared time keep people together but do so to the extent that the experience of these tasks and time expands the partners' self-awareness or sense of shared meaning systems.

Our common-sense conceptualization of relationship management tends to be overly passive and to ignore the trivialities that ultimately paste people together. It is unlikely, then, that the mere longevity of relationships keeps them going, and it is more probable that something else is necessary, something strategic or active or shared jointly that polishes up the relationship. The above suggestion of Dainton and Stafford (1993) is particularly interesting in that it suggests that forms of joint activity are significant in managing relationships when they help to coordinate the partners' feelings that they share a view of the world or understand one another (or one another's system of meaning and priority) more completely than they did before (Duck 1994a).

Nevertheless we should not overlook the fact that in the real world the partners' sense of each other is not all that matters. As intimacy increases, so too do structural constraints and these could become more important in the long run (Milardo and Wellman 1992). They constitute strong barriers to exit from the relationship: it becomes increasingly difficult to leave, so we look into ourselves to see whether we really do want to leave or whether we are prepared to put up with the pain for other reasons ('For the sake of the children'; 'It's not really so bad, some relationships are far worse than this' – although cynics and those who have been through the experience personally might note also the powerful force of continued financial stability in such circumstances, the strong pull of familiar property that might otherwise be lost or given up, and the inestimable value of an organized place from which to operate).

DOES RELATIONSHIP MANAGEMENT SIMPLY SUSTAIN THE STATUS QUO?

It is clear that the management of relationships involves more active processes than we might at first suppose. Another point to bear in mind is the fact that management and development of a relationship are closely tied together in subtle ways: to develop a relationship to a future level of intimacy one first has to be able to sustain it successfully at a lower and previous level of intimacy. Thus successful management will also be affected by the processes concurrently occurring in the development of the relationship. The ability to manage a relationship might be influenced by, for example, the level of uncertainty about the partner and the corresponding ability to reduce that uncertainty.

As Van Lear and Trujillo (1986) have pointed out, decreases in uncertainty about a partner do not occur as consistently as we might expect. These authors had 80 undergraduates take part in a five-week study of acquaintanceship where subjects talked to another volunteer of the same sex once a week for half an hour. Subjects were unacquainted with their partners before the study, which was concerned with changes in perceptions during acquaintanceship. In the second week of their study, the more trust, the more the uncertainty; and the more the uncertainty, the more attraction! Once again, it seems that we prefer a small amount of instability and uncertainty in our relationships and do not expect to find reduced uncertainty as reassuring as theorists have tended to assume. Uncertainty probably serves to maintain relationships by keeping us interested and on our toes to some extent! Van Lear and Trujillo (1986) note that there is a characteristic exploratory stage to relationship development and while we may need to maintain our interest in the other person, our maintenance of the relationship takes a different tack: we manage the relationship by disturbing and challenging ourselves through finding out new things about our partner at this stage. Uncertainty-reduction maintains the relationship at the earliest stages by reassuring us that we share common ground with the other person, but subsequent relationship management is achieved by novelty and challenge. Given this, it would not be sensible, as work on management of relationships develops, to assume that all management works the same way all the time or takes the same form at all times in a relationship. At different times and stages of relationships it could well be the case that there are different needs for different styles of management, and we should bear that possibility in mind as we review the work. For example, Honeycutt *et al.* (1993) noted that there are rules that couples employ to manage their relationship and conflicts in their relationship that are actually different at different points in its life, as they adapt to different circumstances. Equally, as Vangelisti and Huston (1994) indicate, there are important aspects to marriage that can be differentiated and that change in importance as the relationship progresses (and is managed as a relationship). The focal issue is not how the partners feel about each other but how they organize their lives as the relationship unfolds. Likewise, Trickett and Buchanan (1997) propose that the disequilibrium sometimes created by transitions (for example the transition to parenthood) often demands reorganization of time and interaction patterns both within the couple and with other people.

Since the important influences on a relationship change over time as it, too, changes, the work necessary to run the relationship will also change to reflect and bear upon those influences. For this reason we can safely assume that the management of a relationship will require different actions at different points. In support of this idea, Hays (1984) tracked the development of the relationships of 87 students for three months, administering measures of friendship activities and friendship description (including assessments of intensity and intimacy) every three weeks. He showed that the maintenance of relationships was dependent on partners' abilities to diversify the basis of their relationship and to divide the work of the relationship into its leisure time and tasks. Relationships tended to peak in intimacy surprisingly early (after about six weeks) and the features that changed and developed in depth and degree were behavioural patterns, frequency of meetings, diversity of places for meeting, and breadth of activities performed together. In accordance with Hinde's (1981) scheme, outlined in Chapter 3, the relationship began to move from a uniplex form to a multiplex form and worked forward from the base provided by the level previously established. Management and development thus intertwine very clearly and significantly. One cannot develop a newer and more intense form of relationship without successfully first managing it at a less intense stage.

Dindia and Baxter (1987) offered one of the first empirically supported considerations of the active strategies by which people sustain and maintain their relationships. It is a matter of fact that most of the time spent in typical relationships is not spent in developing or dissolving them but in simply managing their everyday variability. In contrast to much research, where interest has so far focused on development or dissolution of relationships, our major real-life effort in relationships is probably devoted to relationship management and repair. Dindia and Baxter (1987) examined the strategies for relational maintenance adopted by a sample of 50 couples (i.e., 100 spouses). Their interest centred on the ways in which a person's choice and use of strategies (as well as the range of options at their disposal) influenced marital satisfaction and length of marriage. There are some 49 strategies that people reported, ranging from 'talk about the day', 'share feelings', and 'symbolic contact' (e.g., a ritualistic telephone call at noon to check how things are going) to such strategies as 'reminiscing', 'compliments' and 'gifts'. Other strategies such as 'seeking outside help', 'joint prayer' and 'spending time together with friends' also feature in this long list. The couples showed evidence of more extended lists for maintaining the relationship than for repairing it when it had got into trouble. Obviously, if the management strategies work then repair strategies are unnecessary, so there is considerable overlap between categories. By and large, however, it seems that the maintenance strategies involve collaborative focus on the daily routines of life while the repair strategies target the relationship or the partner or oneself specifically (e.g., 'talk about problem', 'give in', 'ultimatum'). It was also found that the longer a relationship lasts, the fewer strategies are necessary to maintain it. This may mean either that partners get better at understanding each other and managing one another's needs, or that longer term relationships begin to become and remain more stable from their own momentum than from attention and 'interference' by the individuals in the relationship.

ROLES AND RELATIONSHIPS

I have examined the ways in which elements other than emotions might affect the management of a relationship. One further feature that could easily be overlooked is found in the roles that the relationship demands and the ability of the partners to perform them in complementary ways. The ability to sustain a relationship requires the proper observance and execution of various relational rules but several of these are less general than those researched by Argyle and Henderson (1984), and they apply to performance of specific roles, such as the role of 'husband' or 'wife'. Individuals differ in their perception of the exact elements of these roles (Coleman and Ganong 1995) but they nevertheless see them as important aspects of a relationship and partners will sometimes complain that the other partner, while being a nice person, was an ineffective 'husband' or 'wife'. In such cases the reason for problems in the relationship may be seen as due to poor role performance rather than due to the nastiness of one person, or as due to a poor match between the role needs of the two partners.

Hagestad and Smyer (1982) have shown the importance that we attach to our roles in relationships, the difficulty that we sometimes have in relinquishing these roles even when we want to leave a partner, and the powerful hidden force that the labels 'husband', 'wife' and 'friend' exert in reminding a person of his or her particular involvement in a certain sort of relationship. In considering the break-up of a marriage, the partners will occasionally find it hard to unpick themselves from the role of 'married couple' (see Chapter 6). The performance of the marital role clearly affects a person's self-image and constitutes a large part of the person's view of his or her place in the community. Other people react to single persons in ways that differ from 'proper' reactions to married persons (e.g., you can ask a single person out for a date but you should not invite a married person). Thus the socially approved roles required in the relationship help in some ways to preserve it and maintain the partners as partners in a way that is culturally recognized.

In part the roles work to sustain relationships because of the ways in which they structure time. Clarke *et al.* (1986) studied the ways in which married partners work out the combination of their variously role-required behaviours in order to structure the efforts of their days and weeks together. They found that, in contrast to the husbands' work, the wives' work was spread throughout the week and weekend, and that much of it continued while the husbands were enjoying private leisure time. Husbands' work did not seem to help to relieve the wife from domestic chores or to extend her time for private leisure, except in so far as the husbands released the wives from childcare duties at weekends. An important means of maintaining the relationship thus seems to be achieved (however undesirably) by wives accommodating to husbands' routines, rather than vice versa. As a general point, though, it is clear that management of the role requirements in a relationship necessitates arrangement of, and mutual accommodation to, one another's timetables and preferred activity patterns. Once an arrangement has been worked out (and as we saw in Chapter 4, this can be a stressful, conflicted and time-consuming accommodation), its existence serves to mesh the partners together, to bring them into one another's lives in interconnected ways, and to give them shared experience about which to communicate, common problems to resolve, and joint memories of their relationship to reminisce about, thereby reinforcing the relationship.

ROLE OF THE NETWORK

As we have seen in several places now, an important aspect of relationships is that they are wrapped up in our experience of daily life, our problems and our daily concerns. Large amounts of talk with friends are 'experience swapping' exercises or informal advice giving. Human beings verify their experience of the world by talking or gossiping to friends about it, and find ways of improving an attack on daily issues by hearing friends' advice about them (Bergmann 1993). Gossip often serves a key role as a source of **social comparison** – comparing ourselves with other people – as Suls (1977) has shown, but it often goes beyond that to a point where both formal and informal advice can be shared, problems aired, solved, faced and shelved (Duck 1998). Such advising can be quite indirect; for example, Glidewell *et al.* (1982) found that experienced teachers frequently tell illustrative stories about predicaments they have had and how they solved them and they do this in such a way that novice teachers can work out how to solve the problem depicted in the tale without having to humble themselves by asking directly for help or advice. Hobfoll (1996) indicates that there are many instances of covert social support provided in this way, even though we most often associate our friends with the direct and unambiguous support and help that they provide through performing special tasks like mending a car, as opposed to routine daily choices, reassurances and concerns ('Do you really think these clothes suit me?', 'You've got a cellular phone, do you think I should get one?', 'Do you honestly think I did the right thing?'). We can readily overlook the fact that although we talk to friends at times of particular stress or trouble, their provision of assistance and care is actually rather insubstantial most of the time precisely because it is very regular and pervasive (Leatham and Duck 1990). It takes apparently insignificant forms in the frequent small business of everyday life and is not simply major help with really crucial life decisions but it nevertheless provides important bases for them.

Leatham and Duck (1990) point out that the importance of shared knowledge and of discussion of life or common experience is that it is the continuous basis for personal relationships: it is not just something that comes to the fore when one of the friends has a problem. Sharing of knowledge and experience are happening all the time in unnoticeable ways. Even in our routine daily conversations with friends we unconsciously sustain our experience of the world and thereby maintain our relationship through the commonalities of experience (Morgan 1986). Why else talk about 'the day' and 'the people whom we both know'? In other words, the regular and very tiny routine contacts that we have with our friends every day help us to sustain our relationship not only by allowing us to express emotion, intimacy and feeling, but also because they interweave that person into our daily lives and our human, trivial concerns and make him or her a party to our little projects (Duck 1994c).

As Milardo et al. (1983) showed, there is a certain systematic method to the ways in which we draw ourselves out of old networks and into a new one as we enter a new relationship. In courtship, partners typically pull themselves out of the casual relationships with their network as they develop stronger ties with each other. However, the bonds with close friends are only barely affected by such developments and it seems to be important that we retain contacts with our usual ranks of close confidants when new important relationships begin. On the whole, though, the longer a couple has been a couple, the less they interact with their social network, the smaller the network and the shorter the interactions they have with those few people on the few occasions when they do meet. Klein and Milardo (1993) took the research further and showed that interference and support from the network are both strong. Parents, particularly, try to influence their children as they select marital partners, but the network also serves to sustain and reinforce the relationship by treating the partners as a couple (Stephens and Clark 1996) or by offering aid, support and – curiously – Christmas presents to tie the partnership or the family together: Cheal (1986) shows that Christmas presents are often given to the couple as a partnership rather than to single individuals within it, thus serving to emphasize the 'couplehood' of the pair.

We should recognize the psychological and communicative significance of these network ties in relationships. Not only do they serve to give us all a background against which to understand our experience but they link us directly to those apparently anonymous abstractions, 'society' and 'culture'. Milardo and Wellman (1992) provide a careful analysis of the ties in a small social network and the ways in which they serve to connect the members to the broader community, society, and culture. Every community, society and culture obviously (although it has not always been treated this way) comprises the interlinkages between the groups of people that compose it and the communications that they have with one another – and at the smallest, but probably most important, level that means the interrelationships that pairs of people have with one another. Societies consist of related communities, which in turn consist of networks, which in turn consist of pairs of individuals. By being members of relationships at all these levels, individuals sustain their membership of society and also maintain their other relationships.

A final subtlety is that when married couples are with other people they see the 'playful/social' side of one another to a greater extent than they may do in the day-to-day hassles, routines or boredoms of interaction in the marital home, with tasks to do, sleep to be had, finances to be managed and decisions to be made (Bolger and Kelleher 1993). Thus others in a network can help maintain a relationship by providing opportunities for the two partners to reaffirm their knowledge of the other person's nice and attractive qualities in a variety of settings.

HOW DOES ALL THIS MANAGE RELATIONSHIPS?

In thinking about relationship maintenance and management, then, I have focused not only on the strategies that people use consciously to sustain them – for it is certain that we do think about and plan our relationships to a considerable extent (Berger 1993) – but also on the ways in which relationships are sustained by routine and unnoticed or apparently trivial aspects of ordinary life. For example, Flora and Segrin (1998) note that joint activity time is a relational maintenance behaviour, and so they examined specific qualitative variables that affect the reward value and maintenance potential of joint leisure time. One hundred and four dyads (50 romantics and 54 friends) were videotaped while engaging in one of three activity conditions (game, relax, TV). Results indicated that when participants exhibited good social skills and perceived positivity in their partner, their joint activity time was more satisfying and, vice versa, activity type influenced the opportunities for satisfying interaction.

There are many examples and instances where the little things of life keep us together over and above any deep and careful calculation that we may perform on the costs and benefits of the relationship (Duck 1994c). Also we must not overlook the fact that the 'glue' in a relationship is often ably assisted by the cohesion supplied by the other networks to which we belong: sometimes our relationships are maintained by our membership of groups that meet regularly without our own direct action, and sometimes other members of the network serve as go-betweens or catalysts for the relationship of a given pair of constituent members (for example, Adelman (1987) showed how a network of friends acts as matchmakers in romantic relationships).

However, despite such cohesive pressures adding their weight to the strong individualistic positive affective ties that may already keep a couple together, we sometimes break off relationships, and it is to this interesting and complex topic that we turn in the next chapter.

SUMMARY

Management of relationships is still a relatively neglected topic in research and one that deserves fuller attention. It is too naive to assume uncritically that relationships fall apart unless they are held together and equally unsafe to assume that they hold together unless they are pulled apart. The management of relationships is accomplished by a complex combination of individual strategic inputs, mundane routines, social pressures, ritual behaviours, and communal actions that celebrate the relationship, personal attention to partners' needs, adherence to relational rules, and social skills, among other things. Relationships are sustained not merely by people's personal feelings for one another but also by people's routines, their trivial interconnectedness and presence in one another's spheres of life, by their strategic behaviour intended to sustain the relationships but also by the actions and communications of other friends, mutual acquaintances or colleagues and the partners' embeddedness in a community of ties to others as well as within a set of cultural beliefs about the ways in which relationships 'should' be done. Management of relationships is tied to their development in subtle but important ways in so far as a relationship has to be satisfactorily managed at a given level of intimacy before it can be developed to the next level. There is not, then, a simply new and different set of influences that comes into play at a 'maintenance stage'. Some means for developing relationships are also means for managing them. When relationships break down it may be due to faulty management as much as to increased dislike of a partner's personality or to inadequate development at an earlier stage as much as to failure to carry out the relationships well in the present.

ANNOTATED FURTHER READING

Canary, D. J. and Stafford, L. (eds) (1994) *Communication and Relationship Maintenance*. New York: Academic Press, contains a collection of interesting papers about the ways in which relationships are maintained.

A special issue of *Journal of Social and Personal Relationships* (1993) on relational maintenance was edited by Dindia and Canary.

SIX

WHEN RELATIONSHIPS COME APART

There is very little pain on earth like the pain of a close long-term personal relationship that is falling apart. The unhappiness and the sense of personal rejection and failure are among a whole range of other pains that sear their way into the lives of those in such misfortune. The effects of loss of relationships are sometimes extreme enough to induce severe depression and other psychological traumas (O'Connor and Brown 1984; Hooley and Hiller 1997), and to cause some physical side effects, ranging from sleeplessness to heart failure (Lynch 1977; Bloom *et al.* 1978). Yet a survey of men in the Detroit area found that only 23 per cent of their close relationships had lasted since the age of 18 (Stueve and Gerson 1977). Less than half (only 45 per cent) of romantic partnerships last longer than two years (Hill *et al.* 1976), and the prediction is that some 40–50 per cent of marriages contracted in the USA in the 1990s will end in divorce – and probably half of those that break up will do so within ten years of the marriage (Johnson 1982). There are enormous literatures on divorce and separation – particularly on their consequences (indeed there is a whole *Journal of Divorce*). In the present book I will of necessity deny coverage to much of this material as I cover friendship and romantic break-up, mentioning divorce and separation only occasionally. Readers wishing for more detail on these topics should consult the list of further reading.

A first thought about relational problems is that we should look for those factors that are antecedents of break-up. In the first edition I discussed the limitations of looking at the problem this way and raised some questions about the usefulness of different elements (for example the problems with predictions about break-up that are based only on demographic characteristics; Duck 1988). Early work into break-up developed within the prevailing climate of cultural opinion – where divorce was always 'wrong' and something to be prevented, something rooted as much in moral as in interpersonal problems. For this and other reasons, the research at that time paid most attention to the demographic factors that were correlated with unhappiness in marriages or which seemed to under-lie divorce. The work paints a picture in which breaking parties are either unwilling/unwitting victims of circumstances or victims of moral patho-logy. Their history is 'wrong' or their moral fibre is weak, so they break up. It makes a kind of intuitive sense and a great deal of research successfully explored the sense that it makes.

For instance, it has been shown that marriages where the partners are younger than usual are more unstable (Bentler and Newcomb 1978) and that those between couples from lower socio-economic groups or lower levels of education are more unstable than other marriages (Renne 1970; Mott and Moore 1979). Couples from different demographic backgrounds, such as different races or religions, are more prone to break-up than those of similar origins (Cattell and Nesselroade 1967; Jaffe and Kanter 1979). Equally unstable are marriages between persons who have experienced parental divorce as children (Mott and Moore 1979) or who have had a wider variety of sexual experiences and a greater number of sexual part-ners than average before marriage (Athanasiou and Sarkin 1974). There is also some evidence that marriages between black people are less stable than those of white people, but it is unclear whether this result is robust and it is also unclear exactly how such a finding should be interpreted if it were shown to be true (Ball and Robbins 1984). For instance, it could be the case that economic stability is lower for black people and that this reflects itself in expressed dissatisfaction with everything about life, including marriage; however, Ball and Robbins (1984) indicate that married black men are generally less satisfied with life than are unmarried black men, even when age, health, and socio-economic status are taken into account. Timmer *et al.* (1996), however, examined data from interviews with 115 black and 136 white couples and were able to show differences within a group of black spouses, depending on whether their ties to family networks were strong (which was associated with greater marital stability) or not. Apparently, well-embedded couples benefit from stronger support when they experience marital stress, and that benefit is in turn associated with greater marital happiness. Acitelli *et al.* (1997) also ex-plored the ways in which black people and white people managed their relationships and found that black spouses changed their perceptions from first year to third year according to changes in the management of rela-tionships. These changes were relevant to their satisfaction. In first year black marriages, couples who agree that the husband has the greatest say in decisions are high in stability and satisfaction. By the third year there is greater sharing of decisions and responsibilities. Such changes, rather than race itself *per se*, could underlie the relative satisfaction felt in marriages. It is also important that this study compared the same married couples over a period of time rather than comparing groups of 'black' with groups of 'white' marriages *en masse*, and drawing perhaps overly broad conclusions.

Perhaps for the above reasons, early pieces of research did little to tell us why or how such background demographics would have any specific effects on relationship disintegration. What would make someone from a given age group or socio-economic group or race act in relationships in such a way that would increase the likelihood of relationship break-up? Work identifying the personal characteristics of people whose relationships break up does not of itself help us to predict which, from a given set of demographically comparable marriages, will break up and which will not (Gottman 1994; Stein and Kramer 1996) and takes too little heed of the variety of family and relational forms that can be created to enhance happiness (Adelmann *et al.* 1996; Demo and Allen 1996). Many marriages that started when the partners were relatively young will break up while they are still young, but not all of them will do so; some last until death do the partners part (Dickson 1995; Pearson 1996). Thus the issue for research comes down to focusing on the *processes* by which the lasting and the non-lasting relationships may be distinguished (Gottman 1994; Aldous 1996). The rich and important set of studies on this matter carried out by Veroff and his colleagues (Veroff *et al.* 1993; Crohan 1996; Timmer *et al.* 1996; Acitelli *et al.* 1997; Ruvolo and Veroff 1997; Veroff *et al.* 1997) has begun to lead researchers in much more promising directions therefore.

An additional matter we should think about is whether break-up and divorce really are unequivocally events that we should account for, predict, and prevent or whether they are both extended processes whose prevention may not always be a good thing. Any form of break-up occurs over time and has an extensive history: few divorces are instant consequences of single events. We should also recognize the future extensive consequences for the lives of the partners not only as they negotiate the break-up but also afterwards as they adjust to it. Furthermore, the partners themselves are not the only ones who are involved in their own break-up. Friends, parents, counsellors, judges, and children may also be involved. In accounting for break-up, therefore, we need to consider it as a long-term process in the lives of the partners and their associates (Hayashi and Strickland 1998). Lastly, we should not imagine that people do not sometimes think about or plan their break-up or maybe about how to prevent it: it doesn't always come at people out of the blue or round the corner.

Recently, research has begun, therefore, to look more deeply at the specific relational characteristics of those relationships that break apart. It has turned to such questions as: What is it about the two partners and their behaviour towards one another that accounts for the trouble that they experience? Do troubled couples have particular ways of communicating or relating that are especially ineffective? Research has also begun to explore the break-up of friendships and to look at the actions, strategies and persuasive techniques that people deliberately take to break up relationships. All of the above thus points to the great complexity of relational break-up and its embeddedness in the rest of the participants' lives. Break-up is not just the waning of intimacy or reduction in feelings towards the partner. As Morgan (1986: 412) has observed, the dissolution of relationships highlights the operation of relational processes, such as interpersonal judgements, assessments of social exchange, and interactions, that are present throughout a relationship but go unnoticed in routine interaction.

REASONS FOR FALLING OUT

We can take it for granted that relationships all have good and bad spots that have to be managed (Duck and Wood 1995) and we looked at some of the ways we do this in the preceding chapter. Given all that, then, if we stop to think about the reasons for falling out of a relationship with friends or lovers, we can see that relationship break-up is likely to have many components, particularly if the relationship is a long-term one that has embraced many parts of the person's emotional, communicative, leisure, and everyday life. Virtually any aspect of life could be the reason given for a break-up. Typically, there are more than just a few reasons for break-up, therefore, even though they can be classified into a few general, and obvious, kinds. A question for research is how these classes of causes inter-relate not only with one another but also in their influence on the total impact of the break-up on the persons involved. Further, we should not regard all break-ups as equivalent in other respects. Some relationships break up early in their lives and some break up later; some break up because of problems endemic in the persons in those relationships and some because of partners' interactional incompatibility; still others are broken up by 'catastrophes' like affairs, relocation or death. Some break-ups are eagerly sought, some are regretted and mourned, some are intended, some are not.

Ineptitude or lack of skills in self-expression

Some people find relationships difficult and puzzling, cannot get into them, cannot sustain them, and experience loneliness. Such people usually have atypical ways of thinking about social interaction (Duck *et al.* 1994) and lack social skills – that is to say, they are awkward in physical movements or postures, have odd patterns of eye movements, poor timing of speech, hesitancy, inability to ask interesting questions or make comments that involve another person in their conversations. For instance, lonely persons are well established by many researchers to be poor conversationalists who do not involve the other person in the talk very well (Jones *et al.* 1985), are poor at indicating interest in other people because they often avoid eye contact, do not smile enough and generally signal uninterest (Jones *et al.* 1984), are unrewarding in social interaction (Duck 1991), and display reduced information output in terms of their nonverbal behaviour (Keeley and Hart 1994). In general, Leary *et al.* (1986) have shown that bores also have these poorly developed styles of behaviour and put people off because of their egocentrism and inability to put themselves into another person's shoes.

The people who are lonely thus seem to have a whole range of social skill deficits that make them generally unattractive for other people to talk to, although men and women differ in the ways in which such skills affect their ability to deal with relational stress (Tornstam 1992). One interesting remaining issue concerns the extent to which lonely people relate (or try to relate) to different sorts of relational partners from those that others choose as partners. Perhaps lonely people are just very bad at picking suitable partners. On the other hand, inept behaviours and lack of expressiveness not only make lonely or shy persons somewhat mysterious and unfathomable to outsiders, but also make them appear to intend to show lack of interest, hostility and interpersonal withdrawal, since the signs of lack of interest usually mean that the person really is not interested. When we see such persons appearing uninterested in us, so we are more likely to be uninterested in them.

It is usually clear when you ask shy people, however, that such persons do not *intend* to convey such disaffiliative or unfriendly messages but the messages that are received by outsiders are invariably messages of distance, unconcern and lack of interest in social relationships (Burgoon and Koper 1984). These latter authors had shy subjects interact with strangers and then showed videotapes of that interaction to the shy person's friends and also to strangers. Shy persons were rated as seeming not only distant but actually hostile when their behaviour was observed by people who had not met them before. Their friends and associates, however, saw their behaviour as within the normal range for the circumstances, although at the bottom end of that range. Thus shy and lonely people seem to produce behaviours that put off people who do not yet know them, but once they somehow get past that barrier, their acquaintances come to reinterpret the meaning of their behaviour and to see it in a more positive and attractive light. Until that occurs, however, the behaviours put people off. As such, the social skills deficits perpetuate the person's loneliness since he or she does not encourage others to break through something that appears to be a barrier distancing the person from others. Indeed, Segrin (1993) indicated that depressed persons, who also have 'depressed' skill in interaction, tend to perceive that they are being rejected by others more extremely, and yet tend actually to elicit such rejection from partners – a self-fulfilling vicious cycle.

For such persons imprisoned in the isolating cage of lack of social skill, the initiation of relationships is particularly problematic because no-one else perceives them as being interested in relating. In a sense, then, their relationships usually break down before they get going, but even when they do not, the likelihood is that their potential partners will find them such hard work that the relational soil proves to be unfertile for sustaining living relationships, with the result that their relationships are typically short and unsatisfying (Duck 1991).

Tiredness/boredom and lack of stimulation

We often hear people complain that they are bored in a relationship and need some excitement. A commonly cited reason for starting a new relationship is that the new person has some stimulation value for us and offers novelty and an expansion of our views of the world. We can expect, then, that a reason for breakdown of relationships is that one or both partners feel(s) that the other person no longer provides this type of stimulation. As Wright (1985a) has shown in a series of studies, stimulation value is a major element of friendship and we look to friends and partners for new insights, advice on new ways to approach problems, and challenging suggestions for the progress of our life. If stimulation is a major consideration in the start and maintenance of relationships, we can be fairly certain that lack of stimulation will be a reason for breaking off relationships. Indeed, we find that a frequently cited reason for breaking off a courtship or friendship is that 'I became bored' (Duck 1998) or the relationship 'wasn't going anywhere' (Baxter 1994). In such cases partners could be expressing several things through this simple expression of boredom (e.g., that they had expected things to move more quickly and found that that did not happen, or that the partners could not accommodate to each other, or that their partner was actually a boring person). However, whatever the subtleties of meaning, the fact is that lack of stimulation in the relationship is seen as a sufficient justification for terminating a relationship or starting up a new one, such as an affair. As we have seen in previous chapters, the expectation that a relationship will change and develop is fundamental to its existence, so that its lack of development, particularly in a courtship, is treated as a good enough reason for it to be ended.

'Other' (e.g., relocation or difficulty of maintenance)

Apart from the above factors contributing to the break-up of relationships, there are other elements that can create a climate for dissolution, broadly subsumable under the 'difficulty to maintain' dimension of Wright's (1985b) analysis of friendship. Events such as moving to a new job or home or moving away to attend college can not only strain a relationship but also reduce the intertwining of lives and lower the amount of contact that is possible on a chance or casual basis. Rohlfing (1995) also shows that the sheer stress of maintaining long-distance relationships is sufficient for them to decay, and the greater the frequency of daily contact, the better. Shaver et al. (1985) surveyed 400 members of an entering freshman class of the University of Denver and questioned them about their current relationships, previous transition periods, family background, state and trait loneliness, social skills, typical attributions following social successes and failures, and strategies for coping with loneliness. They noted that one partner's move to college was responsible for the decline of some 46 per cent of pre-college romances and while it may seem 'obvious' that such separations would lead to break-up, there is no very straightforward reason why that should be so. If partners' feelings for one another are the true basis for relationships and if feelings are dependent only on the other person's characteristics as a human being, mere separation should have little effect. However it is clear from the work of Shaver et al. (1985) that the opportunity to be in new relationships is too distracting and the pressures to develop relationships that are convenient ones to sustain are simply too great.

PROCESSES OF FALLING OUT

Given the above as a set of possible reasons for disaffection with a partner or a relationship, what happens when break-up occurs? First, partners have *beliefs* about causes for the actions of breaking up; they have *plans*, intentions, hopes, strategies for bringing it about (or avoiding it); they also have *explanations* for what is occurring, what has occurred, how it has affected them, what they now think of their (ex-)partner, and so on. Breaking up is not only hard to do, but it also involves a lot of separate elements that make up the whole rotten experience.

Rose and Serafica (1986) examined subjects' beliefs about endings of hypothetical relationships as compared with their reports of the endings of actual relationships they had experienced. In the case of hypothetical relationships, subjects expected the relationship to be destabilized by lack of proximity or lack of effort to sustain contact or, in the case of close friendship, by decreases in the quality or quantity of interaction. In the case of real endings, however, subjects were more likely to describe a break-up as due to interference from other relationships and to be an extended – and usually painful – process involving attempts at reconciliation, slow death, and gradual decline of affection, rather than a sudden event. What we cannot, of course, tell from such data is whether that is how things 'really' were or whether that is how people choose to remember it. That is an important point to bear in mind below: it may well be that in the case of break-ups people have an even greater tendency to rewrite history than they usually exhibit (Duck and Sants 1983; Felmlee 1995). All of us reformulate our memories about relationships quite dramatically. In the Duck and Miell (1986) studies, comparing contemporary accounts of first meeting with subsequent retrospective accounts, we found that people even changed their stories about where they had first met. Even more amazing, Surra (1987) reports that about 30 per cent of one of her samples of married couples were in disagreement with their own partner by more than one year about when they first had sexual intercourse together! In the case of relationship break-up we can expect that people will be even more motivated to see things in a particular way and to remember the relationship so that it conforms to that viewpoint (Felmlee 1995), since self-image is very much at stake when relationships break up.

Drawing on the theme of process and sequence in separation, Lee (1984) indicates that premarital romantic break-ups typically have five stages. A person first discovers dissatisfaction (D), then exposes it (E), negotiates about it (N), attempts resolution of the problem (R), and then terminates the relationship (T). Lee found that not all relationships break up by passing through all of these stages: some 'skip' a stage, but for the most part, these stages are intuitively recognizable and familiar. Lee (1984) found, in a survey of 112 such break-ups, that subjects feel that the E and N stages are the most intense, dramatic, and exhausting, as well as the most negative parts of the experience. Subjects who skipped those stages (e.g., by just walking out when they felt dissatisfied) reported having felt less intimate with their partner even while the relationship had been going satisfactorily. In cases where the whole passage from D to T is especially extended in time, the subjects reported that they felt more attracted to their former partner and that they experienced the greatest loneliness and fear during the break-up.

In a study with similar objectives, Baxter (1984) explored the strategies employed by persons intending to dissolve a relationship and found that there are patterned differences among relationships in the ways in which they break up. They do not all follow the same path but they have their own characteristic patterns that fall into several groups. Eight different trajectories for break-up were identified by Baxter (1984), ranging from 'swift implicit mutuality' (or 'sudden death', where both partners agree on the termination) to 'mutual ambivalence', which revealed a set of multiple disengagements mixed in with attempts at repair and reconciliation, or multiple passes through a termination sequence.

In further work on these issues, Baxter (1986) explored the personal expectations that romantic partners have for their relationship and the ways in which these expectations relate to the break-up of the relationship. Eight primary perceived reasons for the break-up of a relationship bear on these expectancies:

- partners feel that each of them should expect a certain amount of autonomy;
- they expect to find a good basis of similarity between the two of them;
- they expect one another to be supportive of each other's self-esteem and feelings;
- they expect the other person to be loyal and faithful;
- they expect the other person to be honest and open;
- they expect to spend time together;
- they expect equitable distribution of effort and resources; and
- they expect there to be some intangible 'magical quality' in the relationship.

Reasons given to Baxter (1986) for breaking up the relationship usually referred to one of these expectations and pinned responsibility for the breakdown on the violation of that expectancy – usually by the former partner, rather than themselves. Presumably a person's choice of strategy for handling the impending or desired break-up would be influenced by his or her perception of the underlying need for break-up and hence by the individualized account of what was the essential problem in the relationship.

In an indirect way, the work of Hagestad and Smyer (1982) bears on this point, since their consideration of different types of divorce echoes not only Baxter's argument that there are different trajectories for the break-up of relationships, but also indicates that a person's way of handling the divorce reflects his or her perception of the flaws in the relationship. Hagestad and Smyer (1982) identified two main types of divorcing: orderly (where both partners fully and satisfactorily disengage from their former positive feelings about their ex-partner, from their feelings about the marriage and its roles, and from the routines of work and daily life that were built into the marriage); and disorderly (where one of the above three disengagements was not successfully accomplished by at least one of the partners). This latter category ranged from cases where one or both partners sincerely and deeply wished that the divorce had not happened and would still like to be married to their former spouse, to cases where the two partners were clear that they no longer loved each other or could not stand the perpetual conflict in the marriage, but nevertheless still wanted to be in the marital role – to be 'a husband' or 'a wife', to share the dreams and the 'walking off into the sunset together'. It is clear from this research that there are many types of divorce, not just one, and that the process of divorcing differs across divorces (see items in the list of further readings for more detail). The key aspect of divorce and relationship loss is quite evidently *the symbolic meaning of the relationship*, something lost along with the relationship itself (Umberson and Terling 1997).

A final point to bear in mind is that people's reflections on their relationships affect their approach to break-up (see Burnett *et al.* 1987). In an intriguing study by Harvey *et al.* (1986), it was found that people have particularly vivid 'flashbulb' memories of past loves and that the memories of those loves serve as important benchmarks in people's constructions of, and approaches to, their lives – and probably their future relationships. Today's break-up sets the scene for tomorrow's relationships, the degree of eagerness with which they are sought, the amount of wariness with which they are approached, and the extent to which the person specifically watches out for or guards against particular features of the new relationship. In brief, past break-ups tune up our awareness of what can go wrong or of which partners do not work for us; we try to learn from that and avoid a repetition of the problem next time.

So, as we move on to reflecting about the nature of the extended process of dissolution of relationships, we should not forget that a person's way of leaving a relationship can set the scene for beliefs about future relationships.

A MODEL OF DISSOLUTION

All of the above considerations help us to move towards a particular overview of the dissolution of relationships, first outlined by Duck (1982a, b). This approach sees relationship dissolution as composed of several different but connected phases, each of which directs a person's thoughts, actions, or interpersonal communications in characteristic ways. It takes account of the fact that a person feels uneasy about a relationship before he or she talks to the partner about it, that there are other persons in a network who contribute to a couple's consideration of break-up, and that a major concern for people is that they want to leave relationships with some feeling that they have acted correctly or in a manner justified by the circumstances they faced or the people they dealt with (see Figure 6.1).

The intrapsychic phase

We frequently complain about people – our partner, boss and colleagues included. It seems that that is a regular part of life, not something special and unusual; but it is sometimes a prelude to a break-up. There is clearly a phase at which individuals reflect on their relationship and prepare a mental list of its deficiencies, along with those of the partner. During such a phase a cost-benefit analysis of a relationship might be assessed but that is not really an automatic cause of the break-up of relationships in the way that some commentators appear to suggest (Huesmann and Levinger 1976). The whining or complaining phase of breakdown is primarily an

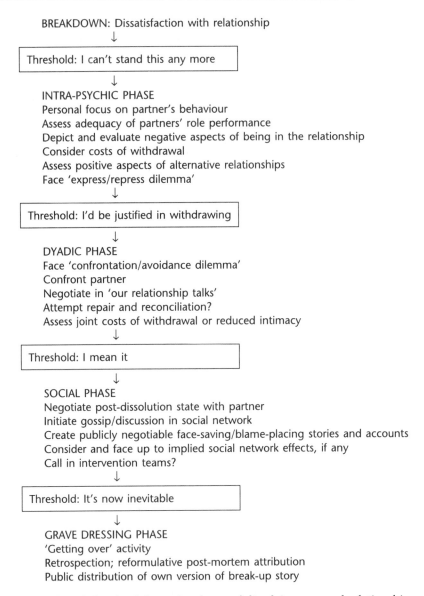

BREAKDOWN: Dissatisfaction with relationship
↓

Threshold: I can't stand this any more

↓

INTRA-PSYCHIC PHASE
Personal focus on partner's behaviour
Assess adequacy of partners' role performance
Depict and evaluate negative aspects of being in the relationship
Consider costs of withdrawal
Assess positive aspects of alternative relationships
Face 'express/repress dilemma'

↓

Threshold: I'd be justified in withdrawing

↓

DYADIC PHASE
Face 'confrontation/avoidance dilemma'
Confront partner
Negotiate in 'our relationship talks'
Attempt repair and reconciliation?
Assess joint costs of withdrawal or reduced intimacy

↓

Threshold: I mean it

↓

SOCIAL PHASE
Negotiate post-dissolution state with partner
Initiate gossip/discussion in social network
Create publicly negotiable face-saving/blame-placing stories and accounts
Consider and face up to implied social network effects, if any
Call in intervention teams?

↓

Threshold: It's now inevitable

↓

GRAVE DRESSING PHASE
'Getting over' activity
Retrospection; reformulative post-mortem attribution
Public distribution of own version of break-up story

Figure 6.1 A sketch of the main phases of dissolving personal relationships
Source: Duck (1982b: 16) Reproduced by permission of Academic Press.

internal phase with little outward show, and a person could decide to do
nothing on the basis of the arrayed deficiencies. This could be because
of a wish to try to put things right, or because of a preference to talk it
through with the partner (or maybe to wait for a suitable alternative
relationship), or because of inertia, lack of willpower, or lack of an appropriate opportunity or mechanism. Whichever is true, break-up is not an

inexorable consequence of an imbalance in the equity of a relationship, and so most researchers have become wary of reporting determinism of causes on effects.

At the point where the complaints build up to a measure beyond a certain threshold, I suspect that the person would begin to communicate the problem indirectly at first, by means of hints or 'needlings' (Duck and Wood 1995). There is some evidence (Duck 1982a, b) that disaffected partners first start to communicate their dissatisfaction this way and then begin a 'talking to a wall' style of communication that involves them expressing their views about the partner to someone who provides the necessary ear, but who is a third party, either neutral and relatively anonymous (such as a bar server or a stranger on the train), or someone who does not know the partner well and will not rush off and relay the information to the partner. At this stage of breakdown, the person is really searching for some self-justification as opposed to any real action to put the relationship right.

The dyadic phase

Once a person feels there are strong enough complaints and grounds for taking things up with the partner, something more has to be done. It is not just a question of weighing up the rewards and costs of a relationship, deciding one does not come out ahead on some simplistic exchange equation, and then 'leaving'. Leaving sounds easy if you say it fast. Actually it involves real confrontations, real arguments, real pain, real attempts at reconciliation and real resolution. After the intrapsychic phase, then, comes the interpersonal mess. A partner has to be argued with face-to-face and not as an abstraction!

It is unlikely, even if they were initially attracted to each other by their similarities, that two persons will take the same view of their relationship (Duck and Sants 1983; Acitelli 1993; Duck 1994a) and it is particularly likely that, when the relationship is to be carved limb from limb, the two partners will disagree about ascription of responsibility for the breakdown. Any revelation of the dissatisfactions mulled over in the intrapsychic phase is likely to cause a certain amount of shock and hurt to the other partner. In turn, it is probable that a person with a problem to discuss will also experience pain, in that if the problem is bad enough to cause the termination of the relationship, then the process of relationship dissolution must be begun; while it is acknowledged but resolvable, both partners may feel the distress of knowing that things are not right for one another. In other words, the possibility, or hope, of 'working it all out' can provide as much distress as balm. The two persons really are psychologically stretched by the simultaneous processes of trying to resolve things with the partner while also delineating their own feelings and general position more precisely, in order to win justice as they see it. Given the uncertainty about whether the relationship really will break up or be repaired, this other process is an added stress.

These are some of the reasons, I believe, why lab and survey research consistently shows real-life oscillation, uncertainty, hesitation, and infirmity of purpose in partners at this point of a break-up (Baxter and Montgomery 1996; Duck 1998). People can often be resentful in a relationship and yet be unwilling to finish it (Duck and Wood 1995). Most of us are people complicated enough to know that it is possible to be deeply in love with someone and yet recognize that they have limitations or occasionally behave in 'difficult' ways. We also know that it is possible to be unhappy in such a relationship without the love ebbing away or without leaving the relationship. Oscillations and weakening of resolve seem to me to be perfectly human vacillations that do not inexorably end relationships, but they are none the more enjoyable for that (Duck 1994b, c). As partners face up to the consequences of deciding between 'break it off' and 'try to repair it', they will inevitably come up against their doubts and anguishes, and will come into conflict with one another – conflict which has to be dealt with in person in addition to other pains. Even if they decide to renegotiate the *form* of the relationship, that negotiation has its problems and unpleasant traps (Lee 1984), and the whole dyadic phase is full of guilt, hostility, resentment, stress and a negative communicative style (Duck 1998).

The social phase

After the partners have done some fighting – and probably even while it is still in progress – there is an important unseen element to break-up. Because no relationship exists independently of its simultaneous connectivity with other people, it is important to gain the support of the networks of friends, relatives, and acquaintances during break-up of a target relationship. It is not satisfactory merely to leave a relationship: it is important not only to feel justified in leaving but also to have one's friends and relatives agree that one was right to leave. For this reason both partners consult friends (and relatives) for advice on the problem and for extra perspectives on the partner and their own actions (La Gaipa 1982). The network becomes involved in relationships that are breaking up and has views about relationships as they spoil (Klein and Milardo 1993). A network also gives support to the fighting partners, takes sides, pronounces verdicts on guilt and blame, and helps to seal the occurrence of the break-up by sanctioning the dissolution (the most obvious example being a courtroom where a divorce decree is pronounced).

The notion that this phase is simply a barrier to relationship dissolution is important but only partly true and misses the point that there are really two roles that the social network serves in the context of breakup (Allan 1998). Yes, the social network probably exerts pressure on a couple to stay together – particularly at the start of a dissolution – and the fear of what parents or neighbours may think could well act as a barrier to some couples splitting up (Klein and Milardo 1993). However, the network also serves a role that facilitates a break-up once the couple seems to be moving towards that. Networks are distributors of gossip (La Gaipa 1982) and that upholds the social norms that provide all relationships with context (Allan 1998). Networks also serve an important role in recovery from relationship break-up, by supporting individuals when break-up has occurred (Harvey *et al.* 1986; Klein and Milardo 1993). Obviously, then, at this point network members do not act as a barrier to break-up, since they actually help people to achieve it.

The grave dressing phase

Getting over a break-up involves not only leaving the relationship – and in some cases dividing up the household, the property and the children's access time – but also a realignment of feelings about the relationship, the partner and the break-up. As La Gaipa (1982) has shown, a necessary part of leaving a relationship is face management: the need for each person to exit with a reputation for relationship reliability still intact. That is to say, in leaving, a person should not acquire a reputation for untrustworthiness or disloyalty, since that would poison the possibility of future relationships. For this reason, for reasons of self-justification, and for the sake of creating an acceptable perspective on the relationship, partners who split up do a lot of 'grave dressing': the relationship is dead and buried so they start to erect a tablet that says important things about its life and death. This tablet takes the form of a good, credible, socially acceptable version of the life of the relationship and the reasons for its death. As Weber (1983) reports, this very often takes the form of a story indicating that the relationship had a fatal flaw right from the start, that the person worked hard to ignore or correct that flaw but, despite commendable efforts, failed: so the relationship had to die (Felmlee 1995). While a primary role of such stories is truly face-saving, it is also clear that the grave dressing phase serves to keep some memories of the relationship alive and to 'justify' the original commitment to the ex-partner (Baxter 1987). Such stories are an integral and important part of the psychology of ending relationships and cannot be written off as inconsequential. By helping the person to get over the break-up they are immensely significant in preparing the person for future relationships as well as helping them out of old ones.

In the field of research on marital and family problems, one growing concern is with 'postmarital relationships', 'remarital relationships' and family reorganization after divorce. Coleman and Ganong (1995), for example, argue that the increasing occurrence of divorce alters people's expectations of married life in that blended families are now becoming normative. Indeed there is 'a shift in ideology – from viewing divorce as pathology to viewing divorce as an institution . . . the study of divorce is no longer narrowly defined within a deviance perspective' (Ahrons and Rodgers 1987: 23). Once divorce is seen as a common transition rather than as pathological, researchers can reasonably begin to attend to a much wider range of issues, such as 'getting over' as well as prevention, and as much to the processes of entering new relationships as to those to do with leaving the old ones (Masheter 1997). With this thought in mind, we can now move on to Chapter 7 on repair of relationships.

SUMMARY

Chapter 6 has examined the process of the break-up of a relationship and explored it as a multifaceted and extended series of psychological and practical activities rather than as a simple event. It is a process that emphasizes the complex functioning of relationships and the management of daily life. There are many elements that relationships require in order to work properly – elements that function quietly and unnoticed until break-up occurs. The present chapter identifies these elements as the internal cognitive evaluation of partner, the behaviour of relating to partner, the embeddedness of relationships in the social network, and the stories that people create in order to explain and justify their relationship's existence and its ending. In the dying and the death of a relationship all of these 'sleeping elements' jerk into vigorous life and make the dissolution of relationships the all-consuming psychological and social experience that it can easily become. However, the ending of relationships is always a fully interactive and communicative social process, not something that happens within the demarcated psychological and cognitive lives of the two partners alone.

ANNOTATED FURTHER READING

Duck, S. W. and Wood, J. T. (1995) *Understanding Relationship Processes 5: Confronting Relationship Challenges*. Newbury Park: Sage, is a set of chapters that deal with the difficulties of relating in various modes, some of which will eventuate in dissolution of the relationship and some of which will not.

Hagestad, G. O. and Smyer, M. A. (1982) Dissolving long-term relationships: patterns of divorcing in middle age, in S. W. Duck (ed.) *Personal Relationships 4: Dissolving Personal Relationships* (pp. 155–87). London: Academic Press, provides an insightful and interesting approach to the complexities of divorce, involving not only the change in feelings towards partner but also sense of self in a role (as discussed in the text here).

Journal of Divorce offers a range of papers on the issues of breakdown of marriage and the recovery therefrom.

SEVEN

PUTTING RELATIONSHIPS RIGHT

There are many important reasons for doing research on friendship and relationships but one that is implicit in much that has been said so far is that personal relationships – whether friendship or marriage – do not have a natural tendency to be conducted successfully even when love and emotion are strongly positive. Yet they can be major sources of our peak life experiences. Researchers therefore often express, but more often merely imply, the hope that the study of friendship and personal relationships will lead to a greater understanding of the ways in which relationships can be repaired, improved or enhanced wherever they are presently unsatisfactory. Despite numerous considerations of marital therapy, there still remains relatively little literature on repairing other kinds of relationships (Duck 1984a), though there is a recent growth of attention to the matter of forgiveness in relationships and to the issue of improving ways of dealing with disloyalty and betrayal (Kelley 1997).

Relationship repair can mean one of three things: helping two people make an unsteady relationship work more satisfactorily (which is usually what people mean by 'repair'); helping one or both persons *out* of a painful relationship that cannot be made to work (this is now receiving more attention than it used to with 'good break-up' being seen to be a mature outcome; Masheter 1997); or helping to 'repair' an individual after the end of a relationship by facilitating the adjustment to the break-up or the loss of a partner (whether that occurs through divorce, separation, bereavement, or some other cause). This latter is now often achieved by support groups of different levels of involvement and usefulness (Morgan *et al.* 1997). This chapter deals with all three kinds of relationship repair, although they are not always as clearly distinct as I have represented them to be here. It should also be noted that one goal of research in relationships may be to make people more aware of the relationship processes which they can influence for themselves (Acitelli 1993) and external intervention is not always either needed or desired. For instance, by drawing on social psychological principles it may be possible to enhance people's self-conscious attempts to work at management and improvement of their relationships whether heterosexual (Kurdek 1991) or homosexual (Kurdek 1992). Repair does not have to be done by outsiders; in reporting mostly on work that examines intervention from outside the relationship I am reflecting the bias of the current (and rather sparse) social psychological literature, but in real life much 'repair' occurs as a result of partners' own cooperation and without things ever getting to the stage where anyone feels that things are serious enough to need 'repair'.

I am also going to deal with only a limited range of approaches, since a thorough consideration of therapeutic interventions in families and marriage is beyond the scope of this volume (but see Mallinckrodt's (1997) comprehensive analysis of therapies for relationships). The present chapter focuses mostly (but not exclusively) on naturally available repairs as may exist from a supportive family or helpful friends or be available to distressed individuals from their own bank of personal resources (Johnson *et al.* 1992), but I will occasionally refer to this large literature on formal therapy.

Thus my approach has a number of personal biases that should be acknowledged. While there are many programmes designed to enhance relationships (e.g., Clements and Markman 1996; Furman and Simon 1998) and while several programmes of premarital counselling and premarital enrichment exist (Notarius 1996; Thomas 1997), it seems unlikely that any such single programme will address all the relevant issues for every type and style of relationship. Just as relationship development, management and breakdown are complicated processes, as we have seen, so the repair of relationships will be complicated (see Duck 1984a for a review). My assumption is that relationship repair will be the more successful the more it takes account of the processes through which the relationship comes to need repair (Duck 1994b). Repair strategies also need to take account of the normal human concerns in which the repair will be embedded, since these broader concerns are not discarded simply because a person focuses on repairing a relationship.

SOME BACKGROUND FOR ENHANCEMENT OR REPAIR OF RELATIONSHIPS

We have seen in Chapters 2–5 that the creation and management of a relationship are processes with many directly and indirectly influential components. For instance, partners have to be competent communicators of their interest in other people, sociable in their interactions with associates, and able to intertwine the parts of their daily activities that, although apparently unrelated to friendship and relationships, nevertheless serve to sustain and enhance the interconnectedness of lives and relationships. We learned also that although relationships are based on feelings of attraction, liking, love and strong affect for one another, there are practical realities of other behaviours and other unrelated feelings and concerns that must be handled well and are essential to the creation of the working entity that makes up a relationship.

If all of these elements are necessary then we can expect Murphy's Law to apply to any of them, such that a relationship could become problematic and need repair in respect of any of them. (Murphy's Law states that 'Anything that can go wrong will go wrong'.) Partners may not be good at showing their liking for one another (Keeley and Hart 1994; Lamke *et al.* 1994), for example, but they may also be poor at coordinating their activities in the relationship especially if one of them is depressed (McCabe and Gotlib 1993; Thompson *et al.* 1995) or very ill (Unger *et al.* 1996). They also may be insufficiently attentive to the leisure time that creates opportunities for strong affect to be developed and sustained (Clarke *et al.* 1986). The comfort of happy times spent in one another's company not only fosters one individual's beliefs in the continuance of the partners' feelings for each other, but also provides context or contrast for understanding the *meaning* of conflict (Crohan 1992). In short, there is *symbolic* meaning derived for the relationship from both happiness and conflict (Umberson and Terling 1997). Burnett (1986) showed that 'contact' – amount, occasion, frequency, or absence – was mentioned more than any other relationship attribute as a significant element and partners' memories for events are very important in affecting their satisfaction – whether or not those memories are 'accurate' (Ross and Holmberg, 1992; Acitelli *et al.* 1993). Clearly, partners may doubt one another's love not because it fails to be expressed verbally, but because they fail to see one another putting the relationship first (Baxter *et al.* 1997), or because they feel that the other person does not *do* the actions of loving by making time to be together (Prager and Buhrmester 1998). If those are the feelings or perspectives that render the relationship unsatisfactory, then some readjustment of them would, by itself, help the persons to repair their relationship by their own efforts. Alternatively, repair can become more difficult when partners, as a result of marital difficulties, also become depressed (Beach and O'Leary 1993). This is because depressed persons tend to become more difficult relational partners and to make more work for their associates.

Accordingly, our consideration of the repair of relationships must have built into it some heed of our theoretical knowledge of how relationships develop and are managed. Researchers also need to attend to beliefs about the matters that are important to individual human beings and also to partners as they develop or manage a relationship. Since relationships break down by stages and phases, as we saw in Chapter 6, it is likely that repair of relationships can also be seen in a stage-like way (Duck 1984b) and that is the way I shall take it here, reflecting the analysis of breakdown discussed in the previous chapter. However, partners could just decide that their relationship needs rejuvenation (Wilmot 1995), and might want to make efforts to enhance or improve it.

Relevant here are not only the underlying human concerns, nor even simply the development of relationships, but also the complexity of the nature of breakdown in relationships. Since not all breakdowns of relationships are the same – and indeed many separable sorts of patterns were identified in the previous chapter – it is very unlikely that one simple method of repairing relationships will be equally and totally effective in every case. If a car breaks down with a clutch problem, it is obviously no use fixing the carburettor. Just as clinical psychologists spend a considerable time identifying the main areas that concern a client in the adjustment to a perceived problem, so too should those trying to repair a relationship first attempt to find out what has gone wrong with that specific relationship and what parts of it have reached breakdown. We should expect it to be reasonable and productive to assume that different repair strategies would have the best effect on different kinds of problem.

We have seen in Chapter 6 that the breakdown of a relationship involves many facets not only of affect, but also of behaviour, communication, and cognition. We have also learned that there are points in the process when one's feelings about one's partner are of secondary significance to the pressures that one feels from the network (Klein and Milardo 1993) or one's desire to have one's own version of the break-up dominate the accounts that circulate about the termination (Weber 1983). In repairing a relationship, then, it is clear that there will be separate but interlocking components, and that dealing with networks or arranging for network support may be as important and as necessary as other actions or cognitive reframes that need to be performed.

For all of the above reasons, repair of relationships will be complex and processual. Much previous work on repair or enhancement of relationships has tended to be conducted as if simple solutions will work across a variety of populations and/or circumstances (see Duck (1984b) for a review). Such approaches probably are too uninterested in the effects of communication and the ways in which two persons must interact socially in order to bring about some cognitively desired outcome. Figure 7.1 represents the different strategies for repairing relationships as they may be mapped onto the model for breakdown of relationships given in Figure 6.1. It provides a schematic representation of the argument elaborated below concerning the different stages of breakdown and how they may be addressed.

Given what we know about the extended processes of development and breakdown of relationships, repair is likely to be complex. It can usefully be viewed as an extended process with components that vary in their style and effectiveness at different points in time and in different sorts of relationships. We need to start by looking at the ways in which problems arise and whether 'special' methods are needed to correct them or whether merely increasing or focusing on 'normal' activity will do the job for us, such as 'being nice', for instance.

THE EMBEDDEDNESS OF BREAKDOWN AND REPAIR IN PEOPLE'S LIVES

In Chapter 1, I indicated the general human concerns that individuals have in entering relationships, bringing with them a desire for order and regularity (Frazier and Cook 1993) or a strong sense of personal rejection (Beach and O'Leary 1993) that implicitly represents a rejection of what a person 'stands for' (Duck 1994a). It seems to me that it is important to regard any attempts at relationship repair as significantly directed by these broad human concerns to establish a sense of control and of self-worth to others as well as by specific concerns that are local to the relationship and its particular issues of the moment.

Dissolution states and thresholds	Person's concerns	Repair focus
1. Breakdown: dissatisfaction with relationship	Relationship process; emotional and/or physical satisfaction in relationship	Concerns over one's value as a partner; relational process
	Threshold: I can't stand this any more	
2. Intrapsychic phase: dissatisfaction with partner	Partner's 'faults and inadequacies'; alternative forms of relationship; relationships with alternative partners	Person's view of partner
	Threshold: I'd be justified in withdrawing	
3. Dyadic phase: confrontation with partner	Reformulation of relationship; expression of conflict; clearing the air	Beliefs about optimal form of future relationship
	Threshold: I mean it	
4. Social phase: Publication of relationship distress	Gaining support and assistance from others; having own view of the problem ratified; obtaining intervention to rectify matters or end the relationship	Either: hold partners together (Phase 1) Or: save face
	Threshold: It's now inevitable	
5. Grave dressing phase: getting over it all and tidying up	Self-justification; marketing of one's own version of the break-up and its causes	Help in getting over; social support for person

Figure 7.1 A sketch of the main concerns at different phases of dissolution
Source: Duck (1984b: 169) Reproduced by permission of Academic Press.

Relationship repair as a project

Just as we may have other plans and projects that influence or even direct our thought and action during the day, so the project of repairing a relationship can soak up a lot of cognitive energy and time. This is not an incidental consequence of relational repair but should be seen as an important component of restructuring the relationship (Guerrero *et al.* 1993). A plan to repair a relationship will clearly bring certain thoughts, representational schemas, and behaviours to the fore in a person's approach to life (Honeycutt *et al.* 1993). For example, a person with a repair plan may choose to adopt reconciliatory strategies in dealing with the partner (Crohan 1996) and may therefore consciously select unprovocative styles of behaviour (McGonagle *et al.* 1993). Clearly, though, one way to repair a relationship is to make it more enjoyable for the partner, by focusing on his or her needs and discouraging cycles of negative interaction (Burleson *et al.* 1996). Such changes and bringing of the relationship to conscious-ness are likely to affect general attitudes and styles through the symbolic meaning that they carry for the relationship (Umberson and Terling 1997). For example, if everyone is usually uncertain about relationships (see Chapter 1), uncertainty about a repaired relationship is likely to be even greater and more fundamental (Birnbaum *et al.* 1997). I suspect that it will increase relational vigilance and make a person more suspicious or careful in a general way and that this vigilance often leads to depression, particularly in women (Assh and Byers 1996). Ehrlich and Lipsey (1969) have shown that such vigilance has detrimental effects on a relationship because it focuses attention too intensely on cues that may be ascribed more significance than they can bear. For instance, every statement made by the partner has meaning wrung out of it, and nonverbal behaviour is also sieved and surveyed for signs of mischief, trickery and betrayal. Such vigilance thus ultimately adversely affects the trust that is a central dynamic of relationships (Boon 1994).

An alternative view, however, is that a certain amount of attentiveness to, or knowledge of, relationship processes will benefit couples in problematic relationships (Burnett 1987). Many commentators argue that communication about relationships is a good thing and that it proffers a correct level of awareness and a helpful enhancement of relationships. I agree that this is possible but the line between awareness and self-consciousness can be very fine and couples are often helped by the presence of a skilled outsider who can guide awareness of the relationship. By this means a person can foster needs for inclusion without inadvertently and unintentionally spoiling the relationship in which revived inclusion is desired.

A related point concerning satisfaction of the need for inclusion is that to express that need too clearly or too forcefully is to invite rejection: one can need to be included but must not be *seen* to have that need too obviously. Lonely people often make the mistake of doing this: they seem too desperate (Wittenberg and Reis 1986; Marangoni and Ickes 1989; Mikulincer and Segal 1990). In repairing a relationship both partners are in effect expressing their need for inclusion quite explicitly and are also breaking one of the implicit rules of relationships discussed earlier (in Chapter 3): 'Don't talk about the state of the relationship directly.' Such a breaking of two important rules of relating itself becomes a problem that has to be overcome before successful repair can be accomplished.

The embeddedness of repair of relationships in such contexts is something that should not be overlooked any more than should some other related contextual and background factors. For instance, through research on the ordinary development of relationships we have learned of the considerable ambiguity of the cues that indicate progress and development of the relationship. Hence the chance that misunderstandings arise from such ambiguity is very large (see Chapters 3 and 4). In repair of relationships the problem is rather different, in that couples focus so – maybe too – directly on the development or enhancement or rejuvenation of their relationship. That is an odd situation, since that topic is usually a stressful one to focus on and indeed too much metacommunication ('talk about talk', or discussion of what you hear your partner 'really saying') can be threatening, especially to men (Acitelli 1988). In the context of their usual real-life expectations, then, a couple's focusing on the mechanics of their relationship during times of stress can be *either* a boon *or* a bane and has no absolute value (Acitelli 1993). What will matter is the way in which they communicate their concerns to one another (Wilmot 1995).

Individual backgrounds

Another general lifestyle issue discussed earlier was the impact of an individual's communication style: if a relationship is problematic because of the ineptitude or lack of skill – or just the simple personal problem – of one of the partners, then it is not the relationship that needs to be fixed but that individual or the behavioural style of that person (Assh and Byers 1996). Communication style is known to be disrupted in distressed couples (Burleson *et al.* 1996) and apart from the fact that husbands' individual styles are often peculiar in distressed marriages since they are more negative or inexpressive than are those of wives (Veroff *et al.* 1993; Ruvolo and Veroff 1997), the interaction patterns in distressed families are characteristically odd, too, with strong patterns of monologue–silence–monologue instead of real dialogue (Ferreira and Winter 1974). Thus the relationship itself is not always the problem; rather the individuals in it could be problematic and in need of 'repair' on an individual basis.

Memory for social events is also relevant to repair of relationships since the partners' memories for relational events will clearly structure their approach to repair, their orientation to one another, and their desire for success in the repair (Crohan 1992; Ross and Holmberg 1992). If memories of the relationship are positive, motivation for repair will obviously be higher than where memories are spoiled or tarnished by grievances (McCall 1982). However, in most relationships where there has been serious conflict, both positive and negative memories are likely to remain side by side. Also, external factors such as those mentioned in Chapter 1 create climates of feeling against which personal experiences are assayed. Thus the fact that it is now widely known that about one in every two Western marriages will end in divorce probably increases a couple's willingness to consider divorce as a solution to their relational problems (Clements and Markman 1996).

These considerations, then, provide a human and societal context against which to examine the phases of repair in relationships, by which I mean to argue that different styles of repair tactic are going to work better at some points in breakdown than at others. So we will first consider personal causes for breakdown – where individualized repair strategies are most effective – and then go on to consider various dyadic and social strategies that follow in the sequence.

INDIVIDUALS' PROBLEMS IN RELATING

Social skills

Among the individual problems that might adversely affect relating are depression (Segrin 1993), inability to express emotions in socially informative ways (King 1993), stigma such as disfigurement (Goffman 1959) or

HIV/AIDS (Crandall and Coleman 1992), unwillingness to accept others (Rotenberg and Kmill 1992), general social avoidance (Duggan and Brennan 1994), and ignorance of the appropriate ways in which to initiate relationships (Vorauer and Ratner 1996). Forty-one per cent of the US population claims to be shy and 24 per cent claims to be lonely (Duck 1998). These are clearly people who find relationships difficult, aversive, or unenjoyable. As Leary (1983) has argued, the whole issue of social/relational anxiety is a complicated one, but in essence it seems that shy and lonely people have developed images of themselves that make them utterly unconfident about entering relationships (Rotenberg and Kmill 1992). In the case of some shy and some lonely people, as we saw previously, they have actually developed styles of communicating and relating which are unhelpful for other people and tend to give off messages that are (mis)-interpreted as showing that the shy person is hostile (Burgoon and Koper 1984; King 1993) or that the lonely person is distant and uninterested in other people (Rotenberg and Kmill 1992). In the case of lonely persons, they may be not only distant but actually incompetent in conversation (Jones *et al*. 1984). Therefore, the usual advice to 'go out and meet more people' is particularly inappropriate as a starting point: it is very likely to increase rather than decrease their experience of rejection unless their problems at conducting relationships satisfactorily are first addressed and diminished (Duck 1991).

In all of these cases, programmes exist to retrain the necessary cognitive attitudes (Young 1982) or social skills – both at the 'macro' level of conversational strategy (Jones *et al*. 1984) and at the 'micro' level of nonverbal behaviour and expression of emotion (Hooley and Hiller 1997). The repair of relating skills in these cases is aimed at making the person more expressive and rewarding to other people, while also giving him or her the experience of feeling better in social situations. That feeling can feed back to an individual's self-concept and help the person to feel more positively disposed towards interaction with other people in general – more affiliative and more inclined to seek affinity towards others.

Problems in developing or keeping relationships

Once such a problem is corrected by therapeutic means or by individual actions, the difficulties in entering a relationship are reduced but the problems of developing relationships are not immediately removed. Some individuals are perfectly comfortable interacting socially with others but find it hard to develop intimate relationships or to keep them once they have begun (Prager 1995). For instance, a large number of people have chronically low self-esteem that renders them uncomfortable in relationships with others (Adler 1929) and they therefore shy away from increasing the intimacy of any relationship (Acitelli and Duck 1987). Low self-disclosers have been implicated in this problem since they fear disclosures that might present themselves in a negative light and, so they think, would put the other person off (Davis and Franzoi 1986). This lack of self-disclosure itself leads to the very lack of intimacy that would be necessary to reassure such persons that they are acceptable to others even with any faults that they may have, and so a vicious circle of withdrawal and distance is established. As Davis and Franzoi (1986) indicate, such private self-consciousness and fear of exposing one's inner thinking lead to low self-disclosure which itself leads to loneliness and a sense of rejection, which keeps the self-esteem low. Thus those who have problems developing relationships should be encouraged to be attentive to their self-disclosure patterns (Duck 1991), to invite others to self-disclose to them, to establish an atmosphere in which they and the other person feel able to self-disclose comfortably and to react to their own and others' self-disclosures in a supportive and accepting way. These ways involve absence of expressed judgement about the material revealed, coupled with a willingness to self-disclose one's own experiences on similar counts, whatever the topic. These techniques will bring about more encouraging experiences of social interaction and will prevent the effects of such individualized problems that can lead to constant experiences of undeveloped relationships.

Further evidence of the same sort of problem comes from research reported by Mehrabian and Ksionzky (1974), who show that neurotics tend to become more insecure and anxious the more intimate and (for most people) 'comfortable' the relationship becomes. A frequent consequence of this is that neurotics are keen to break off relationships before the insecurities are actualized: that is to say, they will break off the relationship in order to prevent the partner doing it first! While such behaviour is understandable from some points of view, it naturally deprives the person of the chance to experience good relationships. It is also insufficiently informed by knowledge that almost everyone feels insecure in developing relationships and it personalizes the feeling as if the (neurotic) person is the only one who has doubts about others' feelings for them. However, recognition of the fact that we all feel doubtful about others' feelings towards us would help all of us deal with the insecurities: they are natural rather than fatal.

There are also some writers (e.g., Lewis and McAvoy 1984) who indicate that drug abuse and alcohol abuse are sometimes means by which certain types of people deal with the problem of uncomfortable relationships – and thereby provide themselves with a handy 'self-handicapping strategy' (that is to say, a self-created problem that provides an apparently valid reason that appears to explain why their relationships collapse). It is more acceptable to people to blame inadequate development of relationships on their abuse of drugs or alcohol, for example, than to have to blame it directly on themselves as inept people.

Dealing with sexual dysfunction and enhancing intimacy

In some cases an individual has no trouble being affiliative, no trouble developing relationships, and no difficulties feeling intimate towards others but has functional or psychological problems when it comes to sexual and other intimate behaviours. Henderson-King and Veroff (1994) used data from a longitudinal study of black and white couples in order to examine how husbands' and wives' feelings of affirmation and tension in their marriage relate to levels of sexual satisfaction. They found that although sexual satisfaction was related to a married couple's sense of 'being affirmed' by the relationship, the relation of sexual satisfaction to marital well-being was not straightforward. The frequency of sexual intercourse, for example, seemed to be a less reliable predictor of marital satisfaction than was the subjective significance of the activity. In any case there were no general rules about this and black and white husbands and wives appear to take different attitudes to the role of sex in marital well-being. In such cases, again, the reparative techniques need to be sensitive to such distinctions and be a mixture of attention to the individual's problems and those that result from the interaction or interplay of the two persons in their intimate behaviour with one another, the racial grouping of the couple, and the number of years that the relationship has lasted. Masters and Johnson (1970) claim to have dealt fairly successfully with hypophilia (i.e., reduced or inappropriately low sexual drive or achievement), and to have done so by several techniques of having one partner service the other person's pleasure needs. However, if the relationship between sexual satisfaction and marital well-being is more complex, it may be that this technique actually works by, for example, reducing sexual anxiety. Several other researchers (e.g., Yaffe 1981) report that there is also a skill-training element, including the assertiveness skills necessary to initiate or decline sexual interaction.

On the other hand, part of the underlying problem which surfaces in the form of sexual dissatisfaction may be that the couple does not communicate intimate feelings in an adequately expressive way. Neimeyer and Hudson (1985) have developed some 'living laboratory' methods for couples that help to improve their intimate interactions with one another, while Dallos (1996) has indicated the ways in which self-disclosure in pairs may be strategically enhanced in order to increase the couple's intimacy. Lewis (1978) also showed how intimacy training can be used to improve a couple's experiences of one another, and his work focused on intimacy between pairs of male friends. All such methods work by improving the efficiency of the expression of emotion and therefore clarifying the couple's feelings for each other in positive, enhancing ways. Under this heading, then, we are dealing with repair of relationships where the partners want to get together and where the problem is essentially the result of one person's habitual social difficulty which is either inherent or generated by the psychological reaction to the partner.

INTRAPSYCHIC PHASE AND INTRAPSYCHIC REPAIR

By contrast, the intrapsychic phase of relationship breakdown is, as we saw in Chapter 6, a complaining/whining/griping/dissatisfaction stage where the only form of repair that matters is making one person feel more positive about the partner. It is essentially a cognitive phase where only beliefs about the partner and the relationship are at issue. The relevant techniques, therefore, will repair the problem by dealing with the person's negative beliefs and trying to change them (Duck 1984b). Bradbury and Fincham (1990) and Fichten and Wright (1985) have indicated that unhappy partners attribute blame unequally and tend to see their partner as responsible for all the conflicts in a relationship. It is unlikely that such a one-sided view is ever accurate and these authors videotaped discussions between the partners in the hope of removing the biases in perception and attribution that exist in the relationship – though I am not sure that there is such a thing as 'bias' in relationships, rather there are different viewpoints. Other techniques involve having the complainer list the positive and pleasing qualities of the partner (Bandura 1977), or having the person keep a diary recording the nice things that the partner does. Yet another possibility is to encourage the person to reinterpret the partner's behaviour in a positive light ('positive altercasting'; Miller and Parks 1982), or to get the person to reflect on the negative feelings of himself or herself and to reassess, therefore, the costs created for the partner in the relationship. Any reassessment of the balance of equity in the relationship will make the person realize that things are not entirely one-sided (Rusbult and Buunk 1993). Any forced recording of one's own negative inputs to the relationship encourages the person to consider the partner's perspective and thereby reach a more balanced and objective view of the complaints made about the partner. This should encourage the individual to take account of that partner's reasonable defences against the complaints. Also as Klein and Lamm (1996) showed, persons who see their own position in a conflict as legitimate are more willing to express themselves openly. Partners who find the other person's position legitimate are more willing to listen to the other side.

DYADIC STAGE AND DYADIC SOLUTIONS

Perhaps the most difficult phase of break-up is that point where both persons realize that there are problems and begin to argue. A person who comments on another's performance of relational interaction is setting himself or herself up for some stormy reactions once the other person starts to justify, explain, excuse, or account for his or her own behaviour and at the same time may challenge, probe, or even attack the commentator's own role in any interactions that were problematic or stressful. As we have repeatedly seen in various ways, it is not socially acceptable to comment either on nonverbal behaviour or on the state of a relationship. To comment on the performance of communication or relating in a partnership is to break several conventions and is clearly unfamiliar for most people. For those reasons we find that partners having relationship problems not only find the discussions themselves hurtful (Baxter 1982) but also find the sheer expression of tension difficult and something that becomes a management issue in its own right (Kaplan 1976). A characteristic style of behaviour in conflicts like this is that partners develop a *cross-complaining cycle* ('You did this', 'Well you did this', 'Well that's because you do this', and so on). Each party counters a complaint with one of his or her own instead of taking the partner's complaint as if it were a reasonable viewpoint to have (Gottman 1994). In short the partners act as if they do not respect one another's different perspectives. Obviously the fact that partners do not acknowledge or respect each other's views will make it even harder for their views to be reconciled.

My point here therefore concerns the process of dyadic interaction in this context. The whole business of dealing with the occurrence of a hurtful argument is a hard one, over and above the content of the argument and what it means to the couple (Duck 1984b). Sometimes the difficulties of talking about the issues cause more hurt than anything that is actually said. At other times, the sheer expression of conflict can be good for couples and can clear the air, for which reason it has been strongly advocated by Kaplan (1984). However, its unskilled or unguided use can be problematic and counsellors therefore usually speak to the partners separately before having them discuss their problems together. Sillars *et al.* (1994) suggest that communication about problems in a conflict has a stronger relationship to the understanding of instrumental perceptions (perceptions of the performance of chores, 'who does what', whether someone is under pressure at work, for example) than to the understanding of abstract relationship perceptions (such as trust, equity, sharing, and indefinite or hard-to-assess issues such as whether a person's interest in the relationship is waning). As I noted in Chapter 5, the practical daily matters represented by instrumental perceptions are distinct from but feed into the more abstract matters. Thus this phase of repair may need to focus on the instrumental and the practical aspect of relational conduct and to translate it into the abstract or more general feelings about the relationship.

SOCIAL SUPPORT AND THE SOCIAL PHASE

The social network serves many unobtrusive functions in the repair or dissolution of relationships although the role of the network does not simply commence only when relational problems begin, as I have been trying to show. Rather, the daily contact with the network provides a sense of reliable alliance and regular ordinary channels of talk through which becomes established a sense of the likelihood of other people's supportiveness and value if ever a crisis should occur (Leatham and Duck 1990). By regular means like this the oncoming problems in a relationship can even be headed off, and the regular daily contact can also serve to sustain the person going through a crisis in a key relationship, by means of advice, gossip and subtle attacks on the other person's version of events. When called into action, such existing companionships also provide support and repairing by means of 'intervention teams' (La Gaipa 1982) which try to give the couple some help in sorting themselves out or try to engineer a more harmonious climate. Friends talk to the partners separately and together, reminding them of their obligations to social norms, and urging them to react to social pressures as well as to their own feelings about each other (La Gaipa 1982). The role of everyday habits of talk is in fact not much altered at this point from the habits of talk that occur in the rest of life, in so far as network members talk to the partners but also talk to one another, making judgements on the partners' behaviour, providing accounts for their problems, offering a background of moral accountability for what is happening, and generally supporting the partners' (or one partner's) worldview and explanation for the problems (Duck 1998). Thus, although the roles of networks in repair may be varied or multifarious (Sarason *et al.* 1997), it is clear that the social phase of repair is a significant one, but not one that differs in its essential features from the routine talk of daily life in other circumstances (Duck 1994a). As Buehler and Legg (1993) indicated, mothers adjusting to marital separation found it much easier to cope when they received practical support as well as psycho-emotional support from their networks and families, again making the point that the practical, mundane daily activities of life are at least as important a factor in feelings about self and relationship as are 'pure emotions'.

GRAVE DIGGING, GRAVE DRESSING, AND RETURN FROM THE GRAVE

Research is now increasingly exploring one of the toughest but most enduring parts of relationship dissolution, namely the period when partners get over the break. Weber (1983) has reported on the ways in which identity management is accomplished in leaving a relationship and the ways in which the partners repair their own self-concepts and their future in relationships. As Weber *et al.* (1987) have suggested, the story told in relationship repair is significant as much for the attitudes that it generates in a person concerning future relationships as for its contribution to an understanding of the past. The role of the grave dressing phase in the repair of ex-partners is probably one of the most exciting areas that remains for future work to explore, as does the role of grief and memory for relationships in getting over the relationship (Harvey *et al.* 1995) – perhaps even in some cases through systematic changes in a person's memory for the nature of the relationship when it was thriving, as we have seen elsewhere in the book (Felmlee 1995).

To focus on such face management issues of relationships is, however, once again to note that the embeddedness of the private lives of two partners in a social network is a very significant part of their enactment of the relationship – the point that started this book and clearly washes over all aspects of relational life, from its birth to its death and beyond.

SUMMARY

Repair of relationships can mean repair of the individuals in a relationship, repair of the mechanics of the relationship, or repair of the person after he or she has left the relationship. This chapter has explored the ways in which the various parts of relationship repair interrelate and serve to enhance a relationship, stabilize it, or satisfactorily extract individuals from unsatisfactory relationships so that they can cast their eyes to the future and new relationships without the same problems as the one they have left. The chapter stressed that the repair of relationships is not a simple process nor one that has only one element (namely the repair of one person's liking for another or both persons' liking for each other). Instead the process involves such complicated issues as face management, network involvement, and self-image as well as the repair of each person's respect and liking for the other. The chapter thus emphasized several of the themes already developed in the earlier parts of the book but applied them to a topic that has not previously had them applied there.

ANNOTATED FURTHER READING

Duck, S. W. (1984b) (ed.) *Personal Relationships 5: Repairing Personal Relationships*. London: Academic Press, is a collection of original chapters to make up just about the only book about relationship repair in general as distinct from the other sources below that deal with specific sorts of relationship such as marriage.

Mallinckrodt, B. (1997) Interpersonal relationship processes in individual and group psychotherapy, in S. W. Duck, K. Dindia, W. Ickes, R. Milardo, R. S. L. Mills and B. R. Sarason (eds) *Handbook of Personal Relationships* (2nd edition) (pp. 671–94). Chichester: Wiley, details some general principles about the role of relationships in helping people recover psychological balance as well as reviewing some repair techniques for relationships.

Notarius, C. (1996) Marriage: will I be happy or sad?, in N. Vanzetti and S. W. Duck (eds) *A Lifetime of Relationships*. Pacific Grove, CA: Brooks/Cole, discusses specifically the issues that deal with marital satisfaction and conflict management.

EIGHT

OVERVIEW

This book might surprise those social psychologists whose views of the area of friendship and personal relationships are shaped by their memories of the work on attraction to strangers that was carried out 20 to 30 years ago. Research on attraction to strangers was abundant in the 1960s and 1970s – indeed it almost defined the field – and that image of the field is retained by many who worked on it in that era, became discouraged, and went on to study other topics yet cannot but see the field as it used to be then (Duck 1995). The present field of personal relationships, by contrast with this heritage, is fundamentally different from the field of interpersonal attraction 20 years ago as recorded in the first edition of this book, both in terms of topics studied and in terms of methods of inquiry (Baxter and Montgomery 1996; Duck et al. 1997a; Fitch 1998). These facts make it easier to respond to the Series Editor's request that this final chapter be my personal overview of the field. As in the first edition of the book, I will draw on a paper that I wrote with Harriet Sants (Duck and Sants 1983) and which I have developed over the intervening period into a book (Duck 1994a) and a chapter in the latest *Handbook of Personal Relationships* (Duck et al. 1997b).

As indicated throughout the book, the emphasis of the best current research on relating to others is cross-disciplinary and process-oriented; it stresses behavioural components of relating in the everyday lives of relational participants in addition to pure cognition, attitudes, or attribution; it is sensitive to the practical contexts where everyday relationships are conducted and especially to the social networks in which they are embedded; and it has a place for the interpersonal communication through which those psychological and cognitive structures act upon this world and by which many relational processes actually operate. It focuses on the strategies and communicative social devices that real people use in real, everyday contexts to achieve real relational goals. It emphasizes the non-automatic nature of relating, its two-sidedness (as distinct from the one-sided impression-formation and judgemental emphasis of much previous work on perception, attribution and attraction) and its embeddedness in the extensive span of people's real lives and social contexts. As such I think the work has, by building on more than social psychology, become truly 'social' and will continue to develop as such.

The reasons for these improvements are to be found in part in the rejection of four unwanted heirlooms inherited from the four ancestors of the study of relationships: interpersonal attraction, the social psychology of impression formation, attribution theory, and the debates about similarity–complementarity of personality. According to Duck and Sants (1983), the four unwanted heirlooms, critiqued in the first edition, are as follows.

1 *Relationships as the chemistry of partner attributes*, i.e., the erroneous view, discussed in Chapters 1 to 4 here, that the satisfactory development of a relationship between two persons can be meaningfully predicted from knowledge of their pre-existing personal characteristics as individuals. As we have seen earlier in the book, the magnetic metaphor underlying such a view of attraction and its aftermath is untenable even though it is still seen as valid by 'common sense'. Even more radically unacceptable is the notion that the success of relationships is predictable from the individual characteristics that two persons take with them into the relationship before they meet.

2 *Relationships as undigested interactions*, i.e., the erroneous assumptions, discussed at several points in this book, that people do not ponder about interactions that have happened, or will happen, do not plan or reminisce, and do not reformulate their understandings of 'what really happened'. The assumption has often been that the behaviour in an interaction is of paramount importance, that people basically agree on 'what happened', and that different interpretations of the 'same event' should not be expected to occur across time for that reason. However as Ross and Holmberg (1992), Honeycutt (1993) and others have shown, relationships *per se* can change without interaction taking place between people, and can be modified just by the thoughts that one person has about the relationship (Acitelli 1993; Duck 1994a).

3 *Relationships as pots of gold at the end of the rainbow*, i.e., the illusory and erroneous assumption implicit in some of the research discussed throughout this book that 'a relationship' is a clear and clearly observable entity that we could bottle and study in the laboratory if we could only identify it by the proper means. Rather we should be realizing that a relationship is an agreement that derives from people's thoughts about interaction, about themselves as individuals, about themselves in relation to one another, and about each other (Acitelli 1993). Such an agreement is open-ended, processual, unfinished, and fluid. For this reason, it is extremely likely that the two partners in a relationship could have quite divergent views of it, as assessed at the same time; that each person could change his/her views of it with time; and finally that any of these views of the relationship could legitimately differ from the observations made of it by third parties, especially by researchers (Duck *et al.* 1997).

4 *Relaters as air traffic controllers*, i.e., the erroneous belief noted in Chapters 2 to 7 that human beings are in perfect control of their actions, that they do everything thinkingly, that when they process information

they do so entirely logically and rationally, that they can hold enormous amounts of relevant detail at their fingertips, and that they are constantly self-aware and competent. (This is different from point 2 above, which argues that people occasionally make plans and have forethought.) It emphasizes the fact that the thoughtless routines of everyday practical life have more significance in the making of relationships than many researchers and relationships scholars have hitherto assumed (Canary and Stafford 1994).

Finally, work since the first edition has exposed the existence of another heirloom, left in a hidden trust and recently rediscovered:

5 *The muting of the social enterprises within which specific relationships are conducted in real life.* I have been exploring in this book the influences not only of networks of friends and relatives in the exercise of normative influences on relationship conduct, but also the role of media and cultural beliefs on the registration and calibration of such things as relationship satisfaction (for example, I have been pointing out that people assess their relationships relative to other people's reports of relationships, as well as in light of their own personal experiences of them). Furthermore, recent development of the sociological understanding of dyadic relationships (Allan 1998) has located all of these activities within the constraints of economic and industrial circumstances, indicating that the form and conduct of relationships – and hence experience of them – are determined by these powerful forces. The social psychology of relating to others is likely to become more credible and predictable to the extent that it is able to place cognitive aspects of relationships within these forces, and in the context of forces that act upon public behaviour.

In brief, all these false assumptions about relating to others come down to a tendency to undervalue the practical aspects of relating in real life and to underestimate the ways in which ideal processes of thought, judgement, and emotion are confined and redirected in the practical circumstances in which they are actually carried out. In part this oversight is a consequence of undue reliance on laboratory methods whose very purpose is to strip away such exterior factors so that a single – but therefore isolated – social psychological process may be examined. The problem comes only when the nude social psychological processes are not reclothed in those exterior influences before being fully interpreted (Duck *et al.* 1997a). What was taken off must be put on again if the interpreter is not to risk misunderstanding the whole process.

DO RELATIONSHIPS RESULT FROM THE CHEMISTRY OF PARTNER ATTRIBUTES?

At first blush, a reasonable assumption is that successful relationships between people are predictable from their 'entry characteristics' – for instance, the personality attributes or looks that partners bring with them to the relationship. A related idea is that a person's relational success can be predicted from his or her pre-existing personality characteristics, attachment styles, or cognitive schemata. To take such a position is to fail to recognize the variability in relationship experiences of a given person, some of whose relationships work and some of which don't. As I showed earlier, the search for the magically influential characteristic or the magically effective type of matching between characteristics will always be unproductive as long as it assumes absolute effects of such factors and takes no account of the ways in which they actually operate in the contingent and particular social and communicative behaviours of real life. By assessing 'objective' personality similarity, or 'objective' physical attractiveness, or 'objective relational styles', experimental studies unintentionally short-circuit the very personal, subjective, and individual reactions to such cues which really are the very stuff that they are trying to assess. They also do not fully recognize the magical interactive effects that can be created in a relationship with that one special soulmate, or the wide variety of relationships that each person has – for most of us have close friends and also enemies. These differences cannot be predicted merely from the pre-existing qualities of the partners since they are *social* relationships – that is to say, relationships that are enacted and have interactive reality – rather than being 'products'. As argued elsewhere (Duck 1994a), even the existence of similarity can be differentiated into four forms (having a common characteristic or experience; mutually declaring that characteristic or experience to one another; evaluating the experience or characteristic equivalently; and sharing the same overall meaning for the characteristic or experience). The progression from the first form to the last can be done only by social interaction, which at any point could change the value placed on the similarity and so render its 'effects' different and contingent rather than absolute.

Not only that, but such approaches also emasculate the social processes that are important in effecting whatever influences such cues have in real life. We should rather be asking how people *behave* when they detect that they are similar, or that X has such-and-such personality style, and how that is different from the way they behave when they detect that they are different. We should also be asking how liking for another person can be facilitated or inhibited by the strategy of searching actively for similarities rather than dissimilarities. This is a different project from merely charting 'the effects' of those similarities and dissimilarities after assuming that they are 'factually established' or as readily provided by the partners to one another in the course of everyday social interaction as they are provided to subjects by the experimenter in the course of an experiment. In real life we do not know about our similarities to someone else this directly; instead we have to make inferences and deductions in the context of real life demands, managements, strategies, and behaviours of others (which often include deliberate concealment of the attitudes and beliefs). Detection of similarities and the assessment of their significance are no easy tasks in the hurly-burly of real life and should not be minimized or short-circuited. Accordingly, such similarities and differences have their effects not by reason of their objective qualities but through their interpersonal consequences, as the more recent work described in this book makes increasingly clear.

As I have shown in Chapters 2–4 here, the relevance of partner characteristics is not to be found in the places where it was assumed to be,
namely in creating parts of a jigsaw that jump together almost of their
own accord and 'click'. Rather, it lies in two domains: first, the way in
which such measurable personality characteristics translate into specific
relational behaviours in everyday daily life that influence partners' interactions with one another; and second, the way in which people discover,
and communicate about, one another's characteristics (and, incidentally,
the characteristics of third parties, since gossip about others serves a very
important bonding function in everyday social life). All this occurs in a
social context that is larded with evaluation and meanings for such things.

It is quite clear that, as Duck and Sants (1983: 32) put it, 'the mere
juxtaposition of two partners' attributes does not create a relationship . . .
Active social processes do this, the social processes of negotiating, communicating "deep" personal attributes, and creating behavioral consequences
of them.' Fortunately for the field, researchers are beginning to explore
these important social, interpersonal and negotiative processes.

Also important are the sequencing and timing of such interactive processes – filter theorists were right about that – and, as Duck and Sants
(1983) suggest, the analogy is to the mixing of water with concentrated
sulphuric acid. Whichever way the mixing is done, the result is dilute
sulphuric acid; but if the water is poured into the acid there is also violent
and dangerous spitting, while the other way of doing things produces
only a gentle warming of the solution. Even if theorists adhere to the idea
that mixing of attributes is influential on relationships, we need to do
more careful work to clarify the means by which the mixing is best achieved
in real social lives and we should not assume that there are simple and
equally balanced effects of *any* order or *any* method of achieving the mix.
In everyday relationships, partners carry out a great deal of negotiating
and compromising, as well as simply being impressed by and attracted
towards one another. Even if initial attraction causes the coming together
of two possible partners on the basis of their relative or absolute characteristics, that in itself can never make a working, living relationship.

ARE RELATIONSHIPS SIMPLY UNDIGESTED INTERACTIONS?

The interpretative digestion of interactions seems to me to be a key aspect
of the relational enterprise, and researchers should not assume that 'the
relationship' is a product of interaction or behaviour alone; rather, it
emerges in part from the independent and combined thinking and talking that the two partners do in relation to those interactions (Acitelli
1993; Miell and Croghan 1996; Duck et al. 1997a). Relationships, then (as
distinct from the interactions, interaction sequences, and interaction patterns that are constructs imposed by researchers), are mental associations
made by people as much as they are behavioural associations, and are
historically-derived representations of experience as much as they are
interpersonally communicative entities with existence independent of
the people treated as being 'in' them. As Duck et al. (1997a: 11) noted, 'the

evidence is that relationships are not simply monolithic *containers* of invariant persons (Baxter and Montgomery 1996) – the most common expression of which view is found in phrases about people *in* relationships. Relationships do not simply surround, encase, or enclose the two individuals who are "in" them. It is misleading to describe development of *relationships*, rather than of partners, and to assess the changes in closeness of the relationship rather than the changes occurring in the persons themselves as they alter their view of themselves together.'

We have a relationship if we both *think* that we have one and can construct a mental history of it. The type of relationship that we experience is in part a type of thinking and a type of locating of self and relationship within a social pattern of thought (e.g., recognizing that what you and I are doing corresponds to a socially identifiable class of action, namely 'being friends'). As previously noted, such thinking is important not only because it invokes the creation of a narrative about the previous development of the relationship but also because it creates a form for an expected future for the relationship and thereby provides both a context for its continuing development and a subtle type of routine: things will continue, for the time being at least, as they are. The stories that we tell now about the present form and nature of the relationship are really also stories with implications for the future of the relationship built into them, and as such they serve to recreate the relationship in its own form and project it into the future. It is important for future work on relationships to explore the role of such narratives in the creation of the 'sense of being in a relationship' that makes such a substantial contribution to the existence of the relationship (Bochner *et al.* 1997). Such a view might also help us to eliminate the rather naive general assumption that retrospective accounts of relational events are necessarily and merely 'biased'. *If* it is true that retrospections are biased, then it is certainly equally true that researchers have not yet shown with any certainty the nature, form and predictable patterns of such biases. On the other hand, I prefer to believe that 'bias' here is a rather interesting social psychological phenomenon and one that will repay the attention that researchers should be devoting to it. The ways in which partners create a sense of their own history as partners are not predetermined by preceding events but rather are constructed ways of creating an interpretative pattern within which to place those events.

Our task in future should be to gain understanding of how retrospective accounts both differ from, and yet project towards, present experience or future expectations or contemporary accounts of the same things, since the differences are surely psychologically informative, not merely indicative of error. In coming to understand changes in accounts we will, I believe, come to understand some key psychological processes that drive relational experience.

If it were self-evident what 'a relationship' is, the present number of researchers working on relationships would by now have agreed on a definition and would use it in a standard way in all of their research, just as other scientists do when writing about 'polymers' and 'DNA'. Yet this does not happen. As I noted some years ago (Duck 1990) a key question in the field still is 'What is a relationship?' My prediction is that a relationship is truly a narrative compilation of experiences by a given reporter and that reports will differ according to the person doing the reporting and the time at which they make the report, as well as the purpose for which they do so (Duck 1994a).

ARE RELATIONSHIPS 'POTS OF GOLD AT THE END OF THE RAINBOW'?

The pot of gold at the end of the rainbow is an illusory item since the rainbow's end moves as the observer moves, and it is therefore never reached. Relationships are similar in that their substance changes with the perspective of the observer (Olson 1977), which is one important reason why researchers need to be careful before assuming that their view of a relationship is the only one or the only correct one. It may be a correct one for a given but restricted purpose but should not be mistaken for the only true perspective for other purposes. Secondly, if partners think about relationships and can plan them or develop strategies for coping with them, they may each reach utterly different conclusions about the success of an interaction and even about the nature of the relationship, despite the fact that, in some other sense, they were 'in' the same relationship and 'had the same experience'. This is not so much a problem for the relationship or for researchers as a fundamental fact of relational and human life (Olson 1977; Duck and Sants 1983), and one that we do not yet sufficiently understand.

Future work on relationships will clearly need to explore the ways in which relational perspectives differ and what this means for the description of the relationship, both in scientific and in personal terms. Clearly the creation (by partners) of a jointly accepted account of the relationship is an important part of its existence, especially with respect to issues of relational quality (as distinct from issues of whether or not there is a relationship). A marriage exists if a legal document says that it does, but its meaning could still be different to everyone who looks at it. Yet the evidence seems to be that, even so, partners do not agree on fundamental aspects of the relationship such as the time when the first intercourse occurred (Surra 1987; see also Chapter 7) or where they first met (Duck and Miell 1986). A couple in which one partner claims that they met in a coffee bar and the other claims that they met at a lecture may both assert confidently 15 weeks later that they met just as one of them was going from a coffee bar to a lecture, for instance (cf. Duck and Miell 1986). As researchers we need to explore the meaning of such divergence and subsequent convergence of narratives in the creation of the sense of being in a relationship and we need to dispense with our present assumption that both partners will agree with one another and with us as researchers unless they are somehow 'biased' or 'wrong'.

We need also to be circumspect and cautious before assuming that the insiders will necessarily agree with outsiders who witness the relationship. Particularly during relationship distress, people go to a lot of trouble to conceal the dynamics of their relationship from the outside world, but the very fact that observers may characterize a relationship in one way and the partners in another is an interesting phenomenon that may or may not indicate erroneous perception, and still less does it show the superiority of one view over another for all purposes. I doubt whether the two partners will agree with an 'objective' observer about all aspects of their relationship. Once again, the existence of such discrepancies and differences is not merely an irritating problem for researchers, but also a very profound truth about relating to others, and a truth that we should seek to comprehend more fully.

ARE RELATERS REALLY 'AIR TRAFFIC CONTROLLERS'?

The common view of air traffic controllers is that they are perfectly rational beings capable of processing vast amounts of information under extreme stress and nevertheless getting it right most of the time, whatever is going on around them. The mistake still made in much literature on relationships is precisely that we assume too easily that information processing is rational and intelligent in relationships when much of the time our research participants and our own personal lives reveal that it is not so. People are naturally confused and puzzled about life and it is time we recognized that in our formal theorizing (Duck 1994a). A large part of what we observe when we look at relationships as open-ended human processes is the manner in which human beings strive perpetually to impose a sense of order and meaning on the flow of experience (Duck 1994a). Various attempts at imposing such order are possible as a function of many influences (for example, mood, time of day, time of week, most recent experience, conversation with others, and so on) and it would be more remarkable to find someone whose view of a relationship was always the same and always reported the same way than it would be to find someone whose was not. Not only do normal human relaters experience normal human doubts and anxieties about many things, including their relationships, but they also, as a natural part of normal human life, are subject to conflicting advice and pressures, in the context of which the advantages of one kind of behaviour over another must be assessed. A great challenge for relationship research and theory is to encompass the variability of experience and reporting about relationships that is self-evident from our daily life.

Sometimes human behaviour has unforeseen consequences and very often our control or influence over a relationship is much less than perfect, so that even if we were perfectly rational, logical information processors, our rationality may be undermined by the unpredictable actions of a relational partner. Why assume that the only person who never does a U-turn or has a change of mind is a relater? Far better to recognize that a part of the excitement of relationships comes from their variability and unpredictability, a variability and unpredictability that researchers somehow have to capture rather than ignore.

The research on attribution and social cognition often seems to represent human beings as the kinds of persons we would like to be rather than the kinds of persons we really are. In relationships, as elsewhere in life, I do not see people being optimally efficient or on top of everything. We all make mistakes and are thoughtless or inconsiderate or sometimes too busy. Rather than relegating such occurrences to mere 'costs' in a relational equation, it is time that we began to understand the chaos in relationships and the flops as well as the strategic successes. No-one has a perfectly successful and satisfactory relational life, not even an air traffic controller.

ARE RELATIONSHIPS HERMETICALLY SEALED INDIVIDUAL EXPERIENCES OF 'THE SOCIAL'?

Although individuals may try to impose their own sense of order and personal meanings on events, the important feature of relationships is that they are conjoint activities where the two partners interpolate and negotiate their own perspective, ideas and views of events. As I indicated above, there is no intuitive surprise to be had in the fact that individuals would occasionally unearth discrepancies of viewpoint that needed to be reconciled. A larger point, however, is that the single individuals and the two partners together must work out such things in the moral and social context provided by a larger society. Virtually no-one is free to construct a relationship in just any manner that they choose without at some point having to account for it to outsiders. Behaviour within a relationship is subject to moral and even legal sanctions, but even in less extreme instances is something about which people are socially aware, with the concern about 'what others will think' being a powerful influence. Even a reference to a moral notion of terms like 'friend' ('That's not how a friend should behave', for example), or a reference to prototypical views of friendship ('Friends should be loyal, trustworthy, helpful, supportive . . .'), or to common wisdom about the rules for friendship ('A friend in need is a friend indeed') is an implicit recognition and internalization of the exterior moral force of a society. Behaviours at the individual and dyadic level are thus influenced at the very least by awareness of the rules of social practice for relationships.

Research in the next 15 years will no doubt pay greater attention to the social contexts in which individual and dyadic action are placed. To overlook such influences would be to detach relating to others from the social environment in which it occurs.

SO . . .

The field of research in personal relationships has witnessed a major boom that will take us comfortably into the next millennium. In order to make the best possible progress at such a time, researchers have to make the kinds of fundamental changes in their approach to the study of relationships that are indicated above. In 20 years we shall look back on a field that has made substantial contributions to the understanding of everyday human and social and communicative life precisely because that, at last, is what it has studied.

GLOSSARY

Affiliation: the tendency or the desire of human beings to belong to, or be accepted by, a group of other people.

Attitude similarity: similarity of opinions, values and beliefs.

Attraction: defined by some writers in the field as an initial attitude towards another person, this term is taken in this text to mean the whole range of behaviours, feelings and practices that are associated with a desire to be in a relationship with another person.

Beauty, dynamic: those aspects of a person's behaviour that make him or her attractive.

Beauty, static: a person's attractive physical appearance.

Cognition: the thoughts and thought structures and processes that a person uses in evaluating situations and people.

Context: the environmental, social, cultural, temporal and attendant conditions surrounding a relationship, the concept of a relationship or the practices of a relationship.

Courtship: the process of developing a long term romantic relationship.

Cultural beliefs about relationships: the prevailing views in a given society or group concerning the manner in which relationships are to be properly conducted.

Cultural norms for relationships: the standards against which the performance or conduct of a relationship is judged in a given society and the prescribed practices for doing relationships 'well'.

Deniability: the availability of a denial that some aspect of behaviour was intended to be interpreted in a particular way and the resources to redefine its intent in a different way (for example, a teasing remark could be taken as an insult by the listener, but the speaker would claim 'deniability' by saying 'Oh, I was only teasing; it was not an insult').

Dialectics: the opposing forces or tensions that pull in different directions in respect of a particular aspect of a relationship (for example the desire to be an autonomous individual pulls against the desire to be connected to other people and hence occasions moments of tension when the individual wants to be a free agent individual but also to be in a relationship, with its attendant obligations to take account of another person's needs and wishes).

Disregard: the tendency to place someone in a category that makes him or her unsuitable as a relationship partner, characterized by not noticing or taking account of him or her as relational partners (for example most of us 'disregard' shop assistants or waiters in this way).

Divided loyalties: the stress that comes from membership in multiple relationships or roles (for example a person may be instructed by the boss to stay longer at work on exactly the evening when she or he had agreed to go out on a special anniversary date and would have to choose to do one or the other).

Ego support value: the extent to which one partner is able to support the other's ego, make him or her feel good as a person, or help him or her to become a better person.

Ethnographic interviews: interviews intended to reach a deep and rich understanding of the experience of the 'native' or the person in the context in which he or she normally lives.

Field of availables: the group of people that we encounter during the course of our lives, and who are available for relationships, whether or not they are regarded as suitable or desirable partners.

Field of desirables: the group of people that we encounter during the course of our lives, and who are regarded as desirable partners.

Field of eligibles: the group of people that we encounter during the course of our lives and who seem on the face of it to be suitable as partners, or who represent realistic choices as romantic or friendship partners for a given person.

Friendship: a non-romantic personal relationship with another person.

Gossip: talk about other people and their behaviour, talk that may or may not be based on truth and which serves the subtle purpose of articulating moral standards by which the alleged behaviour may be judged.

Inclusion: the need for human beings to feel that they belong to or are accepted by a group of other people.

Multiplex relationships: relationships where types of interaction are extremely diverse and focused on many layers of different sorts of activity (for example parent–child relationships where feeding, educating, discipline, play, and physical protection may all occur within the same relationship).

Mundane behaviour: the routine and small behaviours of daily life that are necessary to social functioning but are not necessarily remarked upon by researchers, or by relaters themselves.

Networks: the groups of other people with whom a given person has a connection, the communities to whom the person refers for advice and guidance on relational matters.

Norm of reciprocity: the tendency for people to match something that their partner has done or said (for example, if one person says something private and intimate, then the norm of reciprocity makes it more likely that the other person would respond with some intimate and private disclosure).

NVC (nonverbal communication): the behaviours of social interaction that do not involve words (for example eye movements, bodily movements, degree of physical closeness during an interaction, rate of speech, blushing).

Personal idioms: terms or phrases that have special meaning in a particular relationship but not to anyone else (for example, the nicknames that people may have for sexual behaviour but would not be understood by other people as referring to sexual behaviour).

Personal relationships: relationships between two people who could not be exchanged without changing the nature of the relationship (for example, the two people who are best friends with one another). Distinguish this from 'social relationships' where the two partners in an interaction could be exchanged and the relationship would still be the same (for example a shop assistant and a customer).

Praxis: the practical conduct of relationships and the sets of routines or practices that have to be carried out for the relationship to exist.

Prototypes: the typical assumptions that people make about the features that 'should' be found in a relationship, such as trust, loyalty, and commitment.

Regard: the tendency to notice and take account of someone and so to allow the possibility that the person might become a relational partner.

Relational culture: the unique features and styles of behaviour and interaction in a personal relationship that are particular to that relationship and different from those in other relationships.

Relationship awareness: a person's thinking about interaction patterns, comparisons, or contrasts between himself or herself and the other partner in the relationship.

Routines: practices in a relationship that are typically carried out without much conscious awareness, or else regular styles and practices (such as the 'rules' that govern the conduct of the family evening meal together).

Schemas/schemata: knowledge structures that derive from previous experience and organize the processing of past and future information.

Secret tests: ways of finding out the level of commitment that one's partner feels towards the relationship without actually asking directly (see Chapter 3).

Self-disclosure: the opening up of oneself to other people, usually by allowing them to know private and important things about oneself.

Social comparison: the tendency of human beings to compare their own abilities and opinions with the abilities and opinions of other people.

Social support: the emotional, psychological and physical help that one person gives or is available to (or expected to) offer another person in a personal relationship.

Stimulation value: the extent to which one partner is able to stimulate, inform, or energize the other, by for example providing good new ideas and advice.

Taboo topics: topics that are normally 'off limits' in a relationship, such as detailed recounting of past sexual encounters with other people.

Uncertainty reduction: the systematic attempts to remove ambiguity or incomprehension about another person's behaviour and to reach a deeper understanding of its causes and purposes.

Uniplex relationships: relationships where types of interaction are limited to particular sorts of activity, for example, drinking buddies, who get together merely to drink and talk (compare with multiplex relationships).

Utility value: the extent to which one partner is able to serve the other's needs.

Voluntariness: the assumed freedom of choice to enter and leave relationships.

REFERENCES

Acitelli, L. K. (1988) When spouses talk to each other about their relationship. *Journal of Social and Personal Relationships*, 5: 185–99.

Acitelli, L. K. (1993) You, me, and us: perspectives on relationship awareness, in S. W. Duck (ed.) *Understanding Relationship Processes 1: Individuals in Relationships*. Newbury Park: Sage.

Acitelli, L. K. (1995) Disciplines at parallel play. *Journal of Social and Personal Relationships*, 12: 589–96.

Acitelli, L. K. (1997) Sampling couples to understand them: mixing the theoretical with the practical. *Journal of Social and Personal Relationships*, 14: 243–61.

Acitelli, L. K. and Duck, S. W. (1987) Intimacy as the proverbial elephant, in D. Perlman and S. W. Duck (eds) *Intimate Relationships: Development, Dynamics and Deterioration*. Beverly Hills: Sage.

Acitelli, L. K., Douvan, E. and Veroff, J. (1993) Perceptions of conflict in the first year of marriage: how important are similarity and understanding? *Journal of Social and Personal Relationships*, 10: 5–19.

Acitelli, L. K., Douvan, E. and Veroff, J. (1997) The changing influence of interpersonal perceptions on marital well-being among black and white couples. *Journal of Social and Personal Relationships*, 14: 291–304.

Adams, R. and Blieszner, R. (1996) Midlife friendship patterns, in N. Vanzetti and S. W. Duck (eds) *A Lifetime of Relationships*. Pacific Grove, CA: Brooks/Cole.

Adelman, M. (1987) 'Love's urban agent: social support and the matchmaker'. Paper to Iowa Conference on Personal Relationships, University of Iowa, May–June.

Adelmann, P. K., Chadwick, K. and Baerger, D. R. (1996) Marital quality of black and white adults over the life course. *Journal of Social and Personal Relationships*, 13: 361–84.

Adler, A. (1929) *What Your Life Should Mean to You*. New York: Bantam.

Ahrons, C. and Rodgers, R. (1987) *Divorced Families*. Chicago: Chicago University Press.

Ainsworth, M. D. S., Blehar, M. C., Waters, E. and Wall, S. (1978) *Patterns of Attachment: A Psychological Study of the Strange Situation*. Hillsdale, NJ: Erlbaum.

Aldous, J. (1996) Development, diversity, and converging paths: a commentary. *Journal of Social and Personal Relationships*, 13: 473–9.

Alicke, M. D., Smith, R. H. and Klotz, M. L. (1987) Judgements of physical attractiveness: the role of faces and bodies. *Personality and Social Psychology Bulletin*, 12: 381–9.

Allan, G. A. (1993) Social structure and relationships, in S. W. Duck (ed.) *Understanding Relationship Processes 3: Social Contexts of Relationships*. Newbury Park: Sage.

Allan, G. A. (1995) 'Friendship, class, status and identity'. Paper presented to annual convention of the International Network on Personal Relationships, Williamsburg, VA, June.

Allan, G. A. (1998) Friendship, sociology and social structure. *Journal of Social and Personal Relationships*, 15: 685–702.

Andersen, P. A. (1993) Cognitive schemata in personal relationships, in S. W. Duck (ed.) *Understanding Relationship Processes 1: Individuals in Relationships*. Newbury Park: Sage.

Argyle, M. (1967) *The Psychology of Interpersonal Behaviour*. Harmondsworth: Penguin.

Argyle, M. (1987) *The Psychology of Happiness*. Harmondsworth: Penguin.

Argyle, M. and Henderson, M. (1984) The rules of friendship. *Journal of Social and Personal Relationships*, 1: 211–37.

Argyle, M. and Henderson, M. (1985). The rules of relationships, in S. W. Duck and D. Perlman (eds) *Understanding Personal Relationships: An Interdisciplinary Approach*. London: Sage.

Aron, A. and Aron, E. (1997) Self-expansion motivation and including other in the self, in S. W. Duck, K. Dindia, W. Ickes, R. Milardo, R. Mills and B. Sarason (eds) *Handbook of Personal Relationships* (2nd edition). Chichester: Wiley.

Assh, S. D. and Byers, E. S. (1996) Understanding the co-occurrence of marital distress and depression in women. *Journal of Social and Personal Relationships*, 13: 537–52.

Athanasiou, R. and Sarkin, R. (1974) Premarital sexual behaviour and postmarital adjustment. *Archives of Sexual Behavior*, 3: 207–25.

Bailey, B. (1988) *From Front Porch to Back Seat: Courtship in Twentieth Century America*. Baltimore: Johns Hopkins University.

Baldwin, M. W. (1993) Relational schemas and the processing of social information. *Psychological Bulletin*, 62: 111–12.

Ball, R. E. and Robbins, L. (1984) Marital status and life satisfaction of Black men. *Journal of Social and Personal Relationships*, 1: 459–70.

Bandura, A. (1977) *Social Learning Theory*. Englewood Cliffs, NJ: Prentice Hall.

Barnes, M. L. and Sternberg, R. J. (1997) A hierarchical model of love and its prediction of satisfaction in close relationships, in R. J. Sternberg and M. Hojjat (eds) *Satisfaction in Close Relationships*. New York: Guilford.

Bartholomew, K. (1990) Avoidance of intimacy: an attachment perspective. *Journal of Social and Personal Relationships*, 7: 147–78.

Bartholomew, K. (1993) From childhood to adult relationships: attachment theory and research, in S. W. Duck (ed.) *Understanding Relationship Processes 2: Learning About Relationships*. London: Sage.

Baumeister, R. F. and Leary, M. R. (1995) The need to belong: desire for inter-personal attachments as a fundamental human motivation. *Psychological Bulletin*, 117: 497–529.

Baxter, L. A. (1982) Strategies for ending relationships: two studies. *Western Journal of Speech Communication*, 46: 223–41.

Baxter, L. A. (1984) Trajectories of relationship disengagement. *Journal of Social and Personal Relationships*, 1: 29–48.

Baxter, L. A. (1986) Gender differences in the heterosexual relationship rules embedded in break-up accounts. *Journal of Social and Personal Relationships*, 3: 289–306.

Baxter, L. A. (1987) Symbols of relationship identity in relationship cultures. *Journal of Social and Personal Relationships*, 4: 261–79.

Baxter, L. A. (1992) Root metaphors in accounts of developing romantic rela-tionships. *Journal of Social and Personal Relationships*, 9: 253–75.

Baxter, L. A. (1993) The social side of personal relationships: a dialectical perspective, in S. W. Duck (ed.) *Understanding Relationship Processes 3: Social Contexts of Relationships*. Newbury Park: Sage.

Baxter, L. A. (1994) A dialogic approach to relationship maintenance, in D. J. Canary and L. Stafford (eds) *Communication and Relational Mainten-ance*. New York: Academic Press.

Baxter, L. A. and Montgomery, B. M. (1996) *Relating: Dialogs and Dialectics*. New York: Guilford.

Baxter, L. A. and Widenmann, S. (1993) Revealing and not revealing the status of romantic relationships to social networks. *Journal of Social and Personal Relationships*, 10: 321–38.

Baxter, L. A. and Wilmot, W. (1984) Secret tests: social strategies for acquiring information about the state of the relationship. *Human Communication Research*, 11: 171–201.

Baxter, L. A. and Wilmot, W. (1985) Taboo topics in close relationships. *Journal of Social and Personal Relationships*, 2: 253–69.

Baxter, L. A., Mazanec, M., Nicholson, L., Pittman, G., Smith, K. and West, L. (1997) Everyday loyalties and betrayals in personal relationships: a dialectical perspective. *Journal of Social and Personal Relationships*, 14: 663–78.

Beach, S. R. H. and O'Leary, K. D. (1993) Marital discord and dysphoria: for whom does the marital relationship predict depressive symptomatology? *Journal of Social and Personal Relationships*, 10: 405–20.

Beall, A. and Sternberg, R. (1995) The social construction of love. *Journal of Social and Personal Relationships*, 12: 417–38.

Beck, W. H., Ward-Hull, C. I. and McLear, P. M. (1976) Variables related to women's somantic preferences of the male and female body. *Journal of Personality and Social Psychology*, 34: 1200–10.

Bedford, V. H. and Blieszner, R. (1997) Personal relationships in later life families, in S. W. Duck, (ed.) with K. Dindia, W. Ickes, R. M. Milardo, R. S. L. Mills and B. Sarason, *Handbook of Personal Relationships* (2nd edition). Chichester: Wiley.

Beinstein Miller, J. (1993) Learning from early relationship experiences, in S. W. Duck (ed.) *Understanding Relationship Processes 2: Learning About Relationships*. Newbury Park: Sage.

Bendtschneider, L. and Duck, S. W. (1993) What's yours is mine and what's mine is yours: couple friends, in P. Kalbfleisch (ed.) *Developments in Inter-personal Communication*. Hillsdale, NJ: Erlbaum.

Bentler, P. M. and Newcomb, M. D. (1978) Longitudinal study of marital success and failure. *Journal of Consulting and Clinical Psychology*, 46: 1053–70.

Berger, C. R. (1988) Uncertainty and information exchange in developing relationships, in S. W. Duck, D. F. Hay, S. E. Hobfoll, W. Ickes and B. Montgomery (eds) *Handbook of Personal Relationships*. Chichester: Wiley.

Berger, C. R. (1993) Goals, plans and mutual understanding in personal relationships, in S. W. Duck (ed.) *Understanding Relationship Processes 1: Individuals in Relationships*. Newbury Park: Sage.

Bergmann, J. R. (1993) *Discreet Indiscretions: The Social Organization of Gossip*. New York: Aldine de Gruyter.

Berndt, T. J. (1996) Friendship in adolescence, in N. Vanzetti and S. W. Duck (eds) *A Lifetime of Relationships*. Pacific Grove, CA: Brooks/Cole.

Berscheid, E. (1981) An overview of the psychological effects of physical attractiveness, in G. W. Lucker, K. A. Ribbens and J. A. McNamara Jr (eds) *Psychological Aspects of Facial Form*. Michigan: CHGD.

Berscheid, E. (1994) Interpersonal relationships, in W. Porter and R. Rosenzweig (eds) *Annual Review of Psychology*, 45. Palo Alto: Annual Reviews.

Berscheid, E. (1995) Help wanted: a grand theorist of interpersonal relationships, sociologist or anthropologist preferred. *Journal of Social and Personal Relationships*, 12: 529–33.

Berscheid, E. and Hatfield [Walster], E. (1978) *Interpersonal Attraction* (2nd edition). Reading, MA: Addison-Wesley.

Berscheid, E. and Lopes, J. (1997) A temporal model of relationship satisfaction and stability, in R. J. Sternberg and M. Hojjat (eds) *Satisfaction in Close Relationships*. New York: Guilford.

Berscheid, E., Snyder, M. and Omoto, A. (1989) Issues in studying close relationships: conceptualizing and measuring closeness, in C. Hendrick (ed.) *Close Relationships*. Newbury Park: Sage.

Billig, M. (1987) *Arguing and Thinking: A Rhetorical Approach to Social Psychology*. Cambridge: Cambridge University Press.

Billig, M. (1991) *Ideology and Opinions: Studies in Rhetorical Psychology*. Newbury Park: Sage.

Billig, M., Condor, S., Edwards, D., Gane, M., Middleton, D. and Radley, A. (1988) *Ideological Dilemmas: A Social Psychology of Everyday Thinking*. London: Sage.

Birnbaum, G. E., Orr, I., Mikulincer, M. and Florian, F. (1997) When marriage breaks up – does attachment style contribute to coping and mental health? *Journal of Social and Personal Relationships*, 14: 643–54.

Bloom, B., Asher, S. and White, S. (1978) Marital disruption as a stressor: a review and analysis. *Psychological Bulletin*, 85: 867–94.

Blumstein, P. and Schwartz, P. (1983) *American Couples: Money, Work, Sex*. New York: William Morrow.

Bochner, A. P., Ellis, C. and Tillman-Healy, L. P. (1997) Relationships as stories, in S. W. Duck, K. Dindia, W. Ickes, R. Milardo, R. S. L. Mills and B. R. Sarason (eds) *Handbook of Personal Relationships* (2nd edition). Chichester: Wiley.

Bolger, N. and Kelleher, S. (1993) Daily life in relationships, in S. W. Duck (ed.) *Understanding Relationship Processes 3: Social Contexts of Relationships*. Newbury Park: Sage.

Bookwala, J. and Zdaniuk, B. (1998) Adult attachment styles and aggressive behavior within dating relationships. *Journal of Social and Personal Relationships*, 15: 175–90.

Boon, S. D. (1994) Dispelling doubt and uncertainty: trust in personal relationships, in S. W. Duck (1994) *Understanding Relationships 4: Dynamics of Relationships*. Thousand Oaks: Sage.

Bradbury, T. N. and Fincham, F. D. (1990) Attributions in marriage: review and critique. *Psychological Bulletin*, 107: 3–33.

Bradshaw, S. (1998) I'll go if you will: do shy persons utilize social surrogates? *Journal of Social and Personal Relationships*, 15: 651–69.

Braithwaite, D. O. and Baxter, L. A. (1995) 'I do' again: the relational dialectics of renewing marriage vows. *Journal of Social and Personal Relationships*, 12: 177–98.

Brock, D. M., Sarason, I. G., Sanghvi, H. and Gurung, R. A. R. (1998) The perceived acceptance scale: development and validation. *Journal of Social and Personal Relationships*, 15: 5–22.

Bruess, C. J. S. and Pearson, J. C. (1993) 'Sweet pea' and 'pussy cat': an examination of idiom use and marital satisfaction over the life cycle. *Journal of Social and Personal Relationships*, 10: 609–15.

Buehler, C. and Legg, B. H. (1993) Mothers' receipt of social support and their psychological well-being following marital separation. *Journal of Social and Personal Relationships*, 10: 21–38.

Burger, E. and Milardo, R. M. (1995) Marital interdependence and social networks. *Journal of Social and Personal Relationships*, 12: 403–15.

Burgoon, J. K. and Koper, R. J. (1984) Nonverbal and relational communication associated with reticence. *Human Communication Research*, 10: 601–26.

Burleson, B. R., Kunkel, A. W., Samter, W. and Werking, K. J. (1996) Men's and women's evaluations of communication skills in personal relationships: when sex differences make a difference – and when they don't. *Journal of Social and Personal Relationships*, 13: 143–52.

Burnett, R. (1986) 'Conceptualisation of personal relationships'. Unpub. D.Phil., University of Oxford.

Burnett, R. (1987) Reflection in personal relationships, in R. Burnett, P. McGhee and D. C. Clarke (eds) *Accounting for Relationships: Explanation, Representation and Knowledge*. London: Methuen.

Burnett, R., McGhee, P. and Clarke, D. (1987) *Accounting for Relationships: Explanation, Representation and Knowledge*. London: Methuen.

Byrne, D. (1971) *The Attraction Paradigm*. New York: Academic Press.

Byrne, D. (1997) An overview (and underview) of research and theory within the attraction paradigm. *Journal of Social and Personal Relationships*, 14: 417–31.

Cameron, C., Oskamp, S. and Sparks, W. (1977) Courtship American style: newspaper ads. *Family Coordinator*, 26: 27–30.

Canary, D. J. and Emmers-Sommer, T. (1997) *Sex and Gender Differences in Personal Relationships*. New York: Guilford.

Canary, D. J. and Stafford, L. (eds) (1994) *Communication and Relationship Maintenance*. New York: Academic Press.

Carl, W. J. (1997) 'Relationship gumbo: understanding *bricolage* and the creation of personal relationships as a definitional process'. Paper presented to the Annual Convention of the International Network on Personal Relationships, Oxford University, Ohio, June.

Cate, R. M. and Lloyd, S. A. (1992) *Courtship*. Newbury Park: Sage.

Cate, R. M., Henton, J., Koval, J., Christopher, F. S. and Lloyd, S. A. (1982) Premarital abuse: a social psychological perspective. *Journal of Family Issues*, 3: 79–90.

Cattell, H. and Nesselroade, J. R. (1967) Likeness and completeness theories examined by sixteen personality factor measures on stable and unstable married couples. *Journal of Personality and Social Psychology*, 7: 351–61.

Chan, C-J. and Margolin, G. (1994) The relationship between dual-earner couples' daily work mood and home affect. *Journal of Social and Personal Relationships*, 11: 573–86.

Cheal, D. J. (1986) The social dimensions of gift behaviour. *Journal of Social and Personal Relationships*, 3: 423–39.

Christopher, F. S. and Cate, R. M. (1985) Premarital sexual pathways and relationship development. *Journal of Social and Personal Relationships*, 2: 271–88.

Christopher, F. S. and Frandsen, M. (1990) Strategies of influence in sex and dating. *Journal of Social and Personal Relationships*, 7: 89–106.

Clark, E. M., Morrow, G. D., Brock, K. F., McGaha, A. C. and Frauenhoffer, S. M. (1998) Perceptual accuracy in the balance: the weight of evidence and the evidence of weight. *Journal of Social and Personal Relationships*, 15: 127–36.

Clark, M. S. and Reis, H. T. (1988) Interpersonal processes in close relationships. *Annual Review of Psychology*, 39: 609–72.

Clarke, D. D., Allen, C. M. B. and Salinas, M. (1986) Conjoint time budgeting: investigating behavioral accommodation in marriage. *Journal of Personal and Social Relationships*, 3: 53–70.

Clements, M. and Markman, H. J. (1996) The transition to parenthood: is having children hazardous to your marriage?, in N. Vanzetti and S. W. Duck (eds) *A Lifetime of Relationships*. Monterey, CA: Brooks/Cole.

Coleman, M. and Ganong, L. H. (1995) Family reconfiguration following divorce, in S. W. Duck and J. T. Wood (eds) *Understanding Relationship Processes 5: Confronting Relationship Challenges*. Thousand Oaks: Sage.

Collins, R. and Coltrane, S. (1995) *Sociology of Marriage and Family: Gender, Love and Property*. Chicago: Nelson Hall.

Conville, R. L. (1997) Between spearheads: *bricolage* and relationships. *Journal of Social and Personal Relationships*, 14: 373–86.

Cooney, T. M. (1997) Parent–child relations across adulthood, in S. W. Duck, K. Dindia, W. Ickes, R. Milardo, R. S. L. Mills and B. Sarason (eds) *Handbook of Personal Relationships* (2nd edition). Chichester: Wiley.

Cortez, C. (1986) 'Relationships with media anchors'. Unpublished MS, University of Iowa.

Crandall, C. S. and Coleman, R. (1992) AIDS-related stigmatization and the disruption of social relationships. *Journal of Social and Personal Relationships*, 9: 163–77.

Crohan, S. E. (1992) Marital happiness and spousal consensus on beliefs about marital conflict: a longitudinal investigation. *Journal of Social and Personal Relationships*, 9: 89–102.

Crohan, S. E. (1996) Marital quality and conflict across the transition to parenthood in African American and White couples. *Journal of Marriage and the Family*, 58: 933–44.

Crouter, A. C. and Helms-Erickson, H. (1997) Work and family from a dyadic perspective: variations in inequality, in S. W. Duck, K. Dindia, W. Ickes, R. Milardo, R. S. L. Mills and B. R. Sarason (eds) *Handbook of Personal Relationships* (2nd edition). Chichester: Wiley.

Cunningham, J. D. and Antill, J. K. (1995) Current trends in nonmarital cohabitation: in search of the POSSLQ, in J. T. Wood and S. W. Duck (eds) *Understanding Relationship Processes 6: Under-studied Relationships: Off the Beaten Track*. Thousand Oaks: Sage.

Cupach, W. R. and Spitzberg, B. H. (eds) (1994) *The Dark Side of Interpersonal Communication*. Hillsdale NJ: LEA.

Dainton, M. and Stafford, L. (1993) Routine maintenance behaviours: a comparison of relationship type, partner similarity, and sex differences. *Journal of Social and Personal Relationships*, 10: 255–71.

Dallos, R. (1996) Creating relationships, in D. E. Miell and R. Dallos (eds) *Social Interaction and Personal Relationships*. Milton Keynes: Open University/Sage.

Davis, J. D. (1978) When boy meets girl: sex roles and the negotiation of intimacy in an acquaintance exercise. *Journal of Personality and Social Psychology*, 36: 684–92.

Davis, K. E. and Todd, M. J. (1985) Assessing friendship: prototypes, paradigm cases and relationship description, in S. W. Duck and D. Perlman (eds) *Understanding Personal Relationships*. London: Sage.

Davis, M. H. and Franzoi, S. L. (1986) Adolescent loneliness, self-disclosure and private self-consciousness: a longitudinal investigation. *Journal of Personality and Social Psychology*, 51: 595–608.

Deal, J. and Wampler, K. S. (1986) Dating violence: the primacy of previous experience. *Journal of Social and Personal Relationships*, 3: 457–71.

Delia, J. G. (1980) Some tentative thoughts concerning the study of interpersonal relationships and their development. *Western Journal of Speech Communication*, 44: 97–103.

Demo, D. H. and Allen, K. R. (1996) Diversity within lesbian and gay families: challenges and implications for family theory and research. *Journal of Social and Personal Relationships*, 13: 415–34.

Derlega, V. J., Metts, S., Petronio, S. and Margolis, S. T. (1993) *Self-disclosure*. Newbury Park: Sage.

Dickens, W. J. and Perlman, D. (1981) Friendship over the life cycle, in S. W. Duck and R. Gilmour (eds) *Personal Relationships 2: Developing Personal Relationships*. London: Academic Press.

Dickson, F. C. (1995). The best is yet to be: research on long-lasting marriages, in J. Wood and S. W. Duck (eds) *Understanding Relationship Processes 6: Under-studied Relationships: Off the Beaten Track*. Thousand Oaks: Sage.

Dillard, J. P. and Miller, K. I. (1988) Intimate relationships in task environments, in S. W. Duck (ed.) *A Handbook of Personal Relationships*. New York: Wiley.

Dindia, K. (1994) The intrapersonal–interpersonal dialectical process of self-disclosure, in S. W. Duck (ed.) *Understanding Relationship Processes 4: Dynamics of Relationships*. Newbury Park: Sage.

Dindia, K. (1997) Self-disclosure, self-identity, and relationship development: a transactional/dialectical perspective, in S. W. Duck (ed.) with K. Dindia, W. Ickes, R. M. Milardo, R. S. L. Mills and B. Sarason, *Handbook of Personal Relationships* (2nd edition). Chichester: Wiley.

Dindia, K. and Baxter, L. A. (1987) Strategies for maintaining and repairing marital relationships. *Journal of Social and Personal Relationships*, 4: 143–58.

Dindia, K. and Canary, D. J. (1993) Definitions and theoretical perspectives on maintaining relationships. *Journal of Social and Personal Relationships*, 10: 163–74.

Douglas, W. (1987) Affinity testing in initial interaction. *Journal of Social and Personal Relationships*, 4: 3–16.

Driscoll, R., Davis, K. E. and Lipetz, M. E. (1972) Parental interference and romantic love: the Romeo and Juliet effect. *Journal of Personality and Social Psychology*, 24: 1–10.

Duck, S. W. (1977) *The Study of Acquaintance*. Farnborough: Teakfields (Saxon House).

Duck, S. W. (1980a) Taking the past to heart: one of the futures of social psychology, in R. Gilmour and S. W. Duck (eds) *The Development of Social Psychology*. London: Academic Press.

Duck, S. W. (1980b) Personal relationships research in the 1980s: towards an understanding of complex human sociality. *Western Journal of Speech Communication*, 44: 114–19.

Duck, S. W. (1982a) A topography of relationship disengagement and dissolution, in S. W. Duck (ed.) *Personal Relationships 4: Dissolving Personal Relationships*. London and New York: Academic Press.

Duck, S. W. (1982b) *Personal Relationships 4: Dissolving Personal Relationships*. London and New York: Academic Press.

Duck, S. W. (1984a) A perspective on the repair of personal relationships: repair of what, when?, in S. W. Duck (ed.) *Personal Relationships 5: Repairing Personal Relationships*. London: Academic Press.

Duck, S. W. (ed.) (1984b) *Personal Relationships 5: Repairing Personal Relationships*. London: Academic Press.

Duck, S. W. (1988) *Relating to Others*. London: Open University Press.

Duck, S. W. (1990) Relationships as unfinished business: out of the frying pan and into the 1990s. *Journal of Social and Personal Relationships*, 7: 5–29.

Duck, S. W. (1991) *Friends, for Life*, (2nd revised edition). Hemel Hempstead: Harvester Wheatsheaf. (Published in USA as *Understanding Relationships*. New York: Guilford.)

Duck, S. W. (1993a) Preface on social context, in S. W. Duck (ed.) *Understanding Relationship Processes 3: Social Contexts of Relationships*. Newbury Park: Sage.

Duck, S. W. (ed.) (1993b) *Understanding Relationship Processes 3: Social Contexts of Relationships*. Newbury Park: Sage.

Duck, S. W. (1994a) *Meaningful Relationships: Talking, Sense, and Relating*. Thousand Oaks: Sage.

Duck, S. W. (1994b) Stratagems, spoils and a serpent's tooth: on the delights and dilemmas of personal relationships, in W. Cupach and B. H. Spitzberg (eds) *The Dark Side of Interpersonal Communication*. Hillsdale, NJ: LEA.

Duck, S. W. (1994c) Steady as (s)he goes: relational maintenance as a shared meaning system, in D. J. Canary and L. Stafford (eds) *Communication and Relationship Maintenance*. New York: Academic Press.

Duck, S. W. (1995) Repelling the study of attraction: some recent advances in the study of [heterosexual] relationships. *The Psychologist*, 8: 60–3.

Duck, S. W. (1998). *Human Relationships* (3rd edition). London: Sage.

Duck, S. W. and Craig, R. G. (1978) Personality similarity and the development of friendship: a longitudinal study. *British Journal of Social Clinical Psychology*, 17: 237–42.

Duck, S. W. and Gilmour, R. (eds) (1981) *Personal Relationships 2: Developing Personal Relationships*. London: Academic Press.

Duck, S. W. and Miell, D. E. (1986) Charting the development of personal relationships, in R. Gilmour and S. W. Duck (eds) *Emerging Field of Personal Relationships*. Hillsdale, NJ: LEA.

Duck, S. W. and Pond, K. (1989) Friends, Romans, countrymen, lend me your retrospections: rhetoric and reality in personal relationships, in C. Hendrick (ed.) *Close Relationships*. Newbury Park: Sage.

Duck, S. W. and Sants, H. K. A. (1983) On the origin of the specious: are personal relationships really interpersonal states? *Journal of Social and Clinical Psychology*, 1: 27–41.

Duck, S. W. and Wood, J. T. (1995) *Understanding Relationship Processes 5: Confronting Relationship Challenges*. Newbury Park: Sage.

Duck, S. W., Hay, D. F., Hobfoll, S. E., Ickes, W. J. and Montgomery, B. M. (eds) (1988) *Handbook of Personal Relationships*. Chichester and New York: Wiley.

Duck, S. W., Rutt, D. J., Hurst, M. and Strejc, H. (1991) Some evident truths about communication in everyday relationships: all communication is not created equal. *Human Communication Research*, 18: 228–67.

Duck, S. W., Pond, K. and Leatham, G. B. (1994) Loneliness and the evaluation of relational events. *Journal of Social and Personal Relationships*, 11: 235–60.

Duck, S. W. (ed.) with Dindia, K., Ickes, W., Milardo, R. M., Mills, R. S. L. and Sarason, B. (1997a) *Handbook of Personal Relationships* (2nd edition). Chichester: Wiley.

Duck, S. W., West, L. and Acitelli, L. K. (1997b) Sewing the field: the tapestry of relationships in life and research, in S. W. Duck (ed.) with K. Dindia, W. Ickes, R. M. Milardo, R. S. L. Mills and B. Sarason, *Handbook of Personal Relationships*, (2nd edition). Chichester: Wiley.

Duggan, E. S. and Brennan, K. A. (1994) Social avoidance and its relation to Bartholomew's adult attachment typology. *Journal of Social and Personal Relationships*, 11: 145–53.

Dunn, J. (1996) Siblings: the first society, in N. Vanzetti and S. W. Duck (eds) *A Lifetime of Relationships*. Pacific Grove, CA: Brooks/Cole.

Dunn, J. (1997) Lessons from the study of bi-directional effects. *Journal of Social and Personal Relationships*, 14: 565–73.

Duran, R. and Prusank, D. T. (1997) Relational themes in men's and women's popular non-fiction magazine articles. *Journal of Social and Personal Relationships*, 14: 165–89.

Edwards, D. and Middleton, D. (1988) Conversational remembering and family relationships: how children learn to remember. *Journal of Social and Personal Relationships*, 5: 3–25.

Ehrlich, H. J. and Lipsey, C. (1969) Affective style as a variable in person perception. *Journal of Personality*, 37: 522–40.

Eiser, J. R. and Ford, N. (1995) Sexual relationships on holiday: a case of situational disinhibition. *Journal of Social and Personal Relationships*, 12: 323–39.

Feeney, J. A., Noller, P. and Ward, C. (1997) Marital satisfaction and spousal interaction, in R. J. Sternberg and M. Hojjat (eds) *Satisfaction in Close Relationships*. New York: Guilford.

Fehr, B. (1993) How do I love thee? . . . . let me consult my prototype, in S. W. Duck (ed.) *Understanding Relationship Processes 1: Individuals in Relationships*. Newbury Park: Sage.

Felmlee, D. H. (1995) Fatal attractions: affection and disaffection in intimate relationships. *Journal of Social and Personal Relationships*, 12: 295–311.

Ferreira, A. and Winter, W. (1974) On the nature of marital relationships: measurable differences in spontaneous agreement. *Family Process*, 13: 355–69.

Fichten, C. S. and Wright, J. (1985) Problem-solving skills in happy and distressed couples: effects of videotape and verbal feedback. *Journal of Clinical and Social Psychology*, 39: 157–88.

Fincham, F. (1995) From the orthogenic principle to the fish scale model of omniscience: advancing understanding of personal relationships. *Journal of Social and Personal Relationships*, 12: 523–7.

Fischer, C. (1982) *To Dwell Among Friends*. Chicago: Chicago University Press.

Fisher, S. W. (1996) The family and the individual: reciprocal influences, in N. Vanzetti and S. W. Duck (eds) *A Lifetime of Relationships*. Pacific Grove, CA: Brooks/Cole.

Fitch, K. L. (1998) *Speaking Relationally: Culture, Communication, and Interpersonal Connection*. New York: Guilford.

Fitzpatrick, M. A. and Badzinski, D. (1985) All in the family, in G. R. Miller and M. L. Knapp (eds) *Handbook of Interpersonal Communication*. Beverly Hills, CA: Sage.

Fletcher, G. J. O. and Fitness, J. (1993) Knowledge structures and explanations in intimate relationships, in S. W. Duck (ed.) *Understanding Relationship Processes 1: Individuals in Relationships*. Newbury Park: Sage.

Flora, J. and Segrin, C. (1998) Joint leisure time in friend and romantic relationships: the role of activity type, social skills and positivity. *Journal of Social and Personal Relationships*, 15: 711–18.

Folwell, A. L., Chung, L. C., Grant, J. A., Nussbaum, J. F. and Bethea, L. S. (1997) Differential accounts of closeness in older adult sibling relationships. *Journal of Social and Personal Relationships*, 14: 843–9.

Franzoi, S. L. and Herzog, M. E. (1987) Judging physical attractiveness: what body aspects do we use? *Personality and Social Psychology Bulletin*, 13: 34–44.

Frazier, P. A. and Cook, S. W. (1993) Correlates of distress following heterosexual relationship dissolution. *Journal of Social and Personal Relationships*, 10: 55–67.

Frederickson, B. L. (1995) Socioemotional behaviour at the end of college life. *Journal of Social and Personal Relationships*, 12: 261–76.

Freedman, R. (1986) *Beauty Bound*. Lexington: Gower.

French, D. C. and Underwood, M. K. (1996) Peer relations during middle childhood, in N. Vanzetti and S. W. Duck (eds) *A Lifetime of Relationships*. Pacific Grove, CA: Brooks/Cole.

Fuendeling, J. M. (1998) Affect regulation as a stylistic process within adult attachment. *Journal of Social and Personal Relationships*, 15: 291–322.

Fujino, D. C. (1997) The rates, patterns and reasons for forming heterosexual interracial dating relationships among Asian Americans. *Journal of Social and Personal Relationships*, 14: 809–28.

Furman, W. and Simon, V. A. (1998) Advice from youth: some lessons from the study of adolescent relationships. *Journal of Social and Personal Relationships*, 15: 723–39.

Gaines, S. and Ickes, W. (1997) Perspectives on interracial relationships, in S. W. Duck (ed.) with K. Dindia, W. Ickes, R. M. Milardo, R. S. L. Mills and B. Sarason, *Handbook of Personal Relationships* (2nd edition). Chichester: Wiley.

Ganong, L. H. and Coleman, M. (1998) Grandparents' and stepgrandparents' financial obligations to grandchildren and stepgrandchildren. *Journal of Social and Personal Relationships*, 15: 39–58.

Glidewell, J. C., Tucker, S., Todt, M. and Cox, S. (1982) Professional support systems – the teaching profession, in A. Nadler, J. D. Fisher and B. M. DePaulo (eds) *New Directions in Helping 3: Applied Research in Help-seeking and Reactions to Aid*. New York: Academic Press.

Goffman, E. (1952) *On Cooling the Mark Out*. Harmondsworth: Pelican.

Goffman, E. (1959) *Behaviour in Public Places*. Harmondsworth: Penguin.

Goldstein, J. W. and Rosenfeld, H. M. (1969) Insecurity and preference for persons similar to oneself. *Journal of Personality*, 37: 253–68.

Goodwin, R. (1990) Dating agency members: are they 'different'? *Journal of Social and Personal Relationships*, 7: 423–30.

Goodwin, R. (1995) The privatization of the personal? I: Intimate disclosure in modern-day Russia. *Journal of Social and Personal Relationships*, 12: 121–31.

Goodwin, R. (1998) Personal relationships and social change: the 'realpolitik' of cross-cultural research in transient cultures. *Journal of Social and Personal Relationships*, 15: 227–47.

Gottman, J. M. (1994) *What Predicts Divorce?* Hillsdale, NJ: Erlbaum.

Gottman, J. M., Notarius, C., Gonso, J. and Markman, H. (1976) *A Couple's Guide to Communication*. Champaign, IL: Research Press.

Gouldner, A. W. (1960) The norm of reciprocity: a preliminary statement. *American Sociological Review*, 25: 161–78.

Grote, N. K. and Frieze, I. H. (1998) 'Remembrance of things past': perceptions of marital love from its beginnings to the present. *Journal of Social and Personal Relationships*, 15: 91–109.

Guerrero, L. K., Eloy, S. V. and Wabnik, A. I. (1993) Linking maintenance strategies to relationship development and disengagement: a reconceptualization. *Journal of Social and Personal Relationships*, 10: 273–83.

Guldner, G. T. and Swensen, C. H. (1995) Time spent together and relationship quality: long distance relationships as a test case. *Journal of Social and Personal Relationships*, 12: 313–20.

Hagestad, G. O. and Smyer, M. A. (1982) Dissolving long-term relationships: patterns of divorcing in middle age, in S. W. Duck (ed.) *Personal Relationships 4: Dissolving Personal Relationships*. London: Academic Press.

Haley, J. (1964) Research on family patterns: an instrument measurement. *Family Process*, 3: 41–65.

Harrison, A. A. and Saeed, L. (1977) Let's make a deal: an analysis of revelations and stipulations in lonely hearts advertisements. *Journal of Personality and Social Psychology*, 35: 257–64.

Harvey, J. H., Weber, A. L., Galvin, K. S., Huszti, H. C. and Garnick, N. N. (1986) Attribution and the termination of close relationships: a special focus on the account, in R. Gilmour and S. W. Duck (eds) *The Emerging Field of Personal Relationships*. Hillsdale, NJ: Lawrence Erlbaum.

Harvey, J. H., Barnes, M. K., Carlson, H. R. and Haig, J. (1995) Held captive by their memories: managing grief in relationships, in S. W. Duck and J. T. Wood (eds) *Understanding Relationship Processes 5: Confronting Relationship Challenges*. Thousand Oaks: Sage.

Hatala, M. N., Baach, D. W. and Parmenter, R. (1998) Dating with HIV: a content analysis of gay male HIV-positive and HIV-negative personal advertisements. *Journal of Social and Personal Relationships*, 15: 268–76.

Hayashi, G. M. and Strickland, B. R. (1998) The long-term effects of parental divorce on love relationships: divorce as attachment disruption. *Journal of Social and Personal Relationships*, 15: 23–38.

Hays, R. B. (1984) The development and maintenance of friendship. *Journal of Social and Personal Relationships*, 1: 75–98.

Hays, R. B. (1988) Friendship, in S. W. Duck (ed.) *Handbook of Personal Relationships*. New York: Wiley.

Heller, K. and Rook, K. S. (1997) Distinguishing the theoretical functions of social ties: implications of support interventions, in S. W. Duck, K. Dindia,

W. Ickes, R. Milardo, R. S. L. Mills and B. R. Sarason (eds) *Handbook of Personal Relationships* (2nd edition). Chichester: Wiley.

Henderson-King, D. H. and Veroff, J. (1994) Sexual satisfaction and marital well-being in the first years of marriage. *Journal of Social and Personal Relationships*, 11: 509–34.

Hendrick, C. (1988) Roles and gender in relationships, in S. W. Duck (ed.) with D. F. Hay, S. E. Hobfoll, W. Ickes and B. Montgomery, *Handbook of Personal Relationships*. Chichester: Wiley.

Hendrick, C. and Brown, S. R. (1971) Introversion, extraversion and interpersonal attraction. *Journal of Personality and Social Psychology*, 20: 31–6.

Hendrick, S. S. and Hendrick, C. (1993) Lovers as friends. *Journal of Social and Personal Relationships*, 10: 459–66.

Hendrick, S. S. and Hendrick, C. (1997) Love and satisfaction, in R. J. Sternberg and M. Hojjat (eds) *Satisfaction in Close Relationships*. New York: Guilford.

Hepburn, J. R. and Crepin, A. E. (1984) Relationship strategies in a coercive institution: a study of dependence among prison guards. *Journal of Social and Personal Relationships*, 1: 139–58.

Herold, E. S., Maticka-Tyndale, E. and Mewhinney, D. (1998) Predicting intentions to engage in casual sex. *Journal of Social and Personal Relationships*, 15: 502–16.

Hill, C. T., Rubin, Z. and Peplau, L. A. (1976) Breakups before marriage: the end of 103 affairs. *Journal of Social Issues*, 32: 147–68.

Hinde, R. A. (1981) The bases of a science of interpersonal relationships, in S. W. Duck and R. Gilmour (eds) *Personal Relationships 1: Studying Personal Relationships*. London, New York, San Francisco: Academic Press.

Hobfoll, S. E. (1996) Social support: will you be there when I need you?, in N. Vanzetti and S. W. Duck (eds) *A Lifetime of Relationships*. Monterey, CA: Brooks/Cole.

Hobfoll, S. E. and Stokes, J. P. (1988) The process and mechanics of social support, in S. W. Duck *et al.* (ed.) *Handbook of Personal Relationships*. New York: Wiley.

Honeycutt, J. M. (1993) Memory structures for the rise and fall of personal relationships, in S. W. Duck (ed.) *Understanding Relationship Processes 1: Individuals in Relationships*. Newbury Park: Sage.

Honeycutt, J. M., Woods, B. L. and Fontenot, K. (1993) The endorsement of communication conflict rules as a function of engagement, marriage, and marital ideology. *Journal of Social and Personal Relationships*, 10: 285–304.

Hooley, J. and Hiller, J. (1997) Family relationships and major mental disorder: risk factors and preventive strategies, in S. W. Duck, K. Dindia, W. Ickes, R. Milardo, R. Mills, B. Sarason (eds) *Handbook of Personal Relationships* (2nd edition). Chichester: Wiley.

Hopper, R., Knapp, M. L. and Scott, L. (1981) Couples' personal idioms: exploring intimate talk. *Journal of Communication*, 31: 23–33.

Horton, D. and Wohl, R. R. (1956) Mass communication and parasocial interaction: observations on intimacy at a distance. *Psychiatry*, 19: 215–29.

Huesmann, L. R. and Levinger, G. (1976) Incremental exchange theory, in L. Berkowitz and E. H. Walster (eds) *Advances in Experimental Social Psychology*. New York: Academic Press.

Huston, M. and Schwartz, P. (1995) Lesbian and gay male relationships, in J. T. Wood and S. W. Duck (eds) *Understanding Relationship Processes 6: Under-studied Relationships: Off the Beaten Track*. Thousand Oaks: Sage.

Huston, T. L., Surra, C. A., Fitzgerald, N. M. and Cate, R. M. (1981) From courtship to marriage: mate selection as an interpersonal process, in S. W. Duck and R. Gilmour (eds) *Personal Relationships 2: Developing Personal Relationships*. London and New York: Academic Press.

Jaffe, D. T. and Kanter, R. M. (1979) Couple strains in communal households: a four-factor model of the separation process, in G. Levinger and O. Moles (eds) *Divorce and Separation*. New York: Basic Books.

Johnson, M. (1982) Social and cognitive features of dissolving commitment to relationships, in S. W. Duck (ed.) *Personal Relationships 4: Dissolving Personal Relationships*. London: Academic Press.

Johnson, M. P., Huston, T. L., Gaines, S. O. and Levinger, G. (1992) Patterns of married life among young couples. *Journal of Social and Personal Relationships*, 9: 343–64.

Jones, E. E. and Gordon, E. M. (1972) Timing of self-disclosure and its effects on personal attraction. *Journal of Personality and Social Psychology*, 24: 358–65.

Jones, W. H., Hansson, R. O. and Cutrona, C. E. (1984) Helping the lonely: issues of intervention with young and older adults, in S. W. Duck (ed.) *Personal Relationships 5: Repairing Personal Relationships*. London: Academic Press.

Jones, W. H., Cavert, C. W., Snider, R. L. and Bruce, T. (1985) Relational stress: an analysis of situations and events associated with loneliness, in S. W. Duck and D. Perlman (eds) *Understanding Personal Relationships*. London: Sage.

Jourard, S. M. (1971) *Self-disclosure*. New York: Wiley.

Kamo, Y. (1993) Determinants of marital satisfaction: a comparison of the United States and Japan. *Journal of Social and Personal Relationships*, 10: 551–68.

Kaniasty, K. and Norris, F. H. (1997) Social support dynamics in adjustment to disasters, in S. W. Duck, K. Dindia, W. Ickes, R. Milardo, R. S. L. Mills and B. R. Sarason (eds) *Handbook of Personal Relationships* (2nd edition). Chichester: Wiley.

Kaplan, D. K. and Keys, C. B. (1997) Sex and relationship variables as predictors of sexual attraction in cross-sex platonic relationships between heterosexual adults. *Journal of Social and Personal Relationships*, 14: 191–206.

Kaplan, R. E. (1976) Maintaining interpersonal relationships: a bipolar theory. *Interpersonal Development*, 6: 106–19.

Kaplan, R. E. (1984) Repairing ailing work relationships, in S. W. Duck (ed.) *Personal Relationships 5: Repairing Personal Relationships*. New York: Academic Press.

Keeley, M. and Hart, A. (1994) Nonverbal behavior in dyadic interactions, in S. W. Duck (1994) *Understanding Relationships 4: Dynamics of Relationships*. Thousand Oaks: Sage.

Kelley, D. (1997) 'Forgiveness'. Paper to the annual convention of the National Communication Association, Chicago, November.

Kelvin, P. (1977) Predictability, power and vulnerability in interpersonal attraction, in S. W. Duck (ed.) *Theory and Practice in Interpersonal Attraction*. London: Academic Press.

Kenny, D. A. and Acitelli, L. K. (1989) The role of the relationship in marital decision-making, in D. Brinberg and J. J. Jaccard (eds) *Dyadic Decision Making*. New York: Springer-Verlag.

Kenrick, D. T. and Trost, M. R. (1997) Evolutionary approaches to relationships, in S. W. Duck (ed.) with K. Dindia, W. Ickes, R. M. Milardo, R. S. L. Mills and B. Sarason, *Handbook of Personal Relationships* (2nd edition). Chichester: Wiley.

Kephart, W. M. (1967) Some correlates of romantic love. *Journal of Marriage and the Family*, 29: 470–4.

Kerckhoff, A. C. (1974) The social context of interpersonal attraction, in T. L. Huston (ed.) *Foundations of Interpersonal Attraction*. New York: Academic Press.

Kidd, V. (1975) Happily ever after and other relationship styles: advice on interpersonal relations in popular magazines, 1951–1973. *Quarterly Journal of Speech*, 61: 31–9.

King, L. A. (1993) Emotional expression, ambivalence over expression and marital satisfaction. *Journal of Social and Personal Relationships*, 10: 601–7.

Klein, R. C. A. and Lamm, H. (1996) Legitimate interest in couple conflict. *Journal of Social and Personal Relationships*, 13: 619–26.

Klein, R. and Johnson, M. (1997) Strategies of couple conflict, in S. W. Duck (ed.) with K. Dindia, W. Ickes, R. M. Milardo, R. S. L. Mills and B. Sarason, *Handbook of Personal Relationships* (2nd edition). Chichester: Wiley.

Klein, R. and Milardo, R. (1993) Third-party influences on the development and maintenance of personal relationships, in S. W. Duck (ed.) *Understanding Relationship Processes 3: Social Contexts of Relationships*. Newbury Park: Sage.

Kline, S. L., Stafford, L. and Miklosovic, J. L. (1996) Women's surnames: decisions, interpretations and associations with relational qualities. *Journal of Social and Personal Relationships*, 13: 593–617.

Klinger, E. (1977) *Meaning and Void: Inner Experience and the Incentives in People's Lives*. Minneapolis: University of Minnesota Press.

Knapp, M. L. (1984) *Interpersonal Communication and Human Relationships*. Boston: Allyn and Bacon.

Koestner, R. and Wheeler, L. (1988) Self presentation in personal advertisements: the influence of implicit notions of attraction and role expectations. *Journal of Social and Personal Relationships*, 5: 149–60.

Kovach, S. S. and Robinson, J. D. (1996) The room-mate relationship for the elderly nursing home resident. *Journal of Social and Personal Relationships*, 13: 627–34.

Krauss, R. M. and Fussell, S. R. (1996) Social psychological models of interpersonal communication, in E. T. Higgins and A. W. Kruglanski (eds) *Social Psychology: Handbook of Basic Principles*. New York: Guilford.

Kurdek, L. (1991) The dissolution of gay and lesbian relationships. *Journal of Social and Personal Relationships*, 8: 265–78.

Kurdek, L. A. (1992) Relationship stability and relationship satisfaction in cohabiting gay and lesbian couples: a prospective longitudinal test of the contextual and interdependence models. *Journal of Social and Personal Relationships*, 9: 125–42.

Kurth, S. B. (1970) Friendship and friendly relations, in G. J. McCall, M. M. McCall, N. K. Denzin, G. D. Suttles and S. B. Kurth, *Social Relationships*. Chicago: Aldine.

La Gaipa, J. J. (1982) Rules and rituals in disengaging from relationships, in S. W. Duck (ed.) *Personal Relationships 4: Dissolving Personal Relationships*. London: Academic Press.

Lamke, L., Sollie, D., Durbin, R. G. and Fitzpatrick, J. A. (1994) Masculinity, femininity and relationship satisfaction: the mediating role of interpersonal competence. *Journal of Social and Personal Relationships*, 11: 535–54.

Latty-Mann, H. and Davis, K. E. (1996) Attachment theory and partner choice: preference and actuality. *Journal of Social and Personal Relationships*, 13: 5–23.

Lea, M. and Spears, R. (1995) Love at first byte: relationships conducted over electronic systems, in J. T. Wood and S. W. Duck (eds) *Understanding Relationship Processes 6: Under-studied Relationships: Off the Beaten Track*. Newbury Park: Sage.

Leary, M. L. (1983) *Understanding Social Anxiety*. Beverly Hills: Sage.

Leary, M. R. and Miller, R. S. (in press) Self presentational perspectives on personal relationships, in W. Ickes and S. W. Duck (eds) *The Social Psychology of Personal Relationships*. Chichester: Wiley.

Leary, M. L., Rogers, P. A., Canfield, R. W. and Coe, C. (1986) Boredom in interpersonal encounters: antecedents and social implications. *Journal of Personality and Social Psychology*, 51: 968–75.

Leatham, G. B. and Duck, S. W. (1990) Conversations with friends and the dynamics of social support, in S. W. Duck (ed., with R. C. Silver) *Personal Relationships and Social Support*. London: Sage.

Lee, J. A. (1973) *The Colors of Love: An Exploration of the Ways of Loving*. Ontario: New Press.

Lee, L. (1984) Sequences in separation: a framework for investigating the endings of personal (romantic) relationships. *Journal of Social and Personal Relationships*, 1: 49–74.

Levinger, G. (1965) Marital cohesiveness and dissolution: an integrative review. *Journal of Marriage and the Family*, 27: 19–28.

Levinger, G. (1996) 'My view of relationships'. Paper presented to the Society for Experimental Social Psychology, Sturbridge, MA, October.

Levitt, M., Silver, M. E. and Franco, N. (1996) Troublesome relationships: a part of the human experience. *Journal of Social and Personal Relationships*, 13: 523–36.

Lewis, R. A. (1978) Emotional intimacy among men. *Journal of Social Issues*, 34: 108–21.

Lewis, R. A. and Lin, L. W. (1996) Adults and their midlife parents, in N. Vanzetti and S. W. Duck (eds) *A Lifetime of Relationships*. Pacific Grove, CA: Brooks/Cole.

Lewis, R. A. and McAvoy, P. (1984) Improving the quality of relationships: therapeutic interventions with opiate-abusing couples, in S. W. Duck (ed.) *Personal Relationships 5: Repairing Personal Relationships*. London and New York: Academic Press.

Lin, Y-H. W. and Rusbult, C. E. (1995) Commitment to dating relationships and cross-sex friendships in America and China. *Journal of Social and Personal Relationships*, 12: 7–26.

Little, B. R. (1984) 'Personal project analysis'. Paper presented to Conference of the Self, Cardiff.

Lloyd, S. A. and Cate, R. M. (1985) The developmental course of conflict in dissolution of premarital relationships. *Journal of Social and Personal Relationships*, 2: 179–94.

Lynch, J. J. (1977) *The Broken Heart: The Medical Consequences of Loneliness*. New York: Basic Books.

Lynn, S. and Bolig, R. (1985) Personal advertisements: sources of data about relationships. *Journal of Social and Personal Relationships*, 2: 377–83.

Lyons, R. F. and Meade, D. (1995) Painting a new face on relationships: relationship remodelling in response to chronic illness, in S. W. Duck and

J. T. Wood (eds) *Understanding Relationship Processes 5: Confronting Relationship Challenges*. Thousand Oaks: Sage.

Lyons, R. F., Mickelson, K. D., Sullivan, M. J. L. and Coyne, J. C. (1998) Coping as a communal process. *Journal of Social and Personal Relationships*, 15: 579–605.

McAdams, D. (1988) Personal needs and personal relationships, in S. W. Duck (ed.) with D. F. Hay, S. E. Hobfoll, W. Ickes and B. Montgomery, *Handbook of Personal Relationships*. Chichester: Wiley.

McCabe, S. B. and Gotlib, I. H. (1993) Interactions of couples with and without a depressed spouse: self report and observations of problem-solving situations. *Journal of Social and Personal Relationships*, 10: 589–99.

McCall, G. J. (1982) Becoming unrelated: the management of bond dissolution, in S. W. Duck (ed.) *Personal Relationships 4: Dissolving Personal Relationships*. London: Academic Press.

McCall, G. J. (1988) The organizational life cycle of relationships, in S. W. Duck, D. F. Hay, S. E. Hobfoll, W. J. Ickes and B. M. Montgomery (eds) *Handbook of Personal Relationships*. Chichester: Wiley.

McGonagle, K. A., Kessler, R. C. and Gotlib, I. H. (1993) The effects of marital disagreement style, frequency and outcome on marital disruption. *Journal of Social and Personal Relationships*, 10: 385–404.

Makepeace, J. M. (1981) Courtship violence among college students. *Family Relations*, 30: 97–102.

Mallinckrodt, B. (1997) Interpersonal relationship processes in individual and group psychotherapy, in S. W. Duck, K. Dindia, W. Ickes, R. Milardo, R. S. L. Mills and B. R. Sarason (eds) *Handbook of Personal Relationships* (2nd edition). Chichester: Wiley.

Mamali, C. (1996) Interpersonal communication in totalitarian societies, in W. Gudykunst, S. Ting-Toomey and T. Nishida (eds) *Communication in Personal Relationships across Cultures*. Thousand Oaks: Sage.

Marangoni, C. and Ickes, W. (1989) Loneliness: a theoretical review with implications for measurement. *Journal of Social and Personal Relationships*, 6: 93–128.

Marshall, L. and Rose, P. (1987) Gender stress and violence in the adult relationships of a sample of college students. *Journal of Social and Personal Relationships*, 4: 299–316.

Masheter, C. (1997) Former spouses who are friends: three case studies. *Journal of Social and Personal Relationships*, 14: 207–22.

Masters, W. H. and Johnson, V. (1970) *Human Sexual Inadequacy*. Boston: Little, Brown.

Mehrabian, A. and Ksionzky, S. (1974) *A Theory Affiliation*. Lexington, MA: Lexington Books.

Metts, S. (1997) Face and facework: implications for the study of personal relationships, in S. W. Duck (ed.) with K. Dindia, W. Ickes, R. M. Milardo, R. S. L. Mills and B. Sarason, *Handbook of Personal Relationships* (2nd edition). Chichester: Wiley.

Miell, D. E. (1984) 'Cognitive and communicative strategies in developing relationships'. Unpublished Doctoral Thesis, University of Lancaster.

Miell, D. E. (1987) Remembering relationship development: constructing a context for interactions, in R. Burnett, P. McGhee and D. Clarke (eds) *Accounting for Relationships*. London: Methuen.

Miell, D. E. and Croghan, R. (1996) Examining the wider context of social relationships, in D. E. Miell and R. Dallos (eds) *Social Interaction and Personal Relationships*. Milton Keynes: Open University/Sage.

Miell, D. E. and Dallos, R. (1996) Introduction: exploring interactions and relationships, in D. E. Miell and R. Dallos (eds) *Social Interaction and Personal Relationships*. Milton Keynes: Open University/Sage.

Miell, D. E. and Duck, S. W. (1986) Strategies in developing friendship, in V. J. Derlega and B. A. Winstead (eds) *Friendship and Social Interaction*. New York: Springer Verlag.

Mikulincer, M. and Segal, J. (1990) A multi-dimensional analysis of the experience of loneliness. *Journal of Social and Personal Relationships*, 7: 209–30.

Milardo, R. M. (1982) Friendship networks in developing relationships: converging and diverging social environments. *Social Psychology Quarterly*, 45: 163–71.

Milardo, R. M. and Allan, G. A. (1997) Social networks and marital relationships, in S. W. Duck (ed.) with K. Dindia, W. Ickes, R. M. Milardo, R. S. L. Mills and B. Sarason, *Handbook of Personal Relationships* (2nd edition). Chichester: Wiley.

Milardo, R. M. and Wellman, B. (1992) The personal is social. *Journal of Social and Personal Relationships*, 9: 339–42.

Milardo, R. M., Johnson, M. P. and Huston, T. L. (1983) Developing close relationships: changing patterns of interaction between pair members and social networks. *Journal of Personality and Social Psychology*, 44: 964–76.

Miller, G. R. and Parks, M. R. (1982) Communication in dissolving relationships, in S. W. Duck (ed.) *Personal Relationships 4: Dissolving Personal Relationships*. London: Academic Press.

Miller, R. S. (1996) *Embarrassment: Poise and Peril in Everyday Life*. New York: Guilford.

Montgomery, B. M. (1986) 'Flirtatious messages'. Paper presented to the Third International Conference on Personal Relationships, Herzlia, Israel, July.

Morgan, D. L. (1986) Personal relationships as an interface between social networks and social cognitions. *Journal of Social and Personal Relationships*, 3: 403–22.

Morgan, D., Carder, P. and Neal, M. (1997) Are some relationships more useful than others? The value of similar others in the networks of recent widows. *Journal of Social and Personal Relationships*, 14: 745–59.

Mott, F. L. and Moore, S. F. (1979) The causes of marital disruption among young American women: an interdisciplinary perspective. *Journal of Marriage and the Family*, 41: 335–65.

Murstein, B. I. (1971) Critique of models of dyadic attraction, in B. I. Murstein (ed.) *Theories of Attraction and Love*. New York: Springer.

Murstein, B. I. (1976) *Who Will Marry Whom?* New York: Springer.

Murstein, B. I. (1977) The Stimulus–Value–Role (SVR) theory of dyadic relationships, in S. W. Duck (ed.) *Theory and Practice in Interpersonal Attraction*. London: Academic Press.

Nardi, P. and Sherrod, D. (1994) Friendship in the lives of gay men. *Journal of Social and Personal Relationships*, 11: 186–99.

Neimeyer, G. J. and Hudson, J. E. (1985) Couple's constructs: personal systems in marital satisfaction, in D. Bannister (ed.) *Issues and Approaches in Personal Construct Theory*. London: Academic Press.

Newcomb, M. D. (1986) Cohabitation, marriage and divorce among adolescents and young adults. *Journal of Social and Personal Relationships*, 3: 473–94.

Norton, A. J. and Moorman, J. E. (1987) Current trends in marriage and divorce among American women. *Journal of Marriage and the Family*, 49: 3–14.

Notarius, C. (1996) Marriage: will I be happy or sad?, in N. Vanzetti and S. W. Duck (eds) *A Lifetime of Relationships*. Pacific Grove, CA: Brooks Cole.

O'Connell, L. (1984) An exploration of exchange in three social relationships: kinship, friendship and the marketplace. *Journal of Social and Personal Relationships*, 1: 333–45.

O'Connor, P. and Brown, G. W. (1984) 'Supportive relationships: fact or fancy?', *Journal of Social and Personal Relationships*, 2: 159–76.

Olson, D. H. (1977) Insiders' and outsiders' views of relationships: research studies, in G. Levinger and H. Raush (eds) *Close Relationships: Perspectives on the Meaning of Intimacy*. Amherst: UMass Press.

Orbuch, T. L. (ed.) (1992) *Relationship Loss*. New York: Springer-Verlag.

O'Sullivan, L. F. and Gaines, M. E. (1998) Decision making in college students' heterosexual dating relationships: ambivalence about engaging in sexual activity. *Journal of Social and Personal Relationships*, 15: 347–64.

Parks, M. R. and Adelman, M. (1983) Communication networks and the development of romantic relationships: an expansion of uncertainty-reduction theory. *Human Communication Research*, 10: 55–80.

Parks, M. R. and Eggert, L. L. (1991) The role of social context in the dynamics of personal relationships, in W. H. Jones and D. Perlman (eds) *Advances in Personal Relationships*, Vol. 1. London: Jessica Kingsley.

Parks, M. R. and Roberts, L. D. (1998) 'Making MOOsic': the development of personal relationships on-line and a comparison of their off-line counterparts. *Journal of Social and Personal Relationships*, 15: 517–37.

Pearson, J. C. (1996) Forty-forever years? Primary relationships and senior citizens, in N. Vanzetti and S. W. Duck (eds) *A Lifetime of Relationships*. Pacific Grove: Brooks/Cole.

Perlman, D. (1986) 'Chance and coincidence in personal relationships'. Paper presented to the Third International Conference on Personal Relationships, Herzlia, Israel, July.

Perrin, F. A. C. (1921) Physical attractiveness and repulsions. *Journal of Experimental Psychology*, 4: 203–17.

Pettit, G. and Lollis, S. (1997) Reciprocity and bidirectionality in parent–child relationships: new approaches to the study of enduring issues. *Journal of Social and Personal Relationships*, 14: 435–40.

Planalp, S. (1985) Relational schemata: a test of alternative forms of relational knowledge as guides to communication. *Human Communication Research*, 12: 1–29.

Planalp, S. and Benson, A. (1992) Friends' and acquaintances' conversations I: Observed differences. *Journal of Social and Personal Relationships*, 9, 483–506.

Planalp, S. and Garvin-Doxas, K. (1994) Using mutual knowledge in conversation: friends as experts in each other, in S. W. Duck (ed.) *Understanding Relationship Processes 4: Dynamics of Interactions*. Newbury Park: Sage.

Planalp, S. and Honeycutt, J. M. (1985) Events that increase uncertainty in personal relationships. *Human Communication Research*, 11: 593–604.

Poulakos, T. (1997) *Speaking for the Polis: Isocrates' Rhetorical Education*. Columbia, SC: University of South Carolina Press.

Prager, K. J. (1995) *The Psychology of Intimacy*. New York: Guilford.

Prager, K. J. and Buhrmester, D. (1998) Intimacy and need fulfillment in couple relationships. *Journal of Social and Personal Relationships*, 15: 435–69.

Prusank, D., Duran, R. and DeLillo, D. A. (1993) Interpersonal relationships in women's magazines: dating and relating in the 1970s and 1980s. *Journal of Social and Personal Relationships*, 10: 307–20.

Putallaz, M., Costanzo, P. R. and Klein, T. P. (1993) Parental childhood social experiences and their effects on children's relationships, in S. W. Duck (ed.) *Understanding Relationship Processes 2: Learning about Relationships.* Newbury Park: Sage.

Rasmussen, J. L., Rajecki, D. W., Ebert, A. A., Lagler, K., Brewer, C. and Cochran, E. (1998) Age preference in personal ads: *two* life history strategies or *one* matching tactic? *Journal of Social and Personal Relationships*, 15: 77–90.

Regan, P. C., Kocan, E. R. and Whitlock, T. (1998) Ain't love grand! A prototype analysis of the concept of romantic love. *Journal of Social and Personal Relationships*, 15: 411–20.

Register, L. M. and Henley, T. B. (1992) The phenomenology of intimacy. *Journal of Social and Personal Relationships*, 9: 467–81.

Reis, H. T. and Shaver, P. R. (1988) Intimacy as an interpersonal process, in S. W. Duck, D. F. Hay, S. E. Hobfoll, W. Ickes and B. M. Montgomery (eds) *Handbook of Personal Relationships: Theory, Research and Interventions.* Chichester and New York: Wiley.

Reis, H. T., Nezlek, J. and Wheeler, L. (1980) Physical attractiveness and social interaction. *Journal of Personality and Social Psychology*, 38: 604–17.

Reisman, J. (1981) Adult friendships, in S. W. Duck and R. Gilmour (eds) *Personal Relationships 2: Developing Personal Relationships.* London: Academic Press.

Reissman, C., Aron, A. and Bergen, M. (1993) Shared activities and marital satisfaction: causal direction and self-expansion versus boredom. *Journal of Social and Personal Relationships*, 10: 243–54.

Renne, K. S. (1970) Correlates of dissatisfaction in marriage. *Journal of Marriage and the Family*, 32: 54–67.

Retzinger, S. M. (1995) Shame and anger in personal relationships, in S. W. Duck and J. T. Wood (eds) *Understanding Relationship Processes 5: Relationship Challenges.* Thousand Oaks: Sage.

Rodin, M. J. (1982) Non-engagement, failure to engage, and disengagement, in S. W. Duck (ed.) *Personal Relationships 4: Dissolving Personal Relationships.* New York: Academic Press.

Rohlfing, M. (1995) 'Doesn't anybody stay in one place any more?' An exploration of the understudied phenomenon of long-distance relationships, in J. T. Wood and S. W. Duck (eds) *Understanding Relationship Processes 6: Under-studied Relationships: Off the Beaten Track.* Newbury Park: Sage.

Rose, S. and Serafica, F. C. (1986) Keeping and ending casual, close, and best friendships. *Journal of Social and Personal Relationships*, 3: 275–88.

Rosen, K. H. and Stith, S. M. (1995) Women terminating abusive dating relationships: a qualitative study. *Journal of Social and Personal Relationships*, 12: 155–60.

Ross, M. D. and Holmberg, D. (1992) Are wives' memories for events in relationships more vivid than their husbands' memories? *Journal of Social and Personal Relationships*, 9: 585–604.

Rotenberg, K. and Kmill, J. (1992) Perception of lonely and nonlonely persons as a function of individual differences in loneliness. *Journal of Social and Personal Relationships*, 9: 325–30.

Rothman, E. (1984) *Hands and Hearts: A History of Courtship in America.* New York: Basic Books.

Rubin, A. M., Perse, E. M. and Powell, R. A. (1985) Loneliness, parasocial interactions and local TV news viewing. *Human Communication Research*, 12: 155–80.

Rusbult, C. E. and Buunk, A. P. (1993) Commitment processes in close relationships: an interdependence analysis. *Journal of Social and Personal Relationships*, 10: 175–203.

Ruvolo, A. P. (1998) Marital well-being and general happiness of newlywed couples: relationships across time. *Journal of Social and Personal Relationships*, 15: 470–89.

Ruvolo, A. P. and Veroff, J. (1997) For better or for worse: real–ideal discrepancies and the marital well-being of newlyweds. *Journal of Social and Personal Relationships*, 14: 223–42.

Sabatelli, R. and Pearce, J. (1986) Exploring marital expectations. *Journal of Social and Personal Relationships*, 3: 307–22.

Sabini, J. and Silver, M. (1982) *Moralities of Everyday Life*. Oxford: Oxford University Press.

Sahlstein, E. (1998) 'Long-distance relationships: What are they?' Paper presented at the annual CSCA convention, Chicago.

Sarason, B. R., Sarason, I. G. and Gurung, R. A. R. (1997) Close personal relationships and health outcomes: a key to the role of social support, in S. W. Duck, K. Dindia, W. Ickes, R. Milardo, R. S. L. Mills and B. R. Sarason (eds) *Handbook of Personal Relationships* (2nd edition). Chichester: Wiley.

Schachter, S. (1959) *The Psychology of Affiliation*. Stanford CA: Stanford University Press.

Segrin, C. (1993) Interpersonal reactions to dysphoria: the role of relationhips with partner perceptions of rejection. *Journal of Social and Personal Relationships*, 10: 83–97.

Shackelford, T. K. and Buss, D. M. (1997) Anticipation of marital dissolution as a consequence of spousal infidelity. *Journal of Social and Personal Relationships*, 14: 793–808.

Shaver, P. R., Furman, W. and Buhrmester, D. (1985) Aspects of a life transition: network changes, social skills and loneliness, in S. W. Duck and D. Perlman (eds) *Understanding Personal Relationships*. London: Sage.

Sher, T. G. (1996) Courtship and marriage: choosing a primary relationship, in N. Vanzetti and S. W. Duck (eds) *A Lifetime of Relationships*. Pacific Grove: Brooks/Cole.

Shotter, J. (1992) What is a 'personal' relationship? A rhetorical–responsive account of 'unfinished business', in J. H. Harvey, T. L. Orbuch and A. L. Weber (eds) *Attributions, Accounts and Close Relationships*. New York: Springer-Verlag.

Shotter, J. (1993) *Conversational Realities: Constructing Life through Language*. Thousand Oaks: Sage.

Sillars, A., Folwell, A. L., Hill, K. C., Maki, B. K., Hurst, A. P. and Casano, R. A. (1994) Marital communication and the persistence of misunderstanding. *Journal of Social and Personal Relationships*, 11: 611–17.

Simmel, G. (1950) *The Sociology of Georg Simmel* (trans. K. Wolff). New York: Free Press.

Snell, W. E. Jr (1988) 'The relationship awareness scale: measuring relationship consciousness, relationship-monitoring, and relationship anxiety'. Paper presented at the 34th annual meeting of the Southwestern Psychological Association, Tulsa.

Solomon, D. H. and Samp, J. A. (1998) Power and problem appraisal: perceptual foundations of the chilling effect in dating relationships. *Journal of Social and Personal Relationships*, 15: 191–210.

Spencer, E. E. (1994) Transforming relationships through ordinary talk, in S. W. Duck (ed.) *Understanding Relationship Processes 4: Dynamics of Relationships*. Newbury Park: Sage.

Spitzberg, B. H. (1993) The dialectics of (in)competence. *Journal of Social and Personal Relationships*, 10: 137–58.

Sprecher, S. (1987) The effects of self-disclosure given and received on affection for an intimate partner and stability of the relationship. *Journal of Social and Personal Relationships*, 4: 115–27.

Sprecher, S. and Duck, S. W. (1993) Sweet talk: the role of communication in consolidating relationship. *Personality and Social Psychology Bulletin*, 20: 391–400.

Stafford, L. (1994) Tracing the threads of spider webs, in D. J. Canary and L. Stafford (eds) *Communication and Relational Maintenance*. New York: Academic Press.

Stein, C. H. (1993) Felt obligation in adult family relationships, in S. W. Duck (ed.) *Understanding Relationship Processes 3: Social Contexts of Relationships*. Thousand Oaks: Sage.

Stein, C. H. and Kramer, L. (1996) Different paths, different voices: rethinking the development of families. *Journal of Social and Personal Relationships*, 13: 323–4.

Stephens, M. A. P. and Clark, S. L. (1996) Interpersonal relationships in multigenerational families, in N. Vanzetti and S. W. Duck (eds) *A Lifetime of Relationships*. Monterey, CA: Brooks/Cole.

Sterk, H. (1986) 'Functioning fictions: the adjustment rhetoric of Silhouette romance novels'. Unpublished PhD thesis, University of Iowa.

Sternberg, R. J. (1995) Love as a story. *Journal of Social and Personal Relationships*, 12: 541–6.

Stiles, W. B., Walz, N. C., Schroeder, M. A. B., Williams, L. L. and Ickes, W. (1996) Attractiveness and disclosure in initial encounters of mixed-sex dyads. *Journal of Social and Personal Relationships*, 13: 303–12.

Stueve, C. A. and Gerson, K. (1977) Personal relations across the life cycle, in C. S. Fischer (ed.) *Networks and Places: Social Relations in the Urban Setting*. New York: Free Press.

Suls, J. (1977) Gossip as social comparison. *Journal of Communication*, 27: 164–8.

Surra, C. A. (1987) Reasons for changes in commitment: variations by courtship style. *Journal of Social and Personal Relationships*, 4: 17–33.

Thomas, K. (1997) The psychodynamics of relating, in D. E. Miell and R. Dallos (eds) *Social Interaction and Personal Relationships*. Milton Keynes: Open University/Sage.

Thompson, J. M., Whiffen, V. E. and Blain, M. D. (1995) Depressive symptoms, sex and perceptions of intimate relationships. *Journal of Social and Personal Relationships*, 12: 49–66.

Timmer, S. G., Veroff, J. and Hatchett, S. (1996) Family ties and marital happiness: the different marital experiences of black and white newlywed couples. *Journal of Social and Personal Relationships*, 13: 335–59.

Tornstam. L. (1992) Loneliness in marriage. *Journal of Social and Personal Relationships*, 9: 197–217.

Trickett, E. J. and Buchanan, R. M. (1997) The role of personal relationships in transitions: contributions of an ecological perspective, in S. W. Duck, K. Dindia, W. Ickes, R. Milardo, R. S. L. Mills and B. R. Sarason (eds) *Handbook of Personal Relationships* (2nd edition). Chichester: Wiley.

Umberson, D. and Terling, T. (1997) The symbolic meaning of relationships: implications for psychological distress following relationship loss. *Journal of Social and Personal Relationships*, 14: 723–44.

Unger, D. G., Jacobs, S. B. and Cannon, C. (1996) Social support and marital satisfaction among couples coping with chronic constructive airway disease. *Journal of Social and Personal Relationships*, 13: 123–42.

Vangelisti, A. L. (1994) Family secrets: forms, functions, and correlates. *Journal of Social and Personal Relationships*, 11: 113–35.

Vangelisti, A. L. and Huston, T. L. (1994) Maintaining marital satisfaction and love, in D. J. Canary and L. Stafford (eds) *Communication and Relational Maintenance*. San Diego, CA: Academic Press.

Van Lear, C. A. Jr and Trujillo, N. (1986) On becoming acquainted: a longitudinal study of social judgement processes. *Journal of Social and Personal Relationships*, 3: 375–92.

Veroff, J., Douvan E. and Hatchett, S. (1995) *Marital Instability: A Social and Behavioral Study of the Early Years*. Westport, CT: Praeger.

Veroff, J., Sutherland, L., Chaidla, L. and Ortega, R. M. (1993) Newly weds tell their stories: a narrative method for assessing marital experience. *Journal of Social and Personal Relationships*, 10: 437–57.

Veroff, J., Young, A. M. and Coon, H. M. (1997) The early years of marriage, in S. W. Duck, K. Dindia, W. Ickes, R. Milardo, R. S. L. Mills and B. R. Sarason (eds) *Handbook of Personal Relationships* (2nd edition). Chichester: Wiley.

Vonk, R. and van Nobelen, D. (1993) Masculinity and femininity in the self with an intimate partner: men are not always men in the company of women. *Journal of Social and Personal Relationships*, 10: 627–30.

Vorauer, J. D. and Ratner, R. (1996) Who's going to make the first move? Pluralistic ignorance as an impediment to relationship formation. *Journal of Social and Personal Relationships*, 13: 483–506.

Weber, A. (1983) 'The breakdown of relationships'. Paper presented to conference on Social Interaction and Relationships, Nags Head, North Carolina, May.

Weber, A., Harvey, J. H. and Stanley, M. A. (1987) The nature and motivations of accounts for failed relationships, in R. Burnett, P. McGhee and D. Clarke (eds) *Accounting for Relationships*. London: Methuen.

Weiss, R. S. (1998) A taxonomy of relationships. *Journal of Social and Personal Relationships*, 15: 671–83.

Werking, K. (1997) *Just Good Friends: Cross-sex Friendships*. New York: Guilford.

Werner, C., Altman, I., Brown, B. and Ginat, J. (1993) Celebrations in personal relationships: a transactional/dialectical perspective, in S. W. Duck (ed.) *Understanding Relationship Processes 3: Social Contexts of Relationships*. Newbury Park: Sage.

West, J. (1995) Understanding how the dynamics of ideology influence violence between intimates, in S. W. Duck and J. T. Wood (eds) *Understanding Relationship Processes 5: Confronting Relationship Challenges*. Thousand Oaks: Sage.

Whitbeck, L. B. and Hoyt, D. R. (1994) Social prestige and assortative mating: a comparison of students from 1956 and 1988. *Journal of Social and Personal Relationships*, 11: 137–45.

Wilmot, W. (1995) *Relational Communication*. New York: McGraw-Hill.

Winstead, B. A., Derlega, V. J., Montgomery, M. J. and Pilkington, C. (1995) The quality of friendship at work and job satisfaction. *Journal of Social and Personal Relationships*, 12: 199–215.

Winters, A. M. (1997) 'Prenuptial contracts'. Unpublished paper, University of Iowa.

Wiseman, J. P. (1986) Friendship: bonds and binds in a voluntary relationship. *Journal of Social and Personal Relationships*, 3: 191–211.

Wiseman, J. P. and Duck, S. W. (1995) Having and managing enemies: a very challenging relationship, in S. W. Duck and J. T. Wood (eds) *Understanding Relationship Processes 5: Relationship Challenges*. Thousand Oaks: Sage.

Wittenberg, M. T. and Reis, H. T. (1986) Loneliness, social skills, and social perception. *Personality and Social Psychology Bulletin*, 12: 121–30.

Wood, J. T. (1982) Communication and relational culture: bases for the study of human relationships. *Communication Quarterly*, 30: 75–83.

Wood, J. T. (1993) Engendered relationships: interaction, caring, power, and responsibility in intimacy, in S. W. Duck (ed.) *Understanding Relationship Processes 3: Social Contexts of Relationships*. Newbury Park: Sage.

Wright, P. H. (1985a) Self referent motivation and the intrinsic quality of friendship. *Journal of Social and Personal Relationships*, 1: 114–30.

Wright, P. H. (1985b) The acquaintance description form, in S. W. Duck and D. Perlman (eds) *Understanding Personal Relationships*. London: Sage.

Wright, R. and Contrada, R. J. (1986) Dating selectivity and interpersonal attraction: toward a better understanding of the 'elusive phenomenon'. *Journal of Social and Personal Relationships*, 3: 131–48.

Yaffe, M. (1981) Disordered sexual relationships, in S. W. Duck and R. Gilmour (ed.) *Personal Relationships 3: Personal Relationships in Disorder*. London and New York: Academic Press.

Yogev, S. (1987) Marital satisfaction and sex role perceptions among dual-earner couples. *Journal of Social and Personal Relationships*, 4: 35–46.

Young, A. M. and Acitelli, L. K. (1998) The role of attachment styles and relationship status of the perceiver in the perceptions of romantic partner. *Journal of Social and Personal Relationships*, 15: 161–74.

Young, J. E. (1982) Loneliness, depression and cognitive therapy: theory and application, in L. A. Peplau and D. Perlman (eds) *Loneliness: a Current Sourcebook of Theory Research and Therapy*. New York: Wiley-Interscience.

Zebrowitz, L. (1989) *Social Perception*. Milton Keynes: Open University Press.

Zeifman, D. and Hazan, C. (1997) A process model of adult attachment formation, in S. W. Duck (ed.) with K. Dindia, W. Ickes, R. M. Milardo, R. S. L. Mills and B. Sarason, *Handbook of Personal Relationships* (2nd edition). Chichester: Wiley.

Zimmer, T. (1986) Premarital anxieties. *Journal of Social and Personal Relationships*, 3: 149–60.

Zorn, T. (1995) Bosses and buddies: constructing and performing simultaneously hierarchical and close friendship relationships, in J. T. Wood and S. W. Duck (eds) *Understanding Relationship Processes 6: Understudied Relationships: Off the Beaten Track*. Thousand Oaks: Sage.

Zvonkovic, A. M., Pennington, D. C. and Schmiege, C. J. (1994) Work and courtship: how college workload and perception of work environment relate to romantic relationships among men and women. *Journal of Social and Personal Relationships*, 11: 63–76.

AUTHOR INDEX

SUBJECT INDEX